MODERN

INSTITUTIONAL

ADVERTISING

GEORGE A. FLANAGAN

Formerly vice-president and copy director
Cunningham & Walsh Inc.

MODERN

ADVERTISING

including corporate, corporate image, association, service, and all other major forms of non-product advertising

McGRAW-HILL BOOK COMPANY

New York   San Francisco
Toronto   London   Sydney

To Marjorie

For a long time, there has been a need for a book on institutional advertising, and recently this need has grown more acute. This is a large subject, an important one, and one of immediate concern to increasing numbers of advertising men (not to mention public relations men, corporate executives, and students). For those who seek information about institutional advertising, the few pages accorded it in general texts on advertising have become clearly inadequate. It is time for a fuller exposition, such as this book attempts to supply.

The examining of the whole field of institutional advertising reveals the true nature of the subject in a way that a few isolated examples cannot do. And its nature is seen to be somewhat different from what some advertising men will expect. We find, for one instance—as noted in Chapter 1—that we are dealing not with a *kind* of advertising, but with a broad *area* of advertising.

We find, too, in this subject, a characteristic tendency to refuse to be exactly defined or exactly categorized. Borderlines merge and overlap. Exceptions to the rule abound. And for purposes of definition, one seeks in vain for a common denominator that can be applied, with precision, to every kind of advertising that professional advertising men, at one time or other, have called *institutional*.

Perhaps the nearest semblance to such a common denominator might be the term, *non-product advertising*. Indeed, for a time, it was intended to make the title of this book *Non-Product Advertising*. But, aside from non-product being almost totally unfamiliar and institutional being *very* familiar, non-product, though *nearly* universal, did not apply in every case.

As will be seen, institutional advertising sometimes does help sell products. And it is frequently combined, in the same ads, with product-selling advertising.

Certain borderline subdivisions of institutional advertising, such as service advertising and association advertising, have troubled those who approach the subject of institutional advertising from a purely semantic point of view.

Service advertising sells no product,[1] but *sometimes* (though not always) sells its services in a manner that is very similar to hard-sell product advertising. Yet, is this enough to disqualify it from a comprehensive discussion of institutional advertising? It hardly seems so, especially when service advertising so often displays other institutional affinities. Surely, in borderline cases, a book of this nature should be of more benefit to its readers by being slightly *over*-inclusive in content, rather than under-inclusive, merely for the sake of semantic symmetry.

Trade associations often sell their industry's product generically. This is product-selling, of course. But at the same time, behind this product promotion, there is almost always a strong *protective* motivation, which is highly institutional in spirit. This, in itself, acts to justify the inclusion of association advertising in the book.

That institutional advertising resists exact definition and orderly subdivision need not worry us, however, much as it may agitate the theorist and perfectionist. Institutional advertising is not a science. It is not a branch of metaphysics. It is a practical, everyday part of the advertising business.

The last thing the advertising business would ever do would be to fence itself in. It is alive, energetic, growing—and constantly changing. It is not always orderly. Its purposes are practical, not theoretical. The form that institutional advertising takes reflects the business that makes it. Institutional advertising is what working advertising men have produced to meet the needs of the corporations they serve or work for.

At its core, institutional advertising is strongly individualistic. The technique and content of its advertisements are determined by the objectives of its advertisers. And, as aptly pointed out by John Sheehan, vice-president of the Television Bureau of Advertising, and a specialist in institutional advertising, the objectives of no two institutional advertisers are ever exactly alike.

This book is based on the practical workings of the advertising business. Its information comes, first of all, from a long personal experience, unusually rich in contacts with many phases of institutional advertising and with many institutional advertisers. To this information has been added the suggestions of numerous colleagues and friends. And finally, a wealth of first-hand data has been generously supplied by the very men—often top executives—who

---

[1] With exceptions. See page 257.

have planned, created, or managed most of the outstanding institutional campaigns presented in these pages.

To these professionals whose assistance has made this book possible, acknowledgment must be made collectively; there are too many of them to list individually. Their counsel has been most helpful. And most flattering—and a hopeful portent—has been the desire, expressed by so many of them, to get a copy of this book when published.

George A. Flanagan

MODERN

INSTITUTIONAL

ADVERTISING

One

The traditional, normal function of advertising is to sell products, or to help sell products. The great bulk of the money spent on advertising is used for that purpose. Nevertheless, today, an impressive segment of advertising expenditure is devoted to advertising that is *not* primarily intended to sell products.

No one has made a formal count of the exact volume of such advertising. To do so would be incredibly difficult, because of the recurring need to decide which advertisements were properly product-selling and which were not. Lacking such a count, one may, however, attempt a rough guess.

A recent thumb-through tally of pages in two or three leading magazines revealed that approximately one-fifth to one-fourth of the page-size advertisements were essentially of the non-product type.

The proportion of non-product advertisements is probably somewhat higher in magazines[1] than in other forms of media, such as newspapers or television. To compensate for this, one might arbitrarily reduce the fraction—to, say, one-sixth or one-seventh. Then, if the annual expenditure of *all* advertising is 14½ billion dollars,[2] the expenditure for non-product advertising might well be estimated at several billion dollars or more.

The advertising that concerns itself with something other than selling a product is usually called *institutional advertising*. This advertising is important in total money value. It has been around quite as long as product-selling advertising, possibly longer. It is regularly employed by the largest corporations. And many people are concerned with its planning and execution. It merits much closer study than has yet been given to it.

A Terra Incognita

Institutional advertising is something that almost everybody in the advertising business knows a little

Chapter 1

INSTITUTIONAL
ADVERTISING—
ITS SCOPE
AND PURPOSE

---

[1] Magazines are the only form of media that permits this convenient and representative thumb-through count.

[2] *Advertising Age*, Mar. 29, 1965.

about, but almost nobody knows very *much* about. This is due, in part at least, to the nature of the subject. It is much bigger, wider and, particularly, much more varied than most advertising people suppose. It is *not* all of one piece. It is not a *kind* of advertising; it is an *area* of advertising.

It is made up of many special kinds of advertising, each different from the other and only loosely related by a few broad general aspects in common. The nature of each kind is determined by the individual advertiser's objectives.

The breadth and diversity of institutional advertising does not always reveal itself to the advertising practitioner who has had only one or two specific experiences with it. Consequently, he tends to exemplify the story of the blind men and the elephant, and he falls into their error of assuming that the *whole* subject is exactly the same as the *part* that he knows about.

Such an incomplete view leads to an eagerness to view institutional advertising through the wrong end of the telescope—to want to see it as something smaller than it is. To a persisting desire to *limit* the boundaries of this advertising to make it more manageable and orderly.

But this never works quite satisfactorily. It is unrealistic. It is not the *whole* elephant. It is only the trunk. Or the tail. Or the side.

Confusion about this broad, variegated area of advertising is also caused by the strange word, *institutional,* that identifies the advertising, but does not clearly describe it.

The Term Institutional

The term *institutional* is a relic of the hazy, early days of advertising. At this late date, nobody knows for sure what institutional originally meant, precisely. Any specific semantic connotation it may have had at the beginning has been forgotten by everybody.

One surmise is that the word was originally a high-sounding advertising smart-aleckism—the kind of word an agent might toss around to impress a client. It was probably intended to be just a little bit mysterious, and the uninitiated were expected to guess at its meaning. As many advertising men have, ever since.

One can guess that institutional referred to a kind of advertising that was different from everyday product-selling advertising. And it could be assumed that the *institution* probably meant the *company.* But in what sense the advertising was applied is not clear.

It is perhaps because of this lack of precise definition that institutional has taken on the loose-fitting meaning it most often wears today. That is, to most practical advertising men, the word institutional serves as a handy catch-all appellation, a broad generic term to denote any and all types of advertising not primarily concerned with selling a product.

An extant definition has described institutional advertising as "advertising for the *institution* rather than the product." This is an obvious attempt to rationalize the unruly word institutional. It is not wrong. But its connotations are overly limiting, and it should not be taken too literally.

It should not be translated, for example, to mean that institutional advertising consists *only* of advertising for the corporation. For, by the common usage of advertising men, institutional has grown to include many special kinds of advertising, not all of which would be necessarily or properly called corporate advertising.

Confusion with Product-selling Advertising

There is a curious misconception about institutional advertising that seems to persist among certain highly sales-minded advertising men. This is the idea that institution-advertising and product-advertising are alternate ways of doing one's selling job. And—since institution-advertising will not sell as many products as product-advertising—therefore institutional advertising can't be much good.

The assumption is unrealistic, and the conclusion is silly. For, except in a few special cases to be discussed later, the purpose of institutional advertising is *not,* normally, to sell products.

One uses product-selling advertising to sell a product. One uses institutional advertising, usually, for something entirely different. The two kinds of advertising serve different purposes, fulfill different functions. Though they may cooperate with each other, and occasionally overlap—*one is not a substitute for the other.*

The Purpose of Institutional Advertising

The purpose of institutional advertising is to fulfill legitimate corporate needs *other* than the business of selling a product.

There have been a great many such advertising needs, and new ones constantly occur. Some are matters of no small importance, such as fighting to protect a company's very existence. Here are just a *few* of the tasks that *have* been assigned to institutional advertising and fulfilled successfully:

- To act protectively, using advertising, where feasible and permissible, to protect a company's business when the company is under political attack

- To acquire a favorable corporate image for purposes of more advantageous financing
- To picture the company in such a way as to more easily recruit desirable personnel
- On the part of a multi-division corporation, to achieve corporate unity, both internally and externally
- To apply institutional advertising as a detached lever to lend assistance, in special areas, to the company's selling effort
- On the part of an entire industry, to protect itself against the competitive inroads of another industry or industries

Functional Areas

This is only a beginning. More applications of this advertising will be found listed in a chart at the end of this chapter. And these are by no means all. The list grows constantly.

In fact, if we try systematically to enumerate institutional advertising's uses and purposes, we may be amazed by their large number and wide variety, and by their multitudinous types and classifications. Trying to categorize them, we may be dismayed further by their persistent resistance to being organized. We can, however, *roughly* group them together under a few basic *functions*.

These functional categories are not hard and fast in their boundaries, nor are they mutually exclusive. Practical advertising programs do not fall into them neatly, like letters sorted into mailbags at the post office. Quite often, a single ad or campaign fulfills several functions at the same time.

Keeping this in mind, the functions might be listed as follows:

The protective function The use of advertising to *protect* the corporation and its way of doing business. Against the effects of adverse governmental action, against the inroads of other industries, against labor, or, on labor's part, against management. Or, in wartime, to protect a company's name and goodwill. Plus many special public-relations variations of these protective operations.

The image-making function To improve a corporate image. To build prestige for financing purposes. To assist in recruiting desirable employees. In retail, to attract customers to the store.

Internal and external functions Advertising intended, at least in part, to unify a company *internally*. To improve employee morale. Or *externally* oriented advertising that performs a service for a customer or a subsidiary, with ultimate benefits accruing to the advertiser.

The service-selling function   Advertising to sell a *service*. Services such as those offered by the telephone company, or by some other utility. Insurance. Banking. To promote a geographical area, either for investment or travel. Travel in general.

The public service function   Advertising devoted to the public good, either selfishly or altruistically. Advertising for non-profit organizations. Religious advertising. Patriotic advertising.

The action-initiating function   Advertising to change industry practices. Win proxies. Promote a cause. Secure favorable legislation. Political advertising.

Good Institutional Advertising Should Be Purposeful

It follows from its functions that—in its planning and execution—good institutional advertising must be strongly *purposeful*. That is its first requirement, and its reason for existence.

It must have an *objective*. It should have an assigned job to do, and the job should be worth the money appropriated for it.

The Kind of Advertising That Sells Ideas

Institutional advertising is the kind of advertising that sells *ideas*. It attempts to influence the minds of people to the advertiser's advantage.

The selling of ideas, however, involves a built-in operational difficulty. Ideas, in varying degree, are *abstract,* whereas products are concrete. People, to whom advertising is addressed, usually respond much more readily to the promotion of a concrete product—particularly one that everybody needs—than to an abstract proposal.

This additional burden of dealing with abstractness profoundly conditions the creative techniques of institutional advertising, and makes them different from those of most product-selling advertising. Attitudes and techniques that quite regularly spell success in hard-sell advertising, for example, often fail when applied to an idea-selling assignment.

In institutional advertising, the need to arouse *interest* becomes vitally important. Abstractions do not usually sell themselves. There *is* such a thing as *product interest,* but there is no *abstraction interest. The interest must be created.*

The requirement to be interesting—in one way or another—becomes a basic need for successful institutional advertising. The first cornerstone requirement of this advertising is to be *purposeful.* The second cornerstone is the obligation to be *interesting.*

Institutional Advertising and Public Relations

A great many of the objectives of institutional advertising are of a type long associated with public relations—PR, as its practitioners like to call it. Is not, then, institutional advertising merely a branch of public relations? Sometimes it could be so considered. And sometimes not. The question is really academic.

For although institutional advertising may often originate in the domain of public relations and be under the direction of public relations men, it is nevertheless *advertising*. It must be created by the use of advertising techniques.

Institutional advertising is an area where public relations and advertising activities not only overlap, but intertwine. There are all sorts of organizational arrangements for managing and producing this type of advertising, and most of them seem to work. Jurisdictional disputes can usually be resolved by common sense. When schedules for product-advertising are added to institutional schedules, one can often earn a reduction in media rates.

The Role of the Agency

More important than the jurisdictional assignment of institutional advertising to PR or advertising is the selection of an agency that is skilled in producing this kind of advertising.

Some advertising agencies know how to create good institutional advertising. Some agencies do not.

It is not a matter of the size of the agency, or of the quality of the personnel hired by the agency. Some very large agencies, super-agencies, show a poor record with institutional assignments. Some others have an excellent record.

It is rather the agency's basic and established advertising philosophy and attitudes, enforced by the agency's principals, that determine whether it will produce good institutional advertising or not. Agencies strongly committed to a hard-sell approach, for example, do not, as a rule, do well with institutional advertising.

The best institutional advertising has been produced by agencies with an outstanding flare for *imagination* and *creativeness*. Their people know how to get ideas, are talented in visualizing and writing, and succeed again and again in creating advertisements that are both interesting and effective.

Agencies do not change their basic attitudes very often. This makes it easy to select one that will do a good job with institutional advertising. One has just to look at the ads an agency has produced for others. If the ads have been dull, one can expect the same. If the ads are imaginative and exciting, that, too, can be expected again. And should be sought over other considerations.

SOME OF THE USES OF INSTITUTIONAL ADVERTISING

- To help protect the company's business when harassed by political attack
- To enhance company prestige for financing purposes
- To protect an entire industry against the competitive inroads of other industries
- To counteract unfavorable publicity; to improve the company image for various reasons
- To unify a multi-division corporate operation
- To picture the meaning of company operations to employees
- To seek favorable action by public officials
- To present the company's position favorably during a strike
- To protect the interests of a labor union, during a strike or at other times
- To render a public or patriotic service
- To present company policies favorably to plant-community neighbors
- To seek support for a charitable organization
- To recruit desirable employees
- To sell a service
- To promote a geographical area to investors or tourists; to promote travel
- To sell indirectly, by assisting or supporting customers in *their* selling efforts
- To elect someone to political office
- To advertise a form of advertising media
- To advertise an advertising agency
- To effect changes in corporate or industry practices; to recruit proxies
- To advertise educational institutions
- To promote a religious faith
- To provide an institutional image for a retail store
- To aid and support the government in wartime
- To keep a company's name before the public during wartime product shortages
- To restrain the buying of products! (during wartime shortages)

Chapter **2**

ADVERTISING'S

TWO

BASIC

WORLDS

Every so often, a successful and highly articulate advertising agent will write a book on his craft that stirs up the whole advertising fraternity. Some recent instances are David Ogilvy's *Confessions of an Advertising Man* and Rosser Reeves' *Reality in Advertising*. Back in 1923, Claude Hopkins wrote his famous *Scientific Advertising,* which still creates ripples of discussion among the older admen.

Although books of this type are susceptible to some criticism on the relatively minor score of some of their mannerisms, there is one way in which they are extremely useful. These writings are important business documents—in a business that is not nearly as well documented as it should be. These books are valuable in that they throw light, from a primary source, not merely on *how* advertising is written, but *why* it is written. They constitute deftly organized and skillfully defended webs of attitude toward advertising in general. They are systems of advertising philosophy.

Although not often as brilliantly expounded, systems of philosophies similar to these govern all advertising. Every agency, certainly, has its own advertising philosophy. And most advertisers have a philosophy of some degree of completeness.

If one surveys the entire field of advertising, he will note what is readily apparent, that these advertising philosophies tend to cluster into two major groups, or schools.

One of these two groups will be quickly identified. Everyone recognizes its banner, bearing the words, *hard sell.* In this group will be found the advertisers of packaged goods—household items, foods, pharmaceuticals, and so on—the products of the supermarket and drugstore.

The other group is less cohesive and more diverse, both in its products and its advertising attitudes. What it seems most to have in common is a tendency to veer away from the cult of hard sell. This group includes institutional advertisers, as well as sellers of products.

The Spectrum of Advertising Philosophies

The use of the word *group* to describe the cleavage in advertising philosophy should be interpreted loosely. There is no fence, or wall, or neat white line, separating the two areas of thought.

Instead, there are gradations of difference—a *spectrum,* as it were, from the ultra-hard-sell philosophies at one end to the anti-hard-sell philosophies at the other.

The hard-sell end of the spectrum seems to be characterized by great competitiveness, with emphasis on promotion of *brands.* The other end of the spectrum is less fiercely competitive and includes products more often sold *generically* or *uniquely.* It also includes non-product institutional advertising.

The concept of hard sell   The concept of hard sell has many shades of meaning. To some advertising men, such as Walter Weir,[1] it means a *manner* of selling—hard-boiled sell. To others, it apparently means the seeking of an irrefutable logic, a black-magic formula, that will *force* the consumer to buy.

A third view of hard sell is the thinking of it as *total sell. Everything* in the copy must be directed at selling the product. *Nothing* else can be permitted. There is no room for any entertainment, or cajoling, or interest-building. Just straight *sell* and nothing but *sell.*

In examining this point of view more closely will be found a simple clue to advertising's division into two different worlds.

Intrinsic-interest products   What separates the advertising philosophies of the hard-sell, packaged-goods world from the philosophies of the *other* than hard-sell world is simply *the nature of the products being sold.*

Some products have an intrinsic generic interest in themselves. With such a product—a food or other familiar necessity, or something generally desired, like a car—there is no great need for additional attention-getting or interest-arousing devices. The consumer-shopper is already interested in the product. The only unresolved question in the prospect's mind is what *brand* to select.

This is the essential problem of packaged-goods advertising. Hence, so-called *hard-sell* copy is clearly indicated—copy that goes right to work to sell a specific brand in detail, as hard as possible, point by point. The copy consists of nothing but direct selling. It wastes no time with attention-getting, or entertainment, or other luring-on devices, *because it does not need them.*

The great battle of the packaged-goods world is between *brands.* In this copy, each brand strikes out against its competitors, and extols its own competitive points of superiority.

[1] *On the Writing of Advertising.* McGraw-Hill Book Company, New York, 1960.

Products without intrinsic interest There are, however, many other products where the above is not true, products that do *not* have the benefit of an immediate intrinsic interest. These are products likely to be found in the advertising world that veers away from the hard-sell formulas.

Here, the prospect's attention must be caught. His interest must be aroused. His desire must be built up emotionally, as well as by logic. He must often be sold on the product *generically* before he can be sold the brand. He must be moved to an action he did not anticipate before starting to read the advertisement.

This is an entirely different problem from that faced by the advertiser of a cake of soap, a can of tuna fish, or a bottle of cough medicine. And it calls for an entirely different copy treatment.

Institutional Advertising Must Work Harder

Thus far, we have been speaking primarily of two kinds of product-advertising. But the problems of institutional advertising are almost identical with those of that second advertising world that must sell products without intrinsic consumer interest. In fact, the problem that has just been outlined applies even more forcefully in the case of institutional advertising, which has ideas to sell.

As noted previously, ideas are abstract and less attractive to the average person than something concrete and usable, like a product. Institutional advertising must work harder. Its attention-getting must be of "stopper" quality. Interest must be aroused and *maintained* while it strives to get its point across.

Why Hard-sell Techniques Often Fail with Institutional Advertising

When the "total-sell" techniques are applied to institutional advertising, they often result in dull, ineffective advertisements. Artwork and headlines are usually inadequate in attention-getting and interest-arousing qualities. The reader flips the page without waiting to get the message.

At the same time, the selling mechanisms that can be so effective in packaged-goods advertising lose much of their magic in idea-selling, because the prospect is not interested in the first place, and not enough has been done to arouse his interest. Indiscriminately offered "benefits" can turn out to be duds. Before any successful selling of any kind can be done, the ad must first establish an interest rapport with the reader.

The Three Basic Differences between Product and Institutional Advertising

It should be clear by now that institutional advertising differs from product-selling advertising—notably hard-sell advertising—in three all-important respects:

1. It is devoted to purposes *other* than that of selling a product.

2. It has a special *obligation to be interesting*, because it is not aided by the intrinsic interest of a needed packaged-goods product.

3. This obligation is increased because institutional advertising sells ideas, which are abstract and, hence, require greater interest-building.

Chapter 3

A great deal can be learned about advertising by clipping out and collecting advertisements that seem interesting for one reason or another.

If this is done regularly for a period of several months, one of the first discoveries one makes is that he finds himself clipping out ads of the same advertiser again and again. Indeed, before long, such a collection is likely to evolve into one of campaigns rather than of individual advertisements.

This should not be too surprising. The ad-maker skillful enough to catch our interest once might well be expected to do it again.

A second discovery that comes, if one looks over his collection, is that a *campaign* reveals much more about the advertiser and what he is trying to do than does an individual ad. By observing what is repeated and what is omitted, what is emphasized and what is passed over lightly, it soon becomes clear what the advertiser is spending his money to achieve.

This simple but surprisingly educational type of study can be developed further. It can be made to cover a whole area of advertising. Advertising agencies often make such clipping collections and pin them up on a corkboard wall, so that many persons can study them at the same time.

On one such occasion, a large collection was made of *institutional* advertisements—gathered for the purpose of studying what was good and bad about this particular type of advertising. Several hundred ads were displayed. The overall effect was somewhat startling.

The Most Common Weakness of Institutional Advertisements

It was almost immediately apparent which ads were good and which were bad—and it was equally clear what was wrong with the poor ones. The relatively few good examples stood out like shining stars. The majority, however, seemed to be suffering from a pallid common sickness.

What was wrong was obvious. It was the prevalent fault of *vagueness*—indirectness, lack of clarity, wishy-washiness, doubtfulness of purpose, confusion of thought. And this weakness was not concealed by the occasional diversionary fireworks of gaudy artwork and self-conscious typography.

The good ads, in contrast, had a definite message and delivered it with a punch.

Vagueness is the most common weakness found in institutional advertisements. Its effect is debilitating; it steals many millions of dollars in advertising effectiveness from well-meaning advertisers. Its presence indicates that something has gone wrong in the development of the advertising.

Vagueness starts at the beginning   The fault of vagueness in a finished advertisement can easily be traced to its origin. It starts at the very beginning of the advertising operation. It is not usually something picked up along the way.

It occurs because the men who are willing to spend hundreds of thousands of dollars, or more, for an advertising campaign are not *precisely sure* what they expect the advertising to do; they have not clearly *defined,* in their own minds, exactly what they are spending their dollars to buy.

In other words, they have not laid down a clear-cut *objective* for their campaign.

The Objective

The indispensable first step to successful institutional advertising is the establishment of a formal *objective.*

Such an objective should be carefully arrived at. It should be possible of achievement. It should be clearly understood and clearly stated in written words. Every effort should be made by the advertising to achieve it.

The objective is the means by which institutional advertising is made *purposeful.* It is the hard backbone of the advertising. In the production of this advertising, no other element is nearly so important. Without it, success is impossible.

Formulating the objective   The objective should be formulated in four steps:

1. A soul-searching self-examination on the part of the highest echelon of management concerned as to whether the advertising is needed in the first place.

2. If it *is* needed, management should estimate the size of the need and the cost. Measure the problem. Analyze it. Decide whether advertising is capable of solving it.

3. Decide what general direction the advertising should take and what it will be expected to accomplish.

4. Write down the objective on paper. Come to an agreement with all concerned as to whether it is correctly stated. Stick to it.

Why the objective should be written down   Putting the objective in a written statement does three desirable things:

1. It clarifies thinking. Just writing it down requires a definite expression of what is wanted.

2. It firms up the objective, states it, and protects it from trivial and damaging changes. It keeps everyone on the track—and also the advertising.

3. It becomes a "package"—easier to understand and easier to sell. And easier to work with in developing the advertising.

In the writing of the objective, a long, wordy statement invites ambiguity and opportunity for misunderstanding, and should be avoided. The objective should be stated succinctly in simple language, preferably in a single sentence.

If additional detail seems absolutely necessary, it should be put in separate, corollary *sub-objectives.*

An objective is not expected to tell *everything* about the proposed advertising. It is merely a statement of what the advertising is intended to accomplish.

This book contains a number of statements of objective, as formalized by specific companies. Some examples of these will be found on pages 38, 139, 164, 175 and elsewhere.

The importance of the objective   The objective, firmly established before any ads are produced, provides an antidote or preventative for the sickness of vagueness and indirectness. Guided by an objective, the advertising knows where to go, and it usually goes there. It does its work.

And because it does, it is likely to earn its keep. Vague, unclear advertisements do not. They waste the money spent on them.

As an additional bonus, a well-constructed objective acts as a springboard for agency creativeness. Instead of fumbling about, trying to guess what the client really wants, agency creative people are given what they like, a clear assignment. This enables them to devote all their creative talents to *dramatizing* the assigned job. The result is more exciting advertising—advertising that gives the advertiser much greater-than-usual value for his dollar.

Two

THE PROTECTIVE FUNCTION

The antagonism between business and government, at a height of bitterness during the New Deal period, has slowly subsided. In 1966, business and government appeared to be getting along together, if not perfectly, at least more smoothly than they had in more than thirty years. In fact, so great has been the change in climate, it is hard to recollect the controversial storminess of spirit that existed as recently as fifteen years ago.

But that spirit did exist. And, over the years, it has given rise to the creation of an enormous amount of institutional advertising. If the protective image-building that is part of many institutional programs today is included, it can be said that the involvement of business with government has probably resulted in the production of a larger volume of institutional advertising than any other single cause.

This advertising has been most evident at certain points of attrition between the forces of government and those of business. These have been:

1. Controversy over "public" versus "private" interests in the electric-light-and-power utility area

2. "Free enterprise" advertising

3. Advertising prompted by antitrust litigation

4. Protective image advertising, designed to forestall adverse governmental or political activity

In those cases where the advertising has been straightforward, with simple and clearly thought-out objectives, it has been surprisingly effective. When it has been devious, vague, or fuzzy-minded, it has yielded low-grade results.

Controversy in the Utility Area

There have been long-continued campaigns in the electric-light-and-power area, in which "investor-owned" and "consumer-owned" have vied for public attention, frequently in an atmosphere of cloak-and-dagger warfare. Although some individual advertisements have been striking in appearance, the overall force of this advertising has been vitiated by

Chapter 4

BUSINESS

VERSUS

GOVERNMENT

the air of secrecy and deviousness surrounding it. An average observer, untutored on the inside story of what the fight is really about, finds these ads puzzling and, eventually, something of a bore. Occasionally, some of these ads take on a strong "free enterprise" tinge.

"Free Enterprise" Advertising

The phrase, "free enterprise," was used, and lauded to the skies, perhaps hundreds of times in a flood of institutional advertising that reached a peak of volume about 1950.

Fortune editor William H. Whyte made a brilliant analysis of this advertising in his aptly titled book, *Is Anybody Listening?*[1] In this book, he first of all called attention to the costliness of the effort. The "free enterprise" crusade, he pointed out, was "accounting for at least $100,000,000 of industry's annual advertising, public relations, and employee relations expenditures."

Then he succinctly summarized its effectiveness in these words: "And it is not worth a damn."

It wasn't. For nobody listened. Except, perhaps, other "free enterprise" crusaders. They were talking to themselves.

Mr. Whyte put his finger on the essential weakness of the advertising, its lack of directness and clarity, when he noted that the businessmen involved were not quite sure *what* they were trying to communicate to their readers.

The *why*, the businessmen's own motivation, seemed obvious. They were worried about the long string of Democratic victories at the polls (this was before the election of President Eisenhower), and they hungered for a Republican victory. But *what* the advertising was trying to say lacked the obviousness and simplicity of the *why*.

Crusade in an echo chamber   Emphasis on the words *"free enterprise,"* the keynote of the advertising, and the attempt to sell the phrase to Americans was and is puzzling. That is, if taken at its apparent face value. For "free enterprise" was something most Americans supposed they already possessed, believed in, and had no intention of losing.

Now, however, it can be suspected that the phrase *free enterprise* had an entirely different meaning to the businessman than it did to his audience. To him it apparently meant *laissez faire,* the philosophy of business not being interfered with at all by government. Or so it would seem.

But the advertising did not say *that*. It did not say anything specific. It dealt in the vaguest of generalities, and its main thesis seemed slightly absurd.

[1] Simon & Schuster, Inc., New York, 1952.

Hence, the advertising failed to communicate. Nobody did anything. Nothing happened. The money spent merely circulated.

The failure, the wastefulness, of the advertising was *not* a result of the businessmen necessarily being wrong in wanting the Republican victory, or a removal of government restraints, or a return to "laissez-faire" old times. The failure arose from the businessmen *not saying* what they did want. They did not even state a case for themselves. If they had, they might have accomplished more.

Interpretation of the Antitrust Laws

The antitrust laws, originally intended to curb the monopolistic practices of the great trusts in the nineteenth century, were purposely drawn broadly and loosely, to give the government adequate powers for enforcement.

As a result, *interpretation* of the law became a matter of prime importance in each individual case. It is in this area of application and interpretation that government and big business have come into sharp collision. As commented upon by *Business Week*:[2] "Any law, of course, means what the courts say it means. But it's not just the courts that define antitrust law. Even more, antitrust law is written by the lawyers who, year after year, decide what cases to bring and how to prosecute them."

It was the nature of such interpretation that seemed to color, in the late 1940s and the 1950s, a series of spectacular antitrust prosecutions of the nation's largest corporations.

The Fear of Bigness

An underlying bone of contention surrounding these mid-century trials was *business bigness*. The trusts had once seemed especially menacing because of their size and power. Yet, individual corporations of the 1950s had grown to such a colossal size that the nineteenth century companies seemed like Pygmies in comparison. Furthermore, in size, the greatest corporations far overshadowed smaller competitors in their own industries.

Certain politico-economic thinkers, influential in government circles, saw in this bigness a dangerous and socially menacing "concentration of economic power." They directly equated bigness with *power* and, in turn, with inherent monopoly (or, on occasion, with monopoly's cousin, *oligopoly*—a sort of group monopoly). Bigness per se was viewed as monopolistic.

The concept, of course, was disputed by businessmen and by intellectual

[2] p. 161, Mar. 15, 1959.

writers who did not see bigness as a menace. The businessmen disclaimed any intent to monopolize, and held that bigness was not harmful, but natural, beneficial, and necessary in the vastly expanded world of the twentieth century.

Nevertheless, some of the country's biggest companies found themselves faced by antitrust actions. Two of these cases will be discussed in succeeding chapters. One case will demonstrate the power of straightforward and purposeful institutional advertising. The other will indicate the value of protective image-building in a political atmosphere.

Image—in a Political Climate

In producing their free-enterprise advertisements, the industrial leaders showed a surprising unawareness of the mass voting public they were trying to influence. Although not as bitterly hostile as it had been a few years before, this public, at the time, was still sullen, unfriendly, and suspicious. Its image of business was negative. It was not in a mood to be propagandized. To have succeeded, the advertising would have had to be almost miraculously persuasive. When it relied on an incomprehensible abstraction, no impression was made whatever.

Numerous researches have shown a progressive improvement in the general public's overall image of business, ranging from the outright hostility of the 1930s, through an era of cold suspicion during the 1940s and 1950s, to a relative friendliness and approval in the more prosperous 1960s. But the favorable regard remains diluted by a pervasive apathy, and very little knowledge of the workings of business, particularly big business.

Later, the concept of image will be discussed at length. One point about it, however, should be made here and now. That is, while the value of the image concept may be open to some question when applied to product-selling, there is no doubt of its potency in the *political* arena. In the atmosphere of politics, image is all-important. For politics itself is nothing if not the art of imagery.

In a political atmosphere, image takes oversimplified and primitive forms, understandable to uneducated people. To borrow from the terminology of the television Western, it is likely to be either the image of a "bad guy," who can do no good, or of a "good guy," who can do nothing bad.

The bad guy image, fastened on business during the depression, has lingered long and has had much to do with business's difficulties with those who seek votes from the public. Business's poor image made it a natural choice for a political scapegoat.

For individual corporations, notably those larger ones operating in a political atmosphere or under political controls, the maintenance of a favorable image is a matter of prime importance. Instances of how such an image can be built will be given in later chapters.

In September, 1949, the Department of Justice, charging monopolistic practices, filed an antitrust civil suit against the Great Atlantic & Pacific Tea Company. The suit asked:

- That the 6,000-store chain be split up into seven separately owned retail businesses
- That the New York A&P holding company be forced to separate its manufacturing and processing business from its buying and selling operations
- That the Atlantic Commission Company of New York, a produce wholesaling-and-sales firm, be dissolved

The suit was launched with "a flurry of statements by prosecution and defence, discanting on the respective wickedness and uprightness of the defendants." [1]

Normally, the case would then have settled down quietly to a routine courtroom action. But in this case, precedent was shattered. Within a week, A&P launched a series of full-page ads in 2,000 daily and weekly newspapers, denying the government charges of monopoly and assailing the "antitrust lawyers from Washington." Oversize posters in the A&P stores reiterated the same story.

The intent of the campaign was to protect retail sales through the preservation of public confidence in the integrity of A&P. The company justified its course by calling attention to the publicity "handed out" by the government lawyers "giving in detail their 'allegations' against the company . . . charges that would seriously endanger our business, if they were believed by the public."

The campaign continued for a little less than a year. Direct, hard-hitting advertisements kept hammering away on a basic theme. "Do You Want Your A&P Put Out of Business?" they asked the public. "Do You Want Higher Prices?" "Who Will Be Hurt?"

The public apparently found the answers quickly. Before long, reports came of thousands of letters

Chapter **5**

PROTECTIVE

INSTITUTIONAL

ADVERTISING

IN ACTION

[1] M. A. Adelman, *A&P, a Study in Price-cost Behavior and Public Policy,* Harvard University Press, Cambridge, 1959.

being received strongly criticising the Justice Department's attempt to break up the A&P. As noted in *Printers' Ink:* "Coming from all classes, they indicate most people are more interested in A&P's influence on prices than in pre-election anti-trust suits. Many are drawn in by full-page advertisements telling the chain's story in forceful, easy-to-read English."

More significant, in view of the campaign's objective, was that A&P's sales, during the advertising period, rose 4 million dollars a week above those of the previous year, whereas general retail-grocery sales were off 7 per cent. And the gain was made despite the diversion of a good deal of newspaper space from product-selling to this non-selling institutional copy.

The case dragged on, for more than four years. Finally, in January, 1954, *Printers' Ink* announced:

> The Department of Justice has closed up its case against A&P.
>
> Backing down on earlier demands that the A&P chain be broken up into seven smaller chains and divorced completely from the manufacturing end of the business, Justice has settled for one act of divestiture . . . A&P is left with its retailing and manufacturing operations intact; only its produce-purchasing arm is lopped off.

Example of Successful Institutional Advertising

Though not totally untouched, A&P did well in its court case. The great corporation was *not* dismembered.

Its advertising was more completely successful. It fully met its objective. It counteracted the adverse effect of the government charges, thereby protecting sales, which went up instead of down. It now appears that it also did something more, something perhaps unpremeditated, yet extremely valuable to the company.

It acted powerfully to change a bad image of the company into a good one.

For years, the large grocery chains, particularly A&P, had been harried by organized associations of smaller competitors. In fact, in this very case, one of these groups had petitioned the government for an investigation of the company.

During the sympathetic early New Deal years,[2] these opponents of A&P managed to fasten on that company, as well as other big chains, the image of a greedy, monopoly-hungry, chain-store monster devouring small businesses. This negative image invited numerous political brickbats.

A&P's antitrust advertising campaign counteracted the derogatory image

[2] For an illuminating presentation of the somewhat ironic relations of the small businessmen and the New Deal, see John H. Bunzel, *The American Small Businessman,* Alfred A. Knopf, Inc., New York, 1962.

with an entirely new one, appealing to a new and larger audience—the price-conscious consumer. The new image pictured the company as a public bene-factor, providing food for all at lower prices than would be possible otherwise.

It was the great triumph and achievement of this campaign—lasting as it did less than a year—that it made the new image stick. Its keynote proposition, "If A&P is put out of business, *Your Food Will Cost More!*" evidently was accepted by the public, who now saw A&P as a friend.

In the public consciousness, the old ogre image of the company faded and the organized efforts to maintain it lost steam. It also lost political potency. Attacks from the political rostrum became fewer.

The new image exerted a protective influence that has continued to this day. After a long period of storm, the great company's public relations entered a sunnier era of relative peace. Other great chains also benefited.

The changing of a corporate image from bad to good, as we shall see in a later chapter, is not as simple or as easy to achieve as is sometimes supposed. In this instance, the task was colossal. That it was accomplished, in such a relatively limited period of time and with such long-lasting benefits, has made this A&P campaign a classic example of institutional advertising success.

No other single campaign has demonstrated as dramatically as this one the *effectiveness* of institutional advertising in fulfilling a difficult, but vitally needed corporate objective.

Why the campaign was effective The A&P institutional campaign was prepared by Carl Byoir and placed by Paris & Peart. Its success was largely due to the masterly conception, planning, and execution of the advertisements by this team.

Five reasons can be given for the campaign's effectiveness:

1. *It was completely purposeful.* It had a clear objective ("to protect retail sales through the preservation of public confidence in the integrity of A&P") and it went right to work to do its job in the most straightforward way possible.

2. *It was brilliantly written for its purpose.*

3. *Its message was presented in an easy-to-grasp News format.*

4. *It sold a powerful idea,* which happened to contain a compelling benefit.

5. *The volume of the advertising was adequate to do the job.* The advertisements were big enough, appeared frequently enough, and reached enough of the right people to do the job assigned to the campaign.

Effective institutional writing The writing of this campaign was a major factor in its success. It still stands out because of its stark simplicity and directness. Every single word was to the point. In spite of the controversial subject it discussed, the copy dodged no issues. Indeed, it met them with a candidness that was in itself disarming.

The skillfully persuasive text exerted a strong pull on the emotions, yet the wording always remained cool and logical. It wanted to sound reasonable and it did.

To appreciate the calm, but powerful persuasiveness of this writing, it will be worthwhile to follow some of the copy down through one of the kick-off ads of the campaign:

DO YOU WANT YOUR A&P
PUT OUT OF BUSINESS?

Last Thursday in New York, the anti-trust lawyers from Washington filed a suit to put A&P out of business.

They asked the court to order us to get rid of most of our stores and also the manufacturing facilities which supply you with A&P coffee, Ann Page products, Jane Parker baked goods, and other quality items we produce.

This would mean higher prices for you. It would mean less food on every dinner table and fewer dollars in every pay envelope.

It would mean the end of A&P as you know it.

This poses a basic question for the American people: Do they want to continue to enjoy lower prices and better living? Or do they want to break up A&P and pay higher prices, and have lower living standards?

What do *you* want?

Dropping down to a smaller type-size, the text goes on to describe the anti-trust laws in primer fashion, saying:

These are good laws. They were passed about fifty years ago to prevent any company, or any group of companies, from getting a monopoly in a field and then raising prices to the public. A&P has never done any of these things.

On the contrary:

This whole attack rises out of the fact that we sell good food too cheap. We would not have had any of this trouble if, instead of lowering prices, we had raised them and pocketed the difference.

To explain why the "anti-trust lawyers" should go to the courts, the text fills in a motive:

Obviously, it is the theory of the anti-trust lawyers . . . that any big business must be destroyed simply because it is big, and even if the public gets hurt in the process.

The copy follows with informative specifics indicating the savings instituted by A&P. A subhead reiterates "Do you want higher prices?" Then the copy concludes by picturing the government as attacking, not really the A&P, but the reader himself:

But we believe this attack is a threat to millions of consumers who rely on us for quality foods at low prices; to farmers who rely on us for fast, low-cost distribution of their products; and to our loyal employees.

Note how the copy uses short, simple words, to make itself understandable to *any* A&P customer who might be able to read at all. With this primer style it nevertheless manages to discuss, quite clearly, a subject as abstruse as the antitrust laws—a remarkable writing feat.

Easy to read, easy to see: News   Just as the wording was simplified for easier readership, the visual treatment was simplified to make the ads easy to *see*.

The all-text messages were presented in an uncomplicated *News* format. The big-type headlines could be read 10 feet away. The text type was large, and spaced openly, making it exceptionally readable, even to someone with weak eyes. Layouts were orderly, without clutter. The advertisements lacked somewhat in aesthetic quality, which, however, was of little value. What was substituted for it was something much more important—*clarity.*

It is well known that the quality of *News* in an advertisement is a great interest-catcher. These ads had that quality in abundance. They *were* news. When they first appeared in the inner pages of newspapers, the very fact of their appearance was often reported on the first page of the same newspaper. The newsworthiness of the campaign increased its attention-value, its penetration, and, ultimately, its success.

An idea with a hook   This campaign sold an idea, one with a powerful benefit-punishment proposition—*"Your Food Will Cost More,* if A&P is put out of business." It struck right at the pocketbook nerve.

Most institutional advertising is not blessed with such a forceful, thoroughly believable proposition. But A&P had it, and made the most of it. Each ad was built around it, it was repeated again and again, and the reader was never allowed to forget it. It was a trump card. A&P played it hard to win. And did.

The A&P Campaign and Other Institutional Advertising

No two institutional situations are exactly alike. The A&P campaign differs from most other institutional campaigns in two important respects. Both its quality of exceptional *news,* and its powerful benefit-proposition, are characteristics that occur either rarely or in diluted form in the institutional area. As a result, *most* institutional advertisers are forced to find other means of creating interest and achieving objectives.

When an institutional advertiser *does* have a strong benefit to offer—or can imbue his campaign with the quality of *news—he should certainly make the most of these valuable assets,* as did A&P.

The writers of the A&P campaign did not have to worry about institutional advertising's obligation to be interesting. Their story was steeped in *news,* which is itself eminently interesting.

Conclusions

The A&P campaign demonstrates the *power* of institutional advertising in achieving a protective objective.

It also demonstrates that the key to *effectiveness* can be found in candidness, directness, and simplicity of approach. These qualities can be applied advantageously to all forms of institutional advertising.

To creative men, a study of the writing style should be rewarding.

Three

PROTECTIVE IMAGE-BUILDING

At approximately the same period that the A&P was fighting its epic battle with the "anti-trust lawyers from Washington," another great company was faced with a similar suit seeking its dismemberment. This was the American Telephone and Telegraph Company, and the suit sought to divorce from the Bell Telephone System its vitally important manufactoring subsidiary, the Western Electric Company, even though that subsidiary had been part of the Bell System since 1881.

Unlike the publicly contentious A&P case, this litigation was conducted quietly. The subject was not mentioned in Bell System advertising, and seldom referred to in the press. After six years, the company emerged with a consent decree that left it untarnished, if not altogether untouched. According to *Business Week*, February 4, 1956: "The anti-trust consent decree against the American Telephone & Telegraph Company, hailed last week by government attorneys as 'a major victory,' turned out on second look to be hardly more than a slap on the wrist for the biggest corporation in the world. . . ."

Western Electric was required to divest itself of a few subsidiary activities. But that company itself was *not* split off from AT&T, nor was it dismembered into three parts, as the suit originally asked. The Bell System's reputation suffered little if any damage from the suit. Its only real punishment was the tiring, costly, and time-and-energy-consuming suit itself.

Although advertising played no active role during the actual trying of the case, it must not be assumed that the force of advertising was absent. It was very much present, and its contribution was to surround the company's good name with a protective mantle.

For the advertising had already run in advance—massively—for more than half a century. From the very beginning (one of the first advertisements, in 1908, even included the word *monopoly*), the Bell System's informative advertising had been clearly designed to help the company defend itself in a permanent political atmosphere that might often be hostile.

Chapter **6**

BUILDING

A LONG-TERM

PROTECTIVE

IMAGE

The need for such a defense was real. The System had to get its rates and charges approved by numerous rate-making commissions which, by their very nature, were ever sensitive to the local and national political scene. In the early years, Bell Telephone's status as a monopoly (which it was indeed, though necessarily and in a limited sense) had to be defended frequently. Later, when the System had grown very large, it had to face the attack on bigness.

A Pioneer in Corporate-image Advertising

Long, long before the term *corporate image* had even been dreamed of, the forward-looking leaders of the telephone company set out to build for their enterprise a favorable popular image that, if it could be made strong enough, might well act as a stout buffer when political winds blew adversely. This would require an advertising effort continuing for years.

The first and foremost job of the advertising was to make friends with the American public and to keep that public friendly. In the first year or two, the company's early attempts at friendliness occasionally faltered and stumbled a bit, because it could not resist a curious propensity to scold and preach. But this aberration was evidently noted, for it was speedily corrected, and the advertising henceforth stayed close to its objective of making friends.

With ever-increasing skill, Bell's ad-makers soon succeeded in picturing the company as friendly and neighborly, and everlastingly *people*-conscious. They told how its linemen went out in raging blizzards to keep communications going, how its operators remained at their posts during floods and other disasters, and how its employees were discovered doing nice things for children, or taking a neighborly part in community activities.

The telephone company not only liked people, and wanted to be liked *by* people, it *was* people (2,800,000 ordinary-folk stockholders—more than three-quarters of a million good-citizen employees). It stood for the old American virtues, for grassroots democracy. It loved to run and rerun (with new faces) its famous "Up from the ranks" advertisement, portraying the dozen or more Bell company presidents *all* of whom started their careers at low wages at the bottom of the ladder.

From time to time in its advertising, the company seemed to take the public into its confidence—told how the Bell System worked, and, of course, why it was so valuable to everybody. In its neighborly manner, it managed to speak frankly, without offending, even about such difficult subjects as rates and taxes and finances.

The voice with a smile   Bell Telephone's face was forever clean and bright, its clothes were always neat and brushed. It was *very* respectable. Yet it was human and friendly. And its invincible motto was the oft-repeated headline of its greatest advertisement: *The Voice with a Smile.*

Patiently, persistently, year after year, the telephone company continued with its image-building. And as it did, the image grew stronger, more solid, more real. Furthermore, the company added immense power to the advertising by living up to its own self-created image. It kept out of trouble, improved its service, trained its people to be courteous and pleasant—tried hard to be a good neighbor in fact.

Gradually, the public began to view the telephone company as somewhat different from most other big companies. Other corporations retained the villain-visage. *They* were mentally linked with sinister Wall Street manipulators, were seen as greedy and predatory, and were noted to be continually in trouble with the government. But the telephone company was not usually seen that way. It had become a "good guy."

The power of image in a political atmosphere There is no doubt that *The Voice with a Smile* had lasting popular appeal. Its popularity, in turn, conferred a measure of political prestige. By the time the antitrust actions materialized, AT&T's image had developed into a protective aura.

Hence, when the trial came, and possessing, as the result indicated, an obviously good case, the AT&T lawyers could well afford to conduct their action quietly and without publicity fanfare.

Western Electric Advertising

Assisting in AT&T's protective advertising program was the advertising of its subsidiary companies, most notably, Western Electric. In advertising continued over many years, Western Electric had strongly emphasized its identity with the Bell System, and had constantly endeavored to explain and elucidate, and quietly justify, its overall function as manufacturing-and-supply unit of the System.

Public Relations Advertising

The American Telephone and Telegraph Company is clearly the largest institutional advertiser. Its annual expenditure, reported to be $69,900,000 in 1965,[1] can be considered as devoted totally to *non-product* advertising. For AT&T has no product to sell to the general public. One does not *buy* his telephone. What the company provides is a *service.*

[1] According to *Advertising Age,* Aug. 29, 1966.

Of course, some of the advertising has a commercial motivation in that it promotes greater usage of the company's service in various ways, thereby contributing to revenue and profits. But the considerable remaining part of the advertising is devoted primarily to corporate purposes, and *all* the advertising, whether usage-increasing or not, takes part in the corporate image-building.

The Bell System's advertising has been described as *public relations advertising*. Here the term is entirely fitting. The objectives, over and above the usage-building section of the copy, are public relations objectives. The careful image-building, the politeness, the low-pressure selling of ideas, the patient repetition of basic themes, the people-conscious manner, and the beaming of the corporate story to the System's many different publics are earmarks of an essentially public-relations point of view.

This is also advertising, and started as advertising at a time when the art of public relations was in its earliest infancy. Today, it is notable that this company's advertising and public relations operations, both exceptionally large, dovetail together in an efficient, cooperative, smooth-working organization.

The advertisements   AT&T's ads are characteristically neat, clean, and orderly in appearance. Layouts are simple and uncluttered. Most often, they consist of a large squared-off picture, headline, and rectangular block of copy. This is perhaps the most basic layout possible—and has been called by advertising creative men, "N. W. Ayer No. 1," because of its early traditional association with that agency.

The format of this advertising has changed very little, and then only gradually, over the years. In the past decade, the photographic illustration has grown a little larger and the text copy a little smaller, following the trend of the times. The spirit remains unchanged.

A peculiarity of AT&T magazine advertising has been its consistent predilection for black-and-white photography, and its apparent reluctance to use full color except to meet a special need, such as portraying color telephones. Evidently, the lower cost of black and white, permitting purchase of a greater number of messages, is an important element in the company's media philosophy.

Though adequately interesting, the Bell advertisements are seldom individually spectacular. They seem to avoid any excess of cleverness or artiness, preferring to stick to their job of carrying out the System's solid, well-understood objectives.

In this respect, the individual advertisements can be compared to building bricks in a towering structure. There are many of them, all with a strong "family resemblance," and they come with a relentless continuity, year after year.

"I can't get my brother's pants over his shoes!"

The young man had a problem. He was quite serious about it as he dialed the telephone operator.

"What's wrong?" she asked.

"Nobody's home and I can't get my brother's pants on over his shoes!"

"Why don't you try taking off his shoes and *then* putting on his pants?" the operator gently suggested.

There was a long pause, some heavy breathing, then finally, "Gee, that works swell! Thanks."

* * *

This little story is true. And it tells something of the spirit that thousands of telephone people bring along with them to their work each day.

There are no written rules in the Bell System on how to assist bewildered small boys, or others in need of some neighborly service that falls in our line.

We just try to be helpful. We don't *always* succeed—but we try.

 BELL TELEPHONE SYSTEM
Owned by more than two million Americans

Bell Telephone System advertisements work continuously to build a favorable public image of the telephone company. The company's existence is dependent on public goodwill. Advertising is friendly, neighborly, people-conscious. (AGENCY: *N. W. Ayer & Son*)

Together, they have created a bulwark of public goodwill that has been invaluable to the company on many occasions.

To estimate the ultimate value of this advertising, it is necessary to think of the numerous times, since 1908, when the political atmosphere was actively hostile to big business, and then speculate on what might have happened to the now largest corporation in the world if this advertising had not run at all.

Chapter 7

POWER OF THE

INFORMATIVE

APPROACH

A feeling of serene calm pervades the beautiful forest land portrayed for years in the advertisements of the Weyerhaeuser Company. A deer stares silently at the reader from behind a clump of rhododendron, against a panoramic background of majestic mountains. A family of raccoons warm themselves on a tree stump in the late afternoon sun. Bright-colored waterfowl glide across a mirror-surfaced lake.

There is something intrinsically restful and attractive in these idyllic pictures of the happy wonderland of nature, found in the timberlands of the Pacific Northwest. Requests to the Weyerhaeuser Company for reprints of the pictures have amounted to more than 1,000 a month for many years.

Yet, in reality, the atmosphere surrounding an important wood-products company in the Northwest timberlands has not been quite as calm and peaceful as this. Instead, the clash of opposing interests, demands for increased conservation, ideological dissension, and the threat of political harassment have swirled through and around the lumber lands like angry storm winds. The lumberman has often found himself the target of attack.

To many people, the wood industry's image was that of a wicked lumber baron, a ruthless destroyer, robbing the country of its natural resources. What was remembered particularly was the old time cut-and-move logger, the denuding of the countryside, and the wasteful lumber practices that made use of only a small percentage of the fallen tree. There was an increasing demand for Federal regulation of all timberland. It seemed that before long the lumbermen would have cut down the last tree, and there would be no more.

But in 1952—when the Weyerhaeuser advertising started—that company had embarked on a course far different from the old methods of wholesale destruction. It had already developed a comprehensive program that had been in operation for more than ten years. It was now time to tell the public about it, employing institutional advertising.

How to Have One's Cake and Eat It, Too. The Tree Farm

Actually, the more progressive companies in the wood-products business have been ahead of most of their critics. For one thing, having grown big, acquired large areas of timberland, and developed an extensive wood-products industry, they were the first to appreciate that their supply of wood must be permanently continuous, if they were to remain in business. They could not afford to have the forests become extinct.

Mineral resources can be exhausted, but a tree is a living thing. It can reproduce itself, many times. Why not reforest? If this were done effectively, the industry could have its cake and eat it, too—by making a cake that grew faster than it could be eaten.

Guided by European experience, a comprehensive concept of tree farming emerged. Tree farming came to mean not only replacing cut-down trees with new seedlings, but treating the whole forest as a farm and growing, managing, and harvesting timber as a *crop*.

By means of the tree farm, a permanent supply of timber could be assured. With enough tree farms, the nation would never run out of timber. At the same time, the forest could be utilized fully, yielding multiple benefits. In addition to lumber, it would produce other forest products and provide recreational facilities, stabilization of water supplies, forage for livestock, and a haven for wildlife. And the forest area could be increased to meet the needs of future generations.

Weyerhaeuser. Tree-farm Problems

The Weyerhaeuser Timber Company, as it was then named, pioneered the tree-farm movement in America with the establishment of its 143,000-acre Clemons Tree Farm in Washington state in 1941.[1] Since then, other units of the timber industry have followed suit. Today, tree farming is a confirmed Weyerhaeuser practice. In 1964, this company planted nearly 12 million seedlings, in addition to which 650 million seeds were sown by helicopter.

The harvest cycle for trees varies from 40 to 120 years. That a tree farm can be possible at all is due to the large timberland holdings of the big companies. Maintenance of such a farm is very expensive and represents a heavy investment in the future. Consequently, the wood industry is highly sensitive to the dangers of governmental interference or of heavy tax pressures that may make the enterprise economically impossible.

The management of a tree farm is far from simple. It presents amazingly

[1] Now grown to 365,668 acres.

complex problems. The natural enemies of the forest—insects, disease, animals, wind, and fire—take a bigger annual toll of trees than do the axes and saws of the lumbermen. A hurricane can cause fantastic havoc, requiring emergency logging of fallen trees to forestall the additional danger of fire.

All this is costly and must be paid for out of the sale of wood products. It represents a continuing expense and investment that will require more than a century to come to full fruition. At the same time, the program promises increasing and immensely valuable benefits not only to the company and the timber industry, but to the nation as well.

In 1952, when mounting political pressure began to threaten the economic basis of this constructive undertaking, the Weyerhaeuser Company decided to pioneer a second time—by publicizing, not only for itself, but for its industry as well, the story of tree farming in an *informative* advertising campaign.

That is, its advertising would be based on *informing* the public about the company's business. In order to hold the public's attention, the advertising was required to be highly *interesting*.

The Weyerhaeuser Advertising Campaign

In addition to protecting its business, the company had something else to gain from such a campaign. Weyerhaeuser sold lumber and plywood products and was diversifying into other areas, including shipping containers, folding cartons, fine papers, etc. Weyerhaeuser was a large company, but it was almost unknown to the general public, and it would benefit from increased name-publicity at a time when it was entering a wider market.

It was hoped that a public-minded campaign would create an image of responsibility and a name-reputation that would assist the company in selling its varied products.

Objectives   The original objectives were:

1. To explain tree farms fully, since the public was ignorant about tree farming

2. To encourage all owners of forest lands, including farmers, to join in the tree-farm movement

3. To make it known that the forest industry, through research and engineering, is making considerable progress toward complete utilization of the timber crop

4. To help stabilize markets and speed the marketing of newly developed products

DOE AND FAWN near a rhododendron, Washington state flower. Wildlife is so abundant on many tree farms that game officials cooperate to keep the population from outstripping its food supply. This also reduces damage to young trees.

trees for tomorrow grow on managed timberlands today

A living mantle of young trees grows on Weyerhaeuser timberlands, obscuring stumps left from earlier harvests. Each tree is needed to supply wood for forest products to serve future generations.

As new trees replace the old on our lands, they begin another cycle in a long-range forestry plan. The plan is built around the concept that forests can both be used and perpetuated. Properly managed and protected, timber can be harvested and replaced in repeated crops. This fact is proved on our tree farms year after year.

A tree farm is a living, dynamic forest unit. From it comes a flow of benefits important to man. Foremost is the wood itself, for this versatile raw material is used in lumber, plywood, pulp, paper... some 5,000 products in all. Other benefits include payrolls, water, wildlife and recreation. Each of these values is being perpetuated on our timberlands by careful forest management. *Write us at Box A, Tacoma,Wn.,for booklet,* **Forest Products from Tree Farm to You.**

 Weyerhaeuser Company

Animals and tree-farmed forest land provide fascinating picture subjects for Weyerhaeuser Company corporate advertising. Copy, telling the story of tree farming, has a protective and image-building purpose. (AGENCY: *Cole & Weber*)

The basic theme was the tree farm and its benefits, especially the benefits of forest management to the national scene. The first advertisement appeared in January, 1952. In 1966, the campaign was still running.

Setting the creative theme   The creative theme was based on a simple idea—"the way to get people interested in trees is to get them into the woods." And this is what the ads succeeded in doing.

Rightly, the great woods of the West were believed to be interesting and romantic to many people. At the time, it seemed impossible to capture this romance with photography, so a very realistic, yet nostalgic art style was devised and adhered to, although there were three artists. The artwork was colorful, slightly formalized in technique, and very successful. Providing a consistent look year after year, the art merited much credit for the success of the campaign.

Each picture included a sympathetically presented representative of forest wildlife—animal, bird, or fish—or *families* of animals or birds. But the real hero of every illustration was the great forest, whether seen in intimate close-up or in distant, sweeping grandeur.

The campaign was developed by the Tacoma agency of Cole & Weber. The ads maintained an air of polite niceness and a simple, low-pressure approach to their job of explaining tree farming. Occasionally they pleaded for "a proper tax climate," saying that "improper tax laws can destroy forests as surely as can forest fires." Some of the headlines were:

GROWING THE NATION'S WOOD SUPPLY ON TREE FARMS

FIRE WEATHER . . . A TIME FOR CARE AND VIGILANCE IN THE FOREST

MANY NEW TREES WHERE ONE GREW BEFORE

HIGH WINDS AND INSECTS ARE FOREST ENEMIES

WATER . . . ONE OF THE ABUNDANT RESOURCES OF WESTERN TREE FARMS

Effectiveness of the advertising   The campaign must be considered highly successful. Millions of people have learned about tree farming *and associate it with Weyerhaeuser*. The timber industry has been given a new defense and a new image. The political-and-governmental-relations benefits to Weyerhaeuser have been considerable, with the company's supporters in government strengthened.

An excellent overall corporate image has been built for Weyerhaeuser. And as a bonus, the once unknown company has made its name so well known that it is now a potent factor in assisting the sales of Weyerhaeuser products.

The Power of Informative Advertising

The Weyerhaeuser campaign is an outstanding example of the *informative* approach to an institutional problem. The informative advertiser *educates* the public to see his side of a controversial situation. He leans on information, rather than on selling argument.

To succeed, informative advertising must meet some basic requirements:

1. It must be sound. If the information is false or misleading, the deception will be found out and the advertising will backfire.

2. The advertising *must* be interesting. It must attract and hold attention.

3. It must be more unselfish than most other advertising. It must give the reader his money's worth—must be *generous* in giving him the information *he* wants to know about and not be confined *solely* to the sales pitch the company wants to get across. It must be genuinely educational.

This type of advertising, well done, has a peculiar penetrating power. It works. It is remembered. It has a definite cumulative effect. This is because many people are hungry for interesting, significant information and respond gratefully when it is proffered generously.

Furthermore, these people usually turn out to be the intelligent, alert, and influential members of the community who are best known as opinion-leaders. They are just the ones whose social influence can be extremely valuable to a company with a problem like that of Weyerhaeuser.

Chapter 8

It has long been a basic public relations concept that a corporation deals with not one, but a number of "publics." These are sizeable groups of people with whom the corporation has contact. Each has its own separate interests in the company, and as a result, the company finds it must usually approach each public in a different way from other groups.

A fairly typical and basic list of publics for an average large corporation might probably include:

1. Consumers, or customers
2. Stockholders
3. Employees
4. Suppliers
5. Community neighbors
6. Financiers
7. The government
8. Distributors and dealers

Not all corporations and businesses are constituted the same way, so that the lists of publics can differ somewhat. For example, in addition to those just listed, there are also such publics as *policyholders, agents, brokers, specifiers* and *prescribers,* unknown *influentials, editors* and *journalists,* and *potential employees.* There are *educational* publics and *international* publics. And so on. With the growing complexity of business, new publics come into being from time to time.

Institutional advertising is being increasingly employed by corporations to address its publics. One factor helping to make this feasible, in terms of cost, is that institutional advertising, cleverly written, can often be directed at several publics at the same time. Or can be combined with a degree of product-selling.

There are two publics to which institutional advertising of a protective nature has been addressed. These two publics are not *of* the corporation, yet know the corporation well and rub shoulders with it every day. Their importance lies in their power to interpret the corporation to the outside world, especially at critical moments. One of these is the company's *suppliers*. The other public is its *community neighbors*—the people who live in the towns where the company plants are located.

Who Are the Suppliers?

Although the nation's largest corporations have the facilities to manufacture anything they need, they nevertheless often find it more economical, or otherwise desirable, to purchase special items from others. In fact, these large companies buy mountains of such items—component parts, machines, fabricated and semi-fabricated materials, etc.—from thousands of suppliers.

Some of the suppliers are big companies, but most of them are likely to be quite small. At various times it was reported that the United States Steel Corporation had 54,000 suppliers; General Electric, 42,000; Western Electric, 40,000; Du Pont, 30,000; and General Motors, 26,000.

The large manufacturers need their many suppliers. Very often, an effective teamwork results, with the manufacturer contributing its expert engineering assistance to help the supplier produce a better product.

The Supplier As a Small Businessman

That major manufacturers call on such *large numbers* of suppliers for assistance is significant from a public relations point of view. The suppliers, mostly small businesses scattered all over the country, constitute an important public.

Also, the typical supplier happens to be a special kind of animal, called *the small businessman*. As such, along with 4 million others, he was discovered long ago by politicians and has become a political force.

And by the same token, the small businessman has discovered the politicians. He has his own organizations and an effective lobby in Washington to advance his cause with legislators and administrators. And, as John Bunzel has indicated in his study of the small businessman,[1] the composite of that businessman, and most certainly his lobbying organizations, have no great love for big business.

Hence, large corporations have good reason to attempt to maintain the best possible relations with their supplier public. In daily operations they need the supplier's assistance and cooperation. They try to woo him away from the influence of his ideological proponents. And they particularly hope to avoid the detrimental government pressures which may be politically motivated to "do something for the small businessman."

[1] *The American Small Businessman*, Alfred A. Knopf, Inc., New York, 1962.

In the middle 1950s and later, major defense contractors, among them General Motors, Chrysler, Boeing, Douglas, and others, were under Federal pressure to extend subcontracting to small business to a much greater degree than the prime contractor companies thought wise, or wanted to do.

In a Senate subcommittee hearing, it was charged that the prime contractors tended to deal only with a limited number of companies, preferring to deal with large companies and discriminating against small businesses. The contractors denied the charge of discrimination and declared that a substantial number of their subcontracts went to small business.

The General Motors Supplier Campaign

In view of this background, and at a time when the drive against bigness had only begun to lessen in intensity, the motivation of General Motors' corporate advertising campaign in 1957 appears less mysterious than it might have otherwise.

The double-spread magazine campaign was directed primarily at General Motors' 26,000 suppliers and their 12 million employees and neighbors. Unquestionably, the first objective of the campaign was to protect and improve relations with the current suppliers, and also to attract new ones.

But it is obvious that General Motors hoped that others would read the advertisements. Otherwise, why should the ads appear in broad-circulation national magazines, instead of local-supplier town newspapers?

If the prime audience was intended to be the supplier public, the copy was nevertheless attractively written to engage the interest of other publics. One of these, apparently, was the broad general public at large. Another, not impossibly, might have been legislators in Washington who would be able to appreciate the widespread impact of the campaign.

All would read the same words. Yet to each public, the words could carry a separate and individual significance.

A typical General Motors supplier advertisement   One ad, typical of the series, had the headline:

HOW THE KOSTRZEWA FAMILY MADE AN
OLD AMERICAN DREAM COME TRUE

The text copy began:

> No matter where you or your family comes from, the old tradition still holds true. This country can be your "land of opportunity"—provided, of course, you're willing to make it so.
>
> At least this is the fervent opinion of Val Kostrzewa, late of our armed forces,

and his dad, Joseph, late of a little town in Poland, who founded the flourishing B&K Tool and Die Company of Saginaw, Michigan.

Ever since he first landed in this country the senior Kostrzewa had yearned for a business of his own. Inspired his son to the same viewpoint.

The text then went on to say how the Kostrzewas bought a turret lathe and started a business. After some mishaps, they started to grow and proved they could meet the requirements of GM's Saginaw Steering Gear Division. Soon they won more and more GM orders, until they had a million-dollar business.

What has happened in Saginaw, Michigan, has happened in hundreds of towns and cities all over the United States.

The caption under a large picture of the Kostrzewa family:

GROWING FAMILY WITH A GROWING BUSINESS—the Kostrzewas of Saginaw, Michigan, whose B&K Tool and Die Company has grown from a "long chance" to a prosperous reality. (Left to right standing: Judith, Val, Mrs. Joseph, Joseph; seated; Kathy, Mrs. Val with Lynne Denise, Connie and Val, Jr.)

Each of the advertisements in the series was a case history of this type. Each case was a Horatio Alger story of success, both for the supplier and his community. Each involved a supplier with less than 500 employees, and the locale was usually a small town. Some of the other headlines were:

HOW A LITTLE WISCONSIN VILLAGE GAVE ITSELF A
BIG BOOST WITH SOME HELP FROM GENERAL MOTORS

WHAT A MODERN MOUNTAINEER HAS DONE FOR
HIS OLD KENTUCKY HOME TOWN

HOW A "SWITCH IN TIME" FOR GENERAL MOTORS
BROUGHT SUCCESS TO A SMALL BUSINESS

HOW MODERN TEAMWORK PAYS OFF
IN AN OLD ONION WAREHOUSE

Of course, General Motors linked itself to the success stories, but it pointedly gave the big credit to the small businessman. It used words and phrases he liked to use himself, and it recognized his aspirations as an individualist. It lauded his independence and initiative. And it pointed out that of its 26,000 suppliers, 22,500 were truly small businesses.

A "people" campaign   This was a *people* campaign, not only in subject and wording, but especially in its illustrations. These were natural, everyday photographs of real people, *very real*. There were no professional models. Photographers were sent out to take pictures of actual people with names, where they lived or worked, and just as they looked. The resulting ads had freshness and interest. It is still apparent in tear sheets viewed years later.

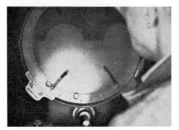

CHECK AND DOUBLE CHECK—B&K expert using comparator to determine accuracy of die for General Motors Safety Power Steering.

How the Kostrzewa family made an old American dream come true

GM BUSINESS—Joseph (in shirt sleeves), Steve Bugai (second from right) and Val (seated right), with top B&K executives, check over new order from Saginaw Steering Gear Division of General Motors.

COOKIE CAMPAIGNERS—Julius Becker, Secretary and Treasurer of B&K, with group of Saginaw Girl Scouts. Typical of company's community interest is Becker's heading up annual cookie and calendar sale.

No MATTER where you or your family comes from, the old tradition still holds true. This country can be your "land of opportunity"—provided, of course, you're willing to make it so.

At least this is the fervent opinion of Val Kostrzewa, late of our armed forces, and his dad, Joseph, late of a little town in Poland, who founded the flourishing B&K Tool and Die Company of Saginaw, Michigan.

Risking a "Nest Egg"

EVER SINCE he first landed in this country the senior Kostrzewa had yearned for a business of his own. Inspired his son with the same viewpoint.

So—when Val finished his war service back in '45—they started on their project—in the smallest possible way. Val used some of his father's savings, bought a turret lathe from the War Assets Administration, set it up in the corner of a local machine shop on a rental deal.

This didn't pan out too well. So the two Kostrzewas built a little garage-like structure in their back yard and moved their lathe into it. There, after hours—for both continued to hold regular jobs—father and son turned out what they could with their one lathe.

But this, they decided, couldn't get them where they wanted to go. They had to have more equipment. So they took the long chance. Joseph cashed all his little $25

Savings Bonds—the family nest egg. They spent this on 6 more machines. Quit their jobs. Sink or swim—they were on their way.

Gaining a Business

BUT they weren't through taking chances. Success in the little back-yard plant was so great—they had to expand into larger quarters. This they did—by getting some co-workers to help them set up a corporation, and renting half of a large manufacturing plant.

Fortunately—the Kostrzewas' new B&K Tool and Die Company quickly proved it could meet the requirements of GM's Saginaw Steering Gear Division. That meant a series of orders—not only from

BORING AHEAD—John Koczenasz, left, operating jig bore; Floyd Tarrant, right, working jig grinder—both on job scheduled for Saginaw Steering Gear Division of General Motors.

GROWING FAMILY WITH A GROWING BUSINESS—the Kostrzewas of Saginaw, Michigan, whose B&K Tool and Die Company has grown from a "long chance" to a prosperous reality. (Left to right standing: Judith, Val, Mrs. Joseph, Joseph; seated: Kathy, Mrs. Val with Lynne Denise, Connie and Val Jr.)

Saginaw but from other General Motors divisions—and from other manufacturers as well.

Result: In five fast years the business that began in a garage on Joseph Kostrzewa's nest egg has become a million-dollar business. The Kostrzewas have a brand-new plant with 60 employes turning out tool jigs, gauges and dies. B&K turns a $475,000 payroll into Saginaw coffers. And you can't sell the U.S.A. short to Val and Joseph Kostrzewa and their associates.

What has happened in Saginaw, Michigan, has happened in hundreds of towns and cities all over the United States. New business has flowed into these communities —and as a result these communities in every state in the Union share in GM's success.

How much they share is shown by the fact that outside sources of materials and services for General Motors receive, in total, close to 50¢ out of every dollar that General Motors takes in.

Michigan Small Business and General Motors

Of the 26,000 business firms from coast to coast supplying GM divisions with goods and services—more than 6,000 of them are in GM's home state of Michigan. Of these, more than 4,500 are small firms—employing less than 100 persons—which, in total, receive more than 350 million dollars a year from General Motors.

GENERAL MOTORS — Good people to work for — Good people to deal with

This General Motors corporate ad carried a goodwill message to the company's supplier public, but told a meaningful story to other publics as well. (AGENCY: *Kudner Agency*)

47

This created a built-in appeal to other people. People are always interested in and curious about each other, particularly when the other people look genuine. Thus, General Motors managed to expand its audience to include not suppliers alone, but the public in general. And its "helping-hand" story could hardly fail to win the sympathetic attention of the larger public, which had additional overtones of value. General Motors improved relations with a nation-wide common-denominator public whom it could deal with as businessmen, hire as employees, sell stock to, and sell cars to—by the millions. A company has no better friends than people.

In 1966, General Motors was running another *people* campaign, signed: *"General Motors Is People . . .* making better things for you."

The Plant Community

Every manufacturing plant lives somewhere. Those living in big cities, like other city dwellers, usually have little communication with their next-door neighbors.

A great many manufacturing plants, however, are located in relatively small cities, where neighbors, both for people and for plants, can be a matter of importance.

For the plant community will probably contain most of the plant's employees, and many of its suppliers. It will include municipal officials with opportunities to make management life difficult. And representatives of the press, or broadcasters, equipped to tell the world about the plant favorably or unfavorably. There will be local bankers and businessmen who might be helpful at times. And clergymen who might comment on plant operations in their sermons.

Very often, the company's plant may be economically dominant in the community. If so, the livelihood of many tradesmen of all kinds will be dependent on the continuance of the company's payrolls. Whether or not the plant considers the community important, the community will certainly consider the plant important and act accordingly.

In times of crisis, such as a hard-fought strike, the attitude of the plant community may play a vital role. At all times, it can have some effect on the plant's operation. Most manufacturers find it pays to have a favorable image in one's own hometown.

Plant-city Advertising

Local plant-city advertising of a friendly, neighborly type confers benefits quickly, such as:

1. The very existence of the advertising helps establish the plant as *local*— not as an outpost of some distant big-city group of money-makers.

2. A channel is opened for communicating with the community.

3. An opportunity is provided for local image-building.

4. The company can build goodwill, in advance, against a crisis that may come in the future.

5. The advertising can contribute to morale of employees.

Make friends early   If a plant is a new arrival in a town, an attitude of aloofness and stiffness breeds lingering dislike. Hence, it becomes wise for a corporation to start early to build an image of warmth, neighborliness, friendliness, and especially, people-consciousness. The cost of so doing can be small compared to the public relations values bought.

Western Electric Plant-city Advertising

Western Electric, the Bell Telephone System's manufacturing subsidiary, has large plants in a number of cities of various sizes. This company quite often runs local advertising campaigns in its plant cities.

When a plant is erected in a new city, the plant usually introduces itself to the community in a local newspaper advertisement. It tells what it is going to make and how this fits in with the service offered by the Bell System. It may conduct an open house, inviting visitors from the community.

Later, the advertising will probably show Western Electric people at their jobs, identify the people by name, and tell something about their jobs. The copy may also mention that this company is a good place to work and that it intends to be a good neighbor in the community.

The importance of doing something important   Long ago, Western Electric discovered that employee morale improved when the worker learned what he was making and what it was used for. And when the employee found that his hands were making something *important,* his job became more important to him, and his attitude toward the company became correspondingly friendlier and more cooperative. As a result, Western Electric plant-community advertising makes a special point to stress the importance of the work being done in the local plant.

Workers in national-magazine advertisements   This same company has often shown pictures of its employees working at their jobs in its full-color national-magazine advertising. These advertisements, too, stressed the importance—to everybody—of the job being done. In justification of using expensive national-magazine pages to picture one's own workers, it should be noted that

Western Electric considers its 160,000 or more workers one of the several major audiences to which its advertising is directed.

Media for plant-city advertising   Local newspapers offer a natural medium for plant advertising in average-size cities. Localized radio and television are also being used increasingly. This use of broadcast media will be discussed in a later chapter.

For industry management, there is no area of advertising more fraught with perils, pitfalls, and traps than that of labor relations. This is largely because of management's frequent overeagerness to use advertising as a battle weapon, as a club to beat the enemy, the labor union, into submission. To aggressive and highly competitive top executives, men who enjoy a fight and go at it wholeheartedly, it seems inconceivable *not* to employ advertising to help win a strike.

But advertising is not a good weapon to use in a strike. It is like a sword that has a way of cutting its owner more often than it hurts the foe.

Unhappy experiences have led to this being generally recognized, and strike advertising is on the wane. Once quite common, it is seldom seen today.

The Case against Strike Advertising

Some of the reasons for *not* advertising in a strike are:

1. There is little or nothing to be gained by it. Most strike issues are properly settled at the bargaining table.

2. Experience shows that attempts to woo the strikers away from their union leadership by advertising amount to little more than an expression of wishful thinking.

3. Very often, the advertising foray against the union is ambushed by a wily foe. Union public-relations men are usually able and highly professional—and especially well versed in strike tactics. They know how to use publicity to turn the advertising claims against the advertising's originators.

4. Print advertising lacks mobility. Statements frozen permanently into print can, in a short time, become embarrassing to the advertisers.

5. The audience reached by the advertising is the *whole community*, not merely the strikers and their unions or management.

The general public normally has little interest in

Chapter 9

LABOR-

RELATIONS

ADVERTISING

the issues of a strike. It merely does not want to be inconvenienced. If it is inconvenienced—and, especially, if it is financially hurt by an overlong strike —its impulse is to call for state or Federal government intervention.

Hence, belligerent advertising thrust at the community at such a time is more likely to generate ill will than goodwill.

6. A peculiar aspect of all advertising in the labor area is that the spending of money for it, and the affixing of the company's or the union's signature to it seems to give the advertising a connotation of special *responsibility*. The advertising becomes a document—on the public record.

Angry statements that have gone on this record have a way of staying there, and can be embarrassing for a long time to come.

There have been a few cases, however, when skilled public relations handling managed to derive a benefit from strike statements. These have occurred when there was an *out-of-town* angle of the controversy, unknown to the community, that affected the community's interests. Revealing such a hidden factor can produce advantageous results.

A New England plant of a large company had been strikebound for a long time. The community became increasingly aroused because the company refused to end the strike by giving in on what seemed to be an obviously minor point. There was a growing clamor for government intervention. The company replied with a diplomatically worded advertisement admitting that the point was indeed minor in this particular plant, but that by giving in on it would set a precedent for its many other and larger plants across the country and would cost the company millions of dollars. This fact had not previously been brought out. It evidently made its point. The uproar subsided. And not long after, the strike was settled.

In a somewhat reverse situation, the Allied Printing Trades Council ran ads in the *New York Times,* charging the New York City Board of Education with buying books from "low-wage, anti-union printers" in Tennessee where a strike had continued for a long time. "Is the Board really anti-union?" asked the politically embarrassing ads.

Constructive Areas for Labor-relations Advertising

Violent, contentious labor-versus-management advertising, whether placed by either side, usually accomplishes little. It is psychologically disturbing to the part of the general public that is neutral and yearns for labor peace. Hence, it may alienate the very section of the public whose goodwill can be of most value to either management or labor.

But this middle, neutral public can be swayed, pro or con, by *another* type of advertising, namely, advertising that is essentially *institutional* in spirit, that is image-improving, and that works to build *goodwill* rather than ill will.

The plant-city advertising described in the previous chapter, for example, can be used by management to improve employee relations in a friendly, constructive manner, without, in any way, incurring conflict with the union.

The opportunity to use institutionally oriented advertising is not confined to management, but is available to labor as well. In fact, labor has already seized this opportunity and has produced at least two sagacious and extremely interesting campaigns.

Advertising by Labor Unions

Traditionally, labor unions have rather consistently refrained from using advertising at all. It has been said that they did not use advertising because they could not afford it. But today, with the considerable funds possessed by the stronger unions, and in view of the fact that they *have* been able to afford *other* costly programs, this statement is not entirely convincing. It would appear that labor's reluctance to advertise must include other factors besides cost.

Possibly, labor's success in using the less costly public relations techniques may be one factor. There are undoubtedly others. One suspects, however, that the ultimate reason for labor's not using advertising was that labor leadership did not see how to get enough solid tangible value from advertising to justify even a modest cost.

Today, such a justification has been discovered. Advertising *can* be of great value to labor. And this is being demonstrated by labor itself.

It is being demonstrated by a radio campaign of labor's parent organization, the AFL-CIO. It is also being demonstrated by the union-label advertising of the International Ladies' Garment Workers' Union.

Edward P. Morgan Broadcast for the AFL-CIO

For more than ten years, the American Federation of Labor and Congress of Industrial Organizations (AFL-CIO) has sponsored an ABC, early evening, national-network radio program featuring the news commentator, Edward P. Morgan.

There is nothing especially remarkable about an advertiser sponsoring a news commentator. But this case is out of the ordinary. It is unusual in that Edward P. Morgan is himself an unusual type of commentator. And it is even more noteworthy that his style should so perfectly fit the needs of the labor organization. The combination has proved exceptionally successful.

Edward P. Morgan differs from the conventional breed of newscaster in a number of ways. He is not after the mass audience. He avoids the mannerisms adopted by other commentators to dramatize their delivery. Instead his approach is calm, gentlemanly, dignified. His diction is cultured, and he does not avoid a long word if that is the one that most precisely expresses his thought.

His material is informative and his presentation consistently interesting. Though sensitively aware of humor and irony in the day's events, Morgan takes his job very seriously. His preparation has obviously been deep and pains-taking. And in his sparkling commentaries that follow the routine recital of news events, his use of language is masterful. At all times, he speaks as an intelligent man, addressing himself to other intelligent men.

Edward P. Morgan is noteworthy for another well-developed trait—his remarkable *objectivity*. Though he sees the world through the eyes of a liberal, he presents his version of it objectively and with much consideration for those who might not agree with him.

Needless to say, this earnest, articulate, yet thoroughly objective commen-tator appeals to intelligent listeners, who are delighted by his adult presenta-tion. These listeners are usually the opinion-makers in each community, exactly the audience most sought by his labor sponsors. Furthermore, Edward P. Morgan's own image of reasonableness rubs off, generously, on his sponsoring organization.

In their accompanying commercials, the AFL-CIO (also the ILGWU, which at times participates in the sponsorship) makes a point to echo the Edward P. Morgan spirit. Everything is presented in broad, social-minded terms, avoiding any nuance of controversy and working, at all times, to build a friendly good-guy image of labor.

The AFL-CIO makes no attempt to influence Edward P. Morgan's program. They accepted him originally as a wholly independent man who was generally in accord with AFL-CIO objectives. And as the long-time sponsorship indi-cates, the labor organization obviously has been happy with its selection.

Earlier in this chapter, it was noted that, in the labor field, the running of paid advertising seemed to confer a connotation of *responsibility*. In the earlier instance mentioned, the connotation had a negative effect, because the advertis-ing was misused. But in *this* instance, with AFL-CIO sponsoring the statesman-like Morgan program, the aura of responsibility projected by this advertising has been immensely beneficial to the union. Among other advantages, it has provided a protective image that effectively refutes the charges of irresponsi-bility so often leveled at union leaders in the past.

Advertising of the ILGWU Union Label

Included in the settlement of the great dress-industry general strike of 1958 was a contract provision for the establishment of a union label, to be sewn into all garments made by members of the International Ladies' Garment Workers' Union (ILGWU). The union had been seeking the adoption of such a label for nearly sixty years, but had heretofore failed to get it, in large part because its previous efforts had been launched on too small a scale to be effective.

The big strike provided an opportunity to establish the label with a major section of the dress industry, and also have it made obligatory through contract provisions. Interestingly, at the same time, because such a label would provide welcome benefits to a large part of the industry as well as to the union, industry negotiators did not oppose the label provision.

They were given an additional incentive to agree—"the union's pledge to finance with 1 million dollars a year the promotion of the union label." The employers "also recognized that the label would provide an additional instrument for combatting non-union, anti-social and chiseling employers who undermine the standards of the garment industry." [1] The word *antisocial* may be taken to connote "racketeering." The agreement was a useful one for both sides.

If the label could obtain any degree of support by the general public, it would obviously become an effective weapon to combat the "fringe of the industry" that sought to undercut both wages and prices through its non-union operation.

Need for promotion of the label   Equal in importance to the establishing of the label was the task of promoting it. In order to function for the benefit of union and unionized industry, it must have some influence on eventual garment purchases by the general public. And it must be remembered that this public consisted of *women,* including women members of the ILGWU and other unions.

Beginning in 1959, a massive, and for a labor union, unprecedented across-the-board program of promotional activities was instituted. Included were public relations and publicity operations, innumerable merchandising and promotion devices, and advertising in newspaper, magazine, trade, and broadcast media. The cost of this, as pledged, has been in excess of 1 million dollars a year.

Research   Wisely, the ILGWU called on a depth research study to orient its major advertising effort, interviewing 1,500 women in ten key metropolitan

---

[1] *Report* of the General Executive Board, ILGWU, May, 1959.

centers from coast to coast. It approached both union and non-union women of all backgrounds and income levels to ascertain what their reactions would be to the new label. Findings of the research served as an important guide for the development of advertising copy.

Development of the ILGWU newspaper campaign   Although the union label was featured in single insertions in women's service magazines and in the commercials of ILGWU's participation in the Edward P. Morgan radio program, the keystone advertising campaign has been that of a series of full-page newspaper ads in leading cities. The campaign has been notable for its creative excellence and for its pioneering in an uncharted area of advertising.

The union's research had indicated that the best appeal for the union label would be its assurance that the labeled garment had not been made in a sweatshop under bad working conditions. This appeared to have a strong emotional impact on women.

Also considered by the advertising agency, the Wexton Company, was the somewhat coldly neutral attitude of much of the general public toward unions, an attitude that when not critical, tended to be apathetic, and anxious not to be put upon. Hence, as a first objective, the agency sought a theme that would provide a "confluence of interest" of the general public with that of the union.

The agency found its theme by recalling "the ugly world of yesterday," the era of sweatshops, excessive homework, and the seven-day working week. In endeavoring to illustrate this theme, the agency made a further, extremely fortunate discovery in coming upon the almost forgotten photographs of Lewis W. Hine. Neglected for years, Hine, who died in 1940, has now belatedly been recognized as one of the greatest camera artists in the history of American photography.

Lewis Hine was the photographer of the poor. He photographed bewhiskered immigrants and workers in factories, including garment-industry sweatshops. Sympathetic to his subjects, he was particularly touched by the plight of child workers in industry and produced many photographic documents of their conditions.

Hine's photographs provided magnificent illustration material. The Wexton agency capitalized on this asset by making the illustration, in each advertisement, part of a powerful picture-headline *idea*, which, in turn, was followed by well-written text copy. All parts of the advertisement worked together to deliver a blockbuster emotional appeal—the very appeal that research had indicated would be most moving to women.

In a later chapter of this book, the role and technique of the picture-headline idea in non-product advertising will be discussed at length. These ILGWU advertisements offer good examples of such ideas. In one ad, an attractive but poorly dressed little girl looks wistfully out of the sunlit window of a factory. The headline is a verse by Sarah N. Cleghorn:

> The golf links lie so near the mill
> That nearly every day
> The laboring children can look out
> And see the men at play.

Another advertisement shows a woman in long skirts carrying a huge pile of garments on her head—work to be done at home. The headline reads:

HEIGHT OF FASHION—1909

After identifying the picture, the text copy continues with the story:

And that was after a full day of work.
A day off? There was no such thing.
Work pursued the worker right around the clock—at home or in the shop.
Happily, times have changed.
Ladies' garment workers can now enjoy their homes, their paid holidays and vacations, their families and their friends.
Seems like a million years ago—the era of the seven-day week and the $5 weekly paycheck.

The copy then tells how the ILGWU brought about security, fair wages, decent working conditions, etc. It next calls attention to the ILGWU label sewn into ladies' and children's garments and asks the reader to look for it:

It is your guarantee that the clothing you buy was made by skilled craftsmen in a shop reflecting the best American standards and conditions.

The ad concludes with a picture of the union label and the words, "Symbol of Decency, Fair Labor Standards and the American Way of Life."

Institutional approach   Though alluding to the accomplishments of the ILGWU, the copy avoids boasting about it and makes no attempt to glorify the union. Its approach is restrained and entirely institutional and seeks to improve the union image in the public mind by placing itself on the side of the greatest good. Narrow-interest controversy is studiously avoided. Nor does the copy press too hard in its selling of the union label. It lets the reader make up her own mind.

In addition to the advertisements recalling the past, the series has included some other advertisements attuned somewhat more to the garment workers' identification with fashion, yet also featuring the union label. These advertisements are "merchandised" by managing to have them displayed, in blow-up form, in retail-store windows. In this evidence of retail support, a new dimension is added to the overall force of the promotion.

Photo: The Bettmann Archive Inc.

"The golf links lie so near the mill
That nearly every day
The laboring children can look out
And see the men at play."

SARAH N. CLEGHORN (1876-1959)

In a matter of days children by the millions will be going back to school. New clothing, school supplies, excitement, anticipation will be the order of the day. That's the way it should be.

And yet—not so many summers ago—it was the lucky child who went back to school. Many just went on with their work—like the 10-year-old girl above in a spinning mill.

Not so long ago child labor, sweatshops, 14-hour-plus working days, seven-day workweeks—were familiar parts of the American landscape.

It took the combined efforts of many organizations, including the great American labor movement, to remove these stains from our society.

American unions, like the International Ladies' Garment Workers' Union, have contributed much beyond their own immediate interests to help make America great.

Laws we all take for granted today like social security, unemployment insurance, workmen's compensation, minimum wages, public school sys-

tems, shorter workweeks didn't just happen. They came because unions like the ILGWU struggled for them.

This is part of what all unions like the ILGWU represent. There are 450,000 members, 80% of them women—many of them mothers, in the ILGWU. Through their union they share the same goals you do. They work for decent shelter, health and education for their families. They measure the future in terms of their children. They contribute to the welfare of their communities and their country.

The label of the ILGWU is their signature in ladies' garments. It is the signature of men and women who, through their union have achieved fair standards, the dignity of a voice in their own conditions of employment and a position of respect in their communities.

Look for it the next time you shop for women's or girls' apparel. It is your guarantee that the clothing you buy was made by skilled craftsmen in a shop reflecting the best American standards and traditions.

UNION LABEL

ILGWU
AFL-CIO

Symbol of Decency,
Fair Labor Standards and the
American Way of Life.

This touching advertisement exerts a strong emotional
appeal, as evidenced by many sympathetic letters of com-
ment and by requests for reprints. It has also won awards
for its excellence. (AGENCY: *The Wexton Company*)

In putting itself on record in sustained advertising, notable for its restrained public-minded copy, the ILGWU builds the same image of *responsibility* that the AFL-CIO (and ILGWU) achieves with the Edward P. Morgan program.

Other Labor Advertising

Although labor union advertising is still something of a rarity, it is on the increase, and more unions are experimenting with it. Among them recently have been the Retail Clerks' International Association (NBC Monitor radio), Amalgamated Clothing Workers' Union, Milk Drivers' Union, the Brotherhood of Locomotive Firemen & Enginemen, and others.

In 1959, the United Steelworkers of America and spokesman organizations for the steel industry fought a 2-million-dollar strike advertising battle in hundreds of newspapers. In advertising technique, in argument, in general appearance—and in emotional heat—the honors were about even. But this was strike advertising, with all the faults of strike advertising. It is doubtful if it had any tangible effect at all on the public to whom it was supposedly addressed. The money might well have been spent in some more constructive way.

Four

THE CORPORATE IMAGE

Sometime between 1955 and 1960, a new phrase, *corporate image*, exploded into the realms of public relations and advertising. PR man David Finn ascribed the first appearance of the word *image*,[1] used in this sense, to a 1955 article in the *Harvard Business Review*.

Indeed, *two* closely related image phrases entered the world at about the same period—*corporate image* and *product image*. Both seem to have been spawned by researchers. Motivational research, especially, appears to have been instrumental in the development of the image concept.

Not everything about the image idea was 100 per cent new. As we have already seen, AT&T had been engaged in actual image-building since 1908, even though the image concept, as such, had not yet been invented. What was new was the phrase itself, and its link with motivational research. It drew attention quickly (1) because of its aptness in describing what had not been well described before and (2) because it seemed to suggest the existence of interesting new advertising opportunities.

When such a provocative term as *corporate image* suddenly sprang into existence, no one in the promotional business just stood there. Immediately, public relations men, advertising agency account representatives, and industrial designers charged in, tucked the new phrase into their attaché cases, and rushed off to sell it to their clients. They found the clients receptive, in fact, fascinated with the new concept.

For the next four or five years, the image-cousins, product and corporate, became the heroes of a sweeping industry fad. The fad's public relations promoters earned the title of "image-merchants." The advertising agencies produced *corporate-image advertising* which often looked, however, suspiciously similar to the institutional advertising of former times. The industrial designers did extremely

Chapter 10

DEVELOPMENT OF THE CORPORATE- IMAGE CONCEPT

[1] "Stop Worrying about Your Image," *Harper's Magazine*, June, 1962.

well redesigning the nameplates and trademarks and much else of the nation's largest corporations.

Then the fad began to subside. This was largely because, as a fad, it had burned itself out. But it was also because the results expected from application of the image concept did not always measure up to the promises of the image-merchants and account executives. Today, the image concept continues to function where needed, but it is no longer the hit performer on the communications stage. In some sectors, it has been returned to the researchers for further improvement.

Corporate image is real. It exists. It *can* be changed advantageously, but the task is difficult, and not all the attempts to effect such a change have succeeded. The failures have been largely due to lack of understanding of the image concept's capabilities and limitations. It has too often been asked to achieve the impossible.

What Is Image?

What is image? *In its simplest possible form,* it is the mental picture of something—a product, a brand, a company, a person—that exists in the mind of *an individual human being.*

Each individual human being sees the object, whether product or corporation, in a different way from any other human being. Within each person, the image he evolves is compounded of his personal experiences, sensations, knowledge, hearsay, prejudice, and fancy.

If an individual's contacts and experience with a corporation are extensive, his personal image of the corporation is likely to be strong, positive, and relatively stable. If the individual's familiarity with the corporation is slight, as is most often the case, his image will probably be weak, hazy, and unstable.

People being people, their images of inanimate objects and abstractions often tend to become personalized. To the stockholder, the company that is generous with its distributions and extras may soon become personalized as a smiling Lady Bountiful. Another, less generous company, might get to be thought of as a tightwad Old Scrooge. Image and personality are very close to being the same thing.

Group image What has been just described is the image that exists in the mind of an *individual.* Although this is the basis of the image concept, it is not in itself of much practical value. What a business wants to know about is the combined image of itself seen by a large number of individuals—a *group,* a public, or the overall general public. Consequently, in speaking of image, a group image is usually meant.

Group images are more complex than they sometimes seem to be, and their apparent nature can be deceptive. Because one individual's image cannot be merely multiplied to get a total image, for no two individual images are alike.

Actually, a total overall group image is like a composite photograph of a number of superimposed faces. As in such a photograph, the overall corporate image is very likely to be blurred. It may have some salient features that stand out from the blur, because some salient aspect of the company may strike many people much the same way, resulting in a fairly unified picture in regard to this aspect. On the other hand there may be deceptive neutral or gray areas caused by conflicting individual images that cancel each other out.

This creates difficulties for the careful research which is the only means of discovering, with any reliability, the nature of a corporate image. The task of research is made easier if it can isolate specific aspects of the total image and focus on these one at a time. And the results are likely to be more usable for advertising or public relations.

Image is not static. Created in the minds of living human beings, it is constantly subject to change and does change. Therefore, it should be checked by research from time to time.

Corporate image is multiple   Because a corporation has many publics, consisting of people with different interests in the company, it projects multiple images—an image for each public. This, too, adds complexity to the company's overall total image.

Management image   Though it may not often be thought of that way, management is also a public of its own corporation, and top executives carry around their own corporate images. These are fully informed images, clear-cut, and as well defined as an image possibly could be.

Partly because of this, when the term *corporate image* burst into the publicity limelight, some top business executives tended to see the corporate-image concept in an oversimplified light. It did not occur to them that the overall image held by the public was, in substance, a far more complicated and elusive thing than their own well-organized view of the corporation. Thus, they were ready to believe that their corporation's image could be easily and quickly changed, if necessary, by deft public relations devices.

But corporate image—a blurred, multiple mosaic of many small, independent images—is not easily manipulated by quick scenery-shifting. There were more failures than successes.

Improper Objectives

Money has been spent dubiously by calling on corporate image to fulfill objectives that are too broad, too vague and general, and too questionable in real value. One example is the frequently noted desire of business executives to make their companies well liked or better liked by the public. Here is an objective as broad and deep as the Pacific Ocean. Large sums of money could be sunk into it indefinitely. And could anyone guarantee that tangible benefits would flow from such an intangible objective?

What is more important to a business is that it not be *disliked*. Dislike can be costly. And since it is usually based on specific causes, it can be corrected. And the cost may not be excessive.

Corporate Image a Function of Public Contact

Corporate image is a function of a company's contacts with the public. Companies with many direct contacts with the public automatically become possessors of a strong corporate image. It is certainly important to these companies that their image be kept favorable.

There are other companies, some of them very big, that are almost totally unknown to the general public and hence project little or no image to that public. Naturally, such a company has no need to worry about its image. And it would be wasting money to try to create an image, except, perhaps, for one or more of its limited, specialized publics.

A Favorable Image Must Be Earned

Through the use of advertising or of public relations operations, a corporation might achieve a favorable image temporarily, but unless it lives up to the promise of its publicity, the good image will soon fade away. Artificial, superficial, and insincere attempts at image-creating usually prove transparent to almost everyone.

Another word for image is *reputation*. Reputation takes a long time to build up. It must be earned by deeds, not words. The resort that publicizes its cleanliness had better make sure that its table linen is spotless and its silverware thoroughly washed. The bank that talks about friendliness would do well to make sure that its employees *act* friendly.

Image in Advertising

The role of image in advertising is auxiliary rather than primary. There is no advertising devoted 100 per cent to image-building, although the advertisements of some of the chemical and electronic companies sometimes come close to it.

Image-building is tied to specific objectives. With AT&T, it helped fulfill a long-range protective function. In subsequent chapters, it will be seen how it plays a part in messages addressed to the financial community—or how it *assists* in recruiting desirable employees. Or how it helps a retail store attract customers. In fact, *most* types of institutional advertising include some degree of image-building.

Image-building is often injected into product-selling advertisements.

Image-building can be thought of as the attempted projection of the *personality* of the corporation into the advertising. It is effected, not directly by the message of the advertisements, but indirectly by means of technique, attitude, tone, and especially, appearance. With these devices, the advertisements try to "act out" the desired corporate image. An excellent example of this "acting out" is the Bell Telephone System campaign discussed earlier in this book.

The Mirror of Research

The Bell Telephone System has been a leader in calling upon research to test its image, to look at itself in a mirror.

The mirror has not always been complimentary. At one time, research used the device of asking telephone users to try and think of the telephone company as a person, and then describe the person. The answers came quickly. The company emerged as a crabby, scolding school teacher.

The research showed that the company had given the impression of always insisting on being right, and being very possessive of its property and jealous of its instruments. Its advertising had a tendency to scold. It almost seemed as if the System did not really want people to *enjoy* telephone service.

One may be sure that the company officials did not delay going to work to correct *this* image.

The Wrong Image

Sometimes a company succeeds in building an image that is clear, strong, and memorable, but, unfortunately, the wrong image.

More than once, executives of the big steel companies have felt that their businesses were aptly symbolized by the burly steel worker—a real he-man "tough guy." In fact, one steel company ran an advertisement picturing such a muscular giant, including a headline that said, almost in the same words, "This is our image."

The psychological self-flattery of such a masculine image is readily apparent. And there *is* some justification for this thinking. Steel *is* a tough metal. Steel-handling machinery *is* gigantic. Steel workers *are* husky. But it is still the wrong image.

To the public, the big boy is likely to loom up unattractively as a brutal bully, which is not at all the best image for the steel industry. Furthermore, the consumer has little reason to be interested in the Tarzans who make the steel, but much reason to be interested in the usefulness of steel. How much more constructive is the image evoked by U.S. Steel's slogan: "Only *steel* can do so many jobs so well!"

Tough, belligerent images are likely to be negative, arousing subconscious resentments. Which is a reminder that when a symbolic character is used, it is always wise to pretest it first with research. Some surprising reactions may turn up.

An obvious image may not always be the most effective one. Most corporations like to *modernize* their images. But when everybody is modern, modernity loses distinction. One manufacturer with a well-established product refused to redesign himself. He preferred to be known as a "crotchety, old-fashioned firm dating back to the Civil War."

Limitations of the Image Concept

A favorable corporate image can be very useful, provided it is exerted in an area where an image *can* have potency. Otherwise, its usefulness may be drastically limited.

It operates, protectively, quite well in a political atmosphere. It also has special values in the financial world. It can be helpful when a company seeks to recruit desirable personnel. And, in special situations, it can help increase sales.

There are, however, limits to its protective power. The finest image in the world cannot save a company caught red-handed in a violation of the law, or in any other clear manifestation of bad citizenship.

Image and "Humanity"

In the past, as indicated by research, one of the most trouble-causing image faults of big business has been its coldness, remoteness, and lack of *"humanity."* As seen by the people, business was not interested in people. This fault contributed to the long-continued negative image of big business.

The need for identification of a corporation with people continues. General Motors, as we have seen, made people, as people, a major keynote of its supplier advertising campaign. Also noted was that the visual success of the campaign was derived from photographing real people on the spot, rather than professional models.

A few words more may be said on the subject. It applies to institutional advertising of any kind. Professional models, however valuable they may be for conventional commercial purposes, should not be used institutionally to portray supposedly plain, everyday people.

As a type, the professional model has become dehumanized by advertising's established practice of selecting too perfect, too beautiful, or even too allegedly "typical" models to sell its wares. The "typical housewife" so often pictured is still too carefully groomed and still looks like a model or an actress.

Real people, the kind we most often see around us, do *not* have consistently regular features, but *do* have little blemishes or just bits of plainness, little deviations from perfection. The same goes for their clothes, their postures, their mannerisms.

These imperfections regularly disqualify their owners from appearing on an advertising page or in a television commercial. Yet these are just the imperfections that make people look real, that give them character and authenticity.

Attention should also be paid to copy. If the characters are supposed to deliver a people-image message, the words put into their mouths should be *people-talk,* and not ad language.

Chapter 11

ADVERTISING TO

THE FINANCIAL

COMMUNITY

Like people, businesses often need money. They get it in an astonishing variety of ways, and in from modest to colossal sums. But no matter how it is done, financing is a constant and universal concern of business.

Some corporations have little trouble raising money. They can borrow at favorable terms; their stock is buoyant in the market. Other corporations do not do so well. Their stock lacks glamour and moves sluggishly.

Of course, purely financial factors such as soundness of management, earnings, and dividend policies may well be at the root of the difference. But even when such factors are about equal, one company still will seem to be able to raise money easier than another.

The reason it can is that *it enjoys a better reputation and has a more favorable image in the financial community.*

Who Is the Financial Community?

The financial community is broader and more heterogeneous than is generally realized. It includes, certainly, banks, investment houses, brokers, etc. But it is bigger than Wall Street, bigger than the downtown financial district.

It includes every person and every organization that can influence the price and salability of a company's securities, or the availability of funds the company can borrow. It includes security analysts and researchers of all types, financial writers and commentators at all levels—including the public press and broadcasters, business magazines, financial data services—and, not unimportant, high-level businessmen chatting over a luncheon table.

It also includes the *influenced,* the readers and listeners. This may be the public pouring over the stock market prices, looking for a buy. Or it may be the managers of great institutional security-buyers— the investment trusts, the insurance companies, or other investing companies.

It extends, geographically, from one end of the country to the other and reaches out, internationally, to foreign countries.

It is this financial community that determines a company's financial reputation—that, in the final analysis, puts a corporation in a spotlight, looks it over, and decides what it is worth.

How Is a Corporation Judged?

Sometimes a corporation is judged very expertly by professionals in the employ of a big investing company. And sometimes the corporation is judged by amateurs with homemade charts, divining rods, and Ouija boards. Both judgments, and every other judgment in between, make up the corporation's total financial community image.

Information on which to base a judgment of this kind comes from a flood of literature of all degrees of authenticity. Some is statistical and technical. Much more is highly "popular."

The judgment of the financial community—aside from that part of it performed by the professionals—is not likely to be overly scientific. Though not necessarily a bad judgment, it will be a broadly based one, leaning on generalities rather than specifics. It will be an *image* judgment.

Advertising to the Financial Community

"Can corporate advertising favorably affect the stability or sale of a company's securities?" *Business Week* asked this question in a survey answered by 1,188 partners and officers of the nation's leading investment banking firms. Of these, 1,046—over 88 per cent—said, "Yes." [1]

With this conclusion, many other business executives would agree. But a more difficult question remains: *How* does one advertise to the financial community?

Should the advertiser concentrate on the "professionals," the analysts and the experts employed by the great institutional traders, whose large-scale buying and selling is said to have an enormous influence on stock market prices? Or should the copy be directed broadly at the *entire* financial community, including the professionals and all others?

Concentrating on the professionals offers a media advantage. The specialized publications, their trade papers, read by the experts are relatively not very costly. To extend the advertising to the whole financial group would require the addition of business magazines, which would add to costs.

At first glance, it would also seem that special copy could be directed at the

[1] From a *Business Week* advertisement, Dec. 14, 1963.

analysts, selling them directly on the corporation and offering them facts and figures. But there is a serious flaw in such a copy approach.

Like the doctor and the architect, the professional security analyst does not want to be told how to do his job. He does not want to be "sold." He wisely prefers to gather his own statistics and make his own analyses. He is paid for being *right*. Hence, such advertising, instead of "selling" him, might incur his annoyance.

Therefore, the advertiser is obliged to fall back on generalized informative institutional advertising, which the analyst *can* read with interest. But this copy would not be very different from any other institutional advertising that could be addressed to the entire financial community.

And inasmuch as it is the entire financial community that defines the image of the corporation, most corporate advertisers, using institutional copy, expand their schedules to include business and opinion-leader magazines, and sometimes even more expensive media.

Image-building Advertisements

Institutional copy written for the financial community usually finds ways to talk about the corporation in an interesting way. As it does this, it tries to fulfill the objective of indicating that this is a company whose stock is bound to increase in value.

In recent years, with many stock buyers seeking capital gains, the financial community has looked favorably on *growth* companies. Rightly or wrongly, many stock buyers tend to equate growth with a strong *research* program, indicating that the company is on its toes and going somewhere. These buyers also think of growth companies as having *aggressive management,* and being *modern* and *progressive* and *diversified.*

All these points have image-value and, accordingly, are incorporated into the institutional copy. Sometimes they are illustrated by pictures. The image of a growth company is the one most often sought by institutional advertisers seeking to influence the financial community.

Multiple objectives As with other image-building efforts, the image-building is usually combined with another advertising objective. Quite often, this may be product-selling, of an informative, generalized nature, of interest to upstairs customer "influentials."

Or, the same advertisement (with a somewhat expanded media schedule) may include several image-building objectives at the same time. Inasmuch as a *growth* company that has *diversified* activities and does plenty of *research* can appeal to bright young college graduates about to embark on a career, the ad designed for a financial community image also can exert a *recruiting* image. The same ad, if it has public service overtones, can have value beamed at a *government* public. A health note can make it interesting to *doctors*.

As the interests of these various publics tend to parallel each other, it is not usually difficult to write a single piece of copy that can appeal to all the groups simultaneously.

Wheeling Steel's Institutional Campaign

In the late 1950s, the Wheeling Steel Corporation, seeking large sums of money under more favorable conditions, felt the need of an improved image in the financial community.

Though a large company, Wheeling was nevertheless dwarfed, for image purposes, by such other steel giants as United States Steel and Bethlehem. To those who knew it, Wheeling was most often remembered as a fabricator of ash cans and garbage cans, in spite of the fact that it produced many other important types of products. And the market for ash cans and garbage cans was a declining one.

Previous advertising had been principally of a trade or industrial nature. Consequently, it was not known in the business and financial communities that Wheeling's business was increasingly diversified—that it sold sheet steel to the automotive industry, tin plate to food canners, corrugated-steel culverts to road builders, and pipe, roofing, lath, and expanded metal to the building industry.

Wheeling's need for funds arose from a comprehensive program of plant improvement and modernization it had inaugurated. Much new machinery was being installed. And one machine in the steel industry can be bigger and more expensive that a whole factory in some other industries. Wheeling was, indeed, tooling itself up as a growth company. What was needed was to tell the world about it.

The advertising   The Wheeling institutional campaign was in reality a generalized product-selling campaign with image-building overtones. It appeared in full color in the *Saturday Evening Post, Business Week,* and *U.S. News and World Report.* A black-and-white linecut version appeared in the *Wall Street Journal.*

The first advertisement pictured an expanse of fiery red, with a white-hot spot in the center, as if one were looking into a furnace full of molten steel. The headline read:

LOOK AT WHEELING STEEL THIS WAY

From wheel to wheel it's Wheeling steel
that's what new cars are made of

Wheeling furnishes steel for many car parts you seldom see! Here are just a few, keyed to show the type of Wheeling steel they're usually made from. ■ *Wheeling* SOFTITE *Galvanized Steel* ■ *Hot-Rolled Steel* ■ *Cold-Rolled Steel* ■ *Long-Terne Steel*

Start at the massive front bumper . . . back to the flaring tail fin. Just about every part in a modern car is fabricated from strong, easily worked sheet steel.

Always a major automotive supplier, Wheeling now furnishes steel that's far superior to any available even a few years ago — strong, ductile steel that frees the imagination of top American stylists.

Wheeling Steel helps the engineer, too. For example, Wheeling's SOFTITE — a long-lasting steel that's protected by the world's tightest zinc coating — successfully combats corrosive exhaust fumes. The result is tougher, safer mufflers for your car.

What's more, Wheeling "Sheet Steel" now co in huge coils that often contain a single mile-length of steel that greatly reduces the scrap formerly encountered during fabrication.

So next time you take a drive in your car, at the strong, tough metal that made it poss Then you'll see why top automotive stylists engineers agree — *you can always rely on steel . . . Wheeling steel.* Wheeling Steel Corporation, Wheeling, West Virginia.

IT'S WHEELING STEEL

Wheeling Steel institutional advertisements contained non-technical selling copy. Purpose was informative, to advise financial community as well as business leaders on scope of Wheeling's business. (AGENCY: *Cunningham & Walsh*)

The text copy pointed out that each heat of steel was *custom-made* from the very beginning for its final use. To be able to do this, Wheeling Steel was integrated from the ore and coal mines to the local sales and distribution offices. And:

> It is because of progressive, integrated operations like this that Wheeling Steel continues to grow. *Bigger? Sure. But more important . . . better.*

Another advertisement showed the parts of a car that were made by Wheeling Steel coming down the road. All the parts were of shining natural steel and comprised most of the car except the tires, steering wheel, upholstery, etc. As there was no driver shown, this near-complete car apparently speeding along the highway created a spooky effect. The illustration (a color photograph of miniature models) was a stopper. The headline:

> FROM WHEEL TO WHEEL IT'S WHEELING STEEL
> THAT'S WHAT NEW CARS ARE MADE OF

Text copy indicated that Wheeling had always been a "major automotive supplier" and now was making new improved steels for automotive use.

One by one, in other advertisements, Wheeling's products were publicized in an interesting way. And most of the ads made a point to end on the note that Wheeling was growing *"Bigger? Sure. But more important . . . better."*

Texaco's Oil-centennial Campaign

During the oil industry's centennial year, 1959, Texaco ran a black-and-white dual-purpose campaign, using both a group of oil industry publications and a group of financial publications, such as *Barron's, Commercial & Financial Chronicle, Financial World, Forbes, ESPA Magazine,* the *Analysts Journal,* and *Magazine of Wall Street.*

The oil industry publications were selected as part of a public relations goodwill gesture to an industry that contains a surprising number of specialized and independent units. The financial publications, obviously, were used to remind the financial community that Texaco was not lagging behind its competitors in research and forward development. The expenditure for the campaign was modest.

Each ad consisted of two photographs, an old one depicting Texaco's early activities and a modern one. All of the text copy was included in the two single paragraph captions. Next to the Texaco signature was the slogan line: "Constant Progress in Oil's First Century."

In one advertisement, the "Yesterday" photograph pictured the famous

Spindletop gusher in 1901. The "Today" photograph depicted a multitude of cars on a great freeway. The headline:

THE GUSHER THAT BROUGHT IN 50,000,000 CARS

One caption noted that Texaco got its start at Spindletop. In the other was stated:

> Today, Texaco is the largest producer of domestic crude oil. Its integrated operations are worldwide in scope. And its laboratories are investigating not only petroleum's valuable energy, but also atomic energy. By keeping in step with the future . . . Texaco continues to grow.

A second ad in the series showed an old-time car being pulled out of a mud-hole on a soggy dirt road by a team of horses. The other picture was an aerial photograph of a superhighway cloverleaf. The headline:

AFTER 5,000 YEARS OF MUD . . . SUPERHIGHWAYS OF PETROLEUM

The word *petroleum* in the headline referred to asphalt, "a non-volatile form of petroleum," a product marketed by Texaco for many years. The series continued with ads indicating progress in research, pipe lines, refining, etc.

The recruiting by business of college graduates and of technically trained personnel is not in itself a new development. For half a century, industry's recruiters have made annual visits to the colleges to sign up, if possible, the cream of the graduating crop.

In recent years, however, the recruiting tempo has begun to accelerate. Recruiting has assumed a new note of urgency. It is the result of the rapid expansion of business itself, plus the scientific explosion. Together, they have created an unprecedented demand for elite personnel.

At times, this has led to dramatic competition between companies to snare the best of the talent available. And not only has it been the college seniors who have been sought; often their professors have been recruited as well.

Two kinds of advertising assist in the recruiting operation.

One kind sells the *job*. It appears most spectacularly in the newspaper classified columns, often in jumbo-size space. Its manner borders on hard sell, and it directly solicits applicants for specific job classifications.

The other kind of advertising sells the *company*. It is image-building. Its manner is relaxed, and it makes a point *not* to offer any specific job. In fact, it is not always apparent that it *has* a recruiting purpose. It seems merely to be general institutional advertising for the company. This advertising usually appears in magazines or on television.

Chapter 12

ADVERTISING

FOR

RECRUITING

Recruiting Advertising Is Selective

Though the two kinds of advertising have very different functions to fulfill, they have one definite characteristic in common—their approach to recruiting is highly *selective*. Each goes after a particular type of employee and carefully avoids attracting hordes of other, unwanted types of employees.

The classified job-selling advertisements make it very clear at the beginning just what job classification is being offered. They then follow up with the benefits that will accrue to the applicant who meets the classification requirements.

The real target of the image-building advertising, on the other hand, is *brains,* wherever they may occur in any capacity useful to the company. Magazine media are carefully selected to reach brainy audiences, and television is programmed for the same purpose.

Copy Appeals for Job-selling Advertising

For advertising to sell a job, copy appeals change from time to time, varying with the current mood of the prospects sought.

A few years back, when there was a fantastic demand for *young* engineers (older ones were not nearly so much in demand), big companies offered the prospect everything his engineer's heart could possibly desire. Dangled before his eyes were glamorous things to work with on the frontiers of science, challenges for eager-beaver problem solvers, free rein for creative imaginations, ultra-modern working conditions, extra on-the-job schooling, and unlimited opportunities for growth and advancement, including, perhaps, a chance to take a crack at management.

The more thoughtful advertisers remembered that the young engineer might be raising a family. They suggested to him that, at *their* plants, he could live in an attractive community of delightful homes, with golf and boating facilities nearby and a cultural atmosphere thrown in, not unlike that of a college campus.

In 1965, five years later, according to industrial relations specialist Lawrence Stessin, the mood of the market had changed. Large percentages of the young graduates intended to stay in college and reach for higher-status degrees. Those who did not had one eye on the Peace Corps and the other on government service.

The old-time good life, the fishing and golfing, was out. What was wanted now was work that was *meaningful,* and truly challenging.

As a result, the up-to-date recruiter stresses what his company is doing for society, how it battles to eradicate disease, or makes equipment to control water pollution, etc.

Recruiting Needs of Large Companies

When a large company needs men in a hurry, or in quantity, it naturally turns to the classified columns. But this emergency situation is relatively rare.

The very large company has a continuing but not an emergency need for a broad range of *many* job classifications. To fill these jobs, it seeks *quality* over quantity. For this, institutional image-building advertising has proved most useful.

One such company, with a general continuing need for young engineers *of many kinds,* ran a series of advertisements in engineering-college publications. With a picture-caption technique, it showed some of its own engineers at work on a *variety* of extremely interesting projects—one in a chemical area, another in electronics, and so on.

The ads made no attempt to solicit job applicants. The low-pressure copy did not even hint that such applicants were needed. It did, however, fulfill the image-making objective of inferring that this was a great place to work, especially for bright young men on the lookout for challenging assignments. The ads also indicated, by their illustrations and situations, that the company offered opportunities in a wide range of directions.

Corporate Image and Recruiting

Just as the corporation undergoes appraisal and judgment by the financial community, so also does it undergo searching appraisal by potential employees. Hence, a good corporate image has obvious value in recruiting.

The corporation with the best image—in the minds of the job-seekers—is likely to get first call on the most desirable talent at the beginning. If, for some reason, the desired talent is not hired, the image *keeps on working* and may bring in the prospect at a later date. A good image may be more influential with older men than with beginners.

As noted in the previous chapter, the same image items that appeal to the financial community are also valuable in recruiting. Too, a company's recruitment image may in part be a rub off of its reputation with the general public. This reputation might have been built up by general corporate advertising. Which, again, underlies the feasibility and usefulness of mutiple-objective, image-building advertisements.

Advertising to Brains

Recruitment interest has expanded to higher-echelon executive and management personnel. At the same time, notably in scientific circles, top-level corporation contacts with the educational and intellectual world have increased enormously.

To reach the common-denominator target of brains, many advertisers use such publications as *Harper's Magazine, Atlantic Monthly, Saturday Review of Literature, Scientific American, Harvard Business Review,* etc.

An outstanding example of the use of television programming to project a brain-appeal image has been the *GE College Bowl.* In this obviously recruiting-minded program, college brain teams compete against each other in answering questions of an intellectual nature.

Retail stores achieve images more quickly than most other forms of business. The stores have many contacts with the public. And their customers naturally compare one store with another, which aids the image-creating process.

Consequently, when a new store advertises for the first time, it automatically finds itself confronted with an image decision. It must decide, then and there, what kind of a store it is going to be. For the appearance and the typographic style of the advertisement have a way of telegraphing to the public a fair idea of the personality of the new store. And the customer, on entering the store, will expect a reflection of the image suggested by the advertising. If disappointed, he might never again patronize the store.

If the store is going to be a price-cutting bargain basement, it would do well to advertise in a bargain-basement manner—purposely clutter its page with products and prices. If it is going to be a high-priced specialty shop, its advertising should put on an air of aloof, aristocratic conservatism. And so on. Whatever the type or personality of the store and the more accurately the advertising reflects it, the better for the store's business. For the projected image will select and attract just those customers most responsive to it.

It is almost impossible for a retail store to avoid developing some kind of an image. The image will be influenced, probably first of all, by the quality and selection of the merchandise offered and the pricing. Next, the appearance of the store and its facilities will be important. Also the service and the spirit of the store's management. Such a basic image is self-creating. It does not depend on advertising. But advertising can build on it. Advertising can publicize the image to a wider public, clarify and interpret it, and enhance it at every opportunity.

Chapter **13**

RETAIL

INSTITUTIONAL

ADVERTISING

Sales Advertising and Institutional Advertising

Retail stores are in business to make money by selling goods at a profit. To help sell goods, a store can use two forms of advertising. Most stores use *both*. These are:

1. Direct product-selling advertising
2. Institutional advertising

The product-selling advertising is traditionally prepared and handled entirely by the store itself, without the assistance of an advertising agency. With institutional advertising, an agency is usually employed. The cost of sales advertising is charged on a pro rata basis against each product. The cost of institutional advertising is charged against the store or, in some cases, against the store's *total* sales.

The sales advertising simply sells products—as directly as possible. It concentrates on product-selling. It is the plain garden variety of store advertising seen in the newspapers every day.

We have already noted that retailing's use of institutional advertising as a *sales builder* differs from the practice of most other forms of business. In retailing, there is a functional reason for this.

The basic purpose of retail institutional advertising is *to get customers to come in to the store*. They can then shop there to their hearts' content.

The customer who does this has an opportunity to select not only from the relatively few products that can be offered in the sales advertising, but from the literally thousands of items presented by the store itself. She or he is almost certain to buy *something* and *may* buy a great deal. In the store, the pressure to buy is greater than when merely glancing through a newspaper. Instead of a picture of the product, the shopper can see the product itself, glamorously displayed. And she will see other wanted products, too, that the newspaper ad forgot to remind her of. The store is taking a part in the sale. So is the customer.

While the customer is in the store, the built-up imagery of the institution takes on a practical turn, because it can psychologically aid in tempting the customer to buy. For example, if the store's image confers a hint of status, that hint, at just the right moment, might tip the scales in selling an expensive item. If the image is of quality and reliability, it might provide assurance when a product is being examined. And if the image is that of a haven for bargains, one may be sure that the customer will be on the lookout for such bargains.

It will be seen, then, that institutional advertising has a substantial meaning for retail establishments. It supplements the work of the product-selling advertising, helps sell the *other* products that were too numerous to be included in the sales advertising, builds store traffic, increases turnover, and brings the customer back another day. The job of the institutional advertising is to make the prospect *think* of the store, *like* the store, want to be *in* the store, *go* to the store, and be happy to *buy* things there.

The World's Largest Store

The institutional note seems less visible today in the advertising of Macy's, "The world's largest store," than it did a generation or two ago. This is probably because Macy's—and almost all of its competitors—have established a ring of branch stores in the prosperous suburbs, with a consequent effect on advertising policies. The super-store has become the bellwether of a regional retailing chain.

The situation was quite different in the days before the advent of the suburban branches. Suburbanites did a much larger share of their department-store shopping in the city, and Macy advertising and image-building strove mightily to capture as much of this lucrative market as possible. Along with product-selling advertising, there was a constant stream of Macy institutional advertisements. These were usually two or three columns in width and were obviously aimed at the full-pursed, educated, quality-conscious, upper-middle-class suburbanite audience.

The ads were bright, sparkling, witty. They were brilliantly written and seemed to emphasize the "smart" rather than the "thrifty" in Macy's slogan: "It's smart to be thrifty." The ads seemed to have a penchant for humor and sophisticated gaiety.

"Not a Head Waiter Knew Him" was the headline of a parody ad spoofing a status-appeal type of advertising prevalent at the time. Another ad, "Imagine our embarrassment!" was a tongue-in-cheek apology for misquoting Charles Lamb's "Neat, not gaudy." In still another instance, in spite of the illustration, Macy's averred that "Though we don't actually bounce babies in our chemises, we do subject our underthings to very arduous and significant tests."

This institutional advertising, well supported by the store's selection and presentation of merchandise, established a strong image of *quality, reliability,* and *adequate good taste* at a reasonable ("6 per cent") price saving. Macy's was not the highest status store in the city, but it was a place where one could shop without *loss* of status, and where one could be confident of the quality of a great many items not easily found elsewhere. The image helped throng Macy's aisles with shoppers, even in Depression years.

Nobody but Nobody but Gimbels

At the very time that the Macy image was riding to glory, that of Gimbel's seemed to be in a decline. Gimbel's was fast becoming the forgotten store. Then Bernice FitzGibbon was called in as advertising director. During her directorship, in the late 1940s and early 1950s, Gimbel's advertising came to life and lifted the Gimbel image to a new eminence in the retailing world.

For the most part, Gimbel's ads remained product-selling ads. But things happened to words and sentences, to headlines and copy, to layout and typography, that began to change the sleepy Gimbel image with a violent alacrity. Ad after ad came out fighting. And the repeated war cry was the slogan: NOBODY BUT NOBODY UNDERSELLS GIMBELS, roared out at the world in over-size type.

Copy, in particular, became livelier, brighter, and more incisive. One ad showed a shadowy-gray silhouette of a good-looking girl with arms outstretched. Superimposed over the figure was the headline:

WHAT'S A POOR GIRL TO DO?

The text copy went on to say:

> Gimbels knows a poor girl is just the same as a rich girl. Is a rich girl's hair any curlier than a poor girl's? Are a rich girl's teeth any pearlier than a poor girl's? Is a rich girl, in short, any girl-ier than a poor girl? Of course not. The only thing that a poor girl doesn't have in the right place is money. Which brings up the question: what's a poor girl to do? Answer: come to *Gimbel's beautiful brand-new fashion floor* . . . .

The copy then talked about Gimbel's thrift and its lower-than-ever prices. It concluded with selling captions and prices for the coats and dresses shown on a frieze of models across the top of the ad.

The world's tallest newspaper typeface   A striking feature of this Gimbel advertising was the increasingly large size of the type used for headlines. When the headline stretched across the page and it didn't seem possible to make the type larger, one word was blown-up still larger, while the rest of the headline was made a little smaller to accommodate the giant-size word.

The letters were simple block letters printed with as dark a gray screen as the newspapers would allow. The lettering grew progressively larger in size as the campaign continued. At the beginning, the letters were about 2 inches high, as used for the word *packed* in the following headline:

GIMBELS IS PACKED . . . JAM PACKED WITH
LUGGAGE FOR CHRISTMAS.

Then, in another ad, the letters of the single word, *Spinets,* spread across the page were 3 inches high. Next came an ad with the word *Here,* more than 4 inches high, then another with the price figure *$5* at least 6 inches high, and still another with the word *More,* in elongated lower case, 7 inches high.

Finally, the ultimate was reached. In the word FURS, the letter "F" extended the full length of the page from top to bottom, more than 21 inches—perhaps the tallest newspaper typeface in history.

It should be said that these huge letters provided tremendous visual impact and attention-value, yet worked well with the product display in the ads. The large letters also quickly came to identify the ads as Gimbel's ads.

Image of Glamour . . . Lord & Taylor

Macy's and Gimbel's talk about thrift. And many of their customers, if not all, characteristically keep an eye on the pennies. But a different atmosphere pervades Lord & Taylor. Here, apparently, the customer is relaxed about price, *expects* to find quality, and looks for glamour. And finds it.

The Lord & Taylor store, a full department store, may at times be surpassed in smartness and expensiveness by her smaller, more specialized rivals near 57th Street. Her location, relatively speaking, is slightly downtown. Yet her appeal to the affluent buyer has never been lessened. In the higher-echelon suburbs, her enthusiastic market, she is regarded almost with reverence. No store in the metropolitan area enjoys such a magnificently favorable image as Lord & Taylor.

The keynote of the Lord & Taylor image is sheer glamour. The store itself is decorated to appear glamorous. The merchandise is nearly always interesting, sometimes truly exciting, and not necessarily expensive. The store's extra departments enhance rather than detract from its intriguing atmosphere. At Christmas, its wonderful window display is one of the sights of the city. Here one finds a bit of pure fairyland—and a very well-to-do fairyland at that. The store's service is gracious. Many a shopper feels a pleasurable thrill in just *being* in Lord & Taylor's.

Lord & Taylor's advertising aptly reflects the personality of the store. *This* advertising never, never looks like a bargain counter. Prices are often nonchalantly omitted. Artists depict products with a few sketchy brush strokes. Lord & Taylor's advertising is utterly relaxed. Its "name" fashion illustrators draw with a loose and carefree style in a sea of white space. And it can devote a whole newspaper page to a puppy with a slipper in its mouth being furiously chased around the page by a Siamese cat which finally captures the slipper.

With this, the only words of copy are:

> The chase really ends in our treasure-packed Slipper Shop.   LORD & TAYLOR

The signature, Lord & Taylor, is not printed, but handwritten with an air of studied swish. Fun abounds on a Lord & Taylor page, and freedom from want. And glamour. It has been this way for many years. And for many years, Lord & Taylor has continued to be a very prosperous store.

Ohrbach's

If Lord & Taylor is a successful example of one kind of store, Ohrbach's can be thought of as a successful example of almost the exact opposite kind. For years, Ohrbach's has been an embodiment of anti-glamour, of indifference to status, and of total disinterest in suburbia.[1] Ohrbach's store decor is plain and practical. It rips the status labels off quality merchandise. And its sharp-eyed customers are very much New Yorkers, very much city dwellers. But it *does* deliver with the incredible bargains its advertising promises.

Ohrbach's started as a grim Fourteenth Street price-cutter, in face-to-face competition with the redoubtable, equally price-cutting S. Klein. Both have prospered. But as time went on, Ohrbach's increasing preoccupation with higher style and with uptown quality items began to give it an individual image: "The fancypants of 14th Street."

Finally, Ohrbach's moved uptown, to the former McCreery location on 34th Street. Here it continues to prosper by offering good-merchandise values at startlingly low prices. It remains primarily a store for women, although there is a men's basement.

The store's clientele is strangely mixed. Some customers come from the lower East Side and some from the fashionable upper East Side. Some are bargain-conscious sales girls from other stores. Some are college graduates from the Village. Some are movie stars. They all have one thing in common—they know what they are about.

Ohrbach's attracts the smart shopper, the inveterate bargain hunter. Its customers can spot quality without the help of a status label. Ohrbach's greatest lure is its ability to offer the same luxury items found in elegant uptown stores at prices averaging 20 to 22 per cent below the uptown prices. And Ohrbach's pays attention to high fashion. It has its buyers in Paris, and its able copiers on Seventh Avenue, and beats the uptown stores in importing the latest mode.

[1] Like other stores, Ohrbach's now has satellite branches elsewhere, at least one of them in a suburb.

LIBERAL TRADE-IN

bring in your wife
and just a few dollars
...we will give you a new woman

Ohrbach's

NEW YORK • NEWARK • LOS ANGELES

"A BUSINESS IN MILLIONS...
A PROFIT IN PENNIES"

Why cheat yourself of the
newest and best just because you
think you can't afford it? At Ohrbach's,
you don't have to pay high prices for beautiful
things. And there are tremendous assortments
to choose from — all new, all exciting. Bring us
the wife you have now and we will transform
her into a lovely new woman —
for just a few dollars. It will be
the easiest payment you ever made!

NEW YORK, 14th ST. FACING UNION SQUARE • IN NEWARK, MARKET & HALSEY STS.

Sparkling ideas get the Ohrbach story across to smart women shoppers. Ohrbach's uses only institutional advertising to get customers into the store. After that, the store's bargains make the sales. (AGENCY: *Doyle Dane Bernbach*)

Accomplishing this has been no simple matter. Achieving Ohrbach's success has required brilliantly expert merchandising skill, inspired buying, incredibly high turnover and incredibly low overhead, and not least, enviable relations with both employees and suppliers.

Ohrbach's advertising   If Ohrbach's store-operating methods are unorthodox, its advertising is even more so. Though one of the most remorseless price-cutters in the city, Ohrbach's never advertises a bargain sale, never advertises its low prices. In fact, it never advertises merchandise at all. It depends entirely on *institutional* advertising! Furthermore, Ohrbach's spends a lower percentage of sales for advertising than any other department store and has an advertising budget one-thirtieth the size of Macy's.

Yet Ohrbach's business has soared to more and more millions of dollars each year. Hordes of women pour into its store aisles and struggle to get at counters to buy. More than once, the police have had to be called in to restore order among the mobs of eager buyers.

Idea-ads at Work

One reason for the economy of the advertising and the happy sales effect that has accompanied it may be found in its obvious creative excellence. Each one of these ads was widely seen and well remembered as they came along. This was because they were *idea*-ads. They had the power to catch attention and to penetrate reader-consciousness.

Nevertheless, the advertisements never ceased to be mindful of their unchanging objectives—(1) to reach out to the smart shopper, (2) to convey to her in a glance the personality of the store, (3) to intrigue her with the selling proposition, "high fashion at low prices," and (4) to get her to walk into the store. After that, the bargains she saw there were expected to sell themselves.

The advertisements were clever, some of them very, very clever. But in this advertising, one rarely finds an instance of cleverness for its own sake. In every case, the cleverness is immediately put to work to fulfill the advertising objectives. It *starts* by being on the track. Consequently, for all their gaiety and exuberance, these ads always work very hard.

One of these ads (page 117), the famous "cat lady" ad, is described in Chapter 16. Another, almost equally famous advertisement, pictured a man carrying his wife under his arm. The headline and subhead read:

LIBERAL TRADE-IN

Bring in your wife and just a few dollars
. . . we will give you a new woman

The text copy:

> Why cheat yourself of the newest and best just because you think you can't afford it? At Ohrbach's, you don't have to pay high prices for beautiful things. And there are tremendous assortments to choose from—all new, all exciting. Bring us the wife you have now and we will transform her into a lovely new woman—for just a few dollars. It will be the easiest payment you ever made! OHRBACH's—*A business in millions . . . a profit in pennies.*

It is a tribute to William Bernbach and the creative people of his agency, Doyle Dane Bernbach, that after fifteen years, this campaign has never seemed to lack for ideas or lose its bounce and freshness, but actually seems to get more interesting and surefooted as time goes on.

Chapter 14

CORPORATE-

IDENTITY

ADVERTISING

Thus far, most of the forms of non-product advertising discussed in this book have concerned very large corporations. But there is one form of institutional advertising, however, that can be of value to smaller companies as well. This is advertising to publicize the company's *name*, per se. It is called *corporate-identity advertising, name-identity advertising,* or *nameplate advertising.*

The purpose of this advertising is to make a company's name broadly known, thereby causing it to stand out from a forest of "unknown" competitors. In certain circumstances, and in certain industries, this name identity can confer definite benefits.

For very small companies, it can be the first step to business growth. It puts the company on the map and widens its circle of prospects for sales. It introduces the formerly obscure company to potential new customers. A known *name* instills confidence, attracts prospects, and makes sales easier.

Name-identity advertising also has value for the larger corporation that has previously remained relatively anonymous, but which decides, for various reasons, to seek name-publicity. A typical example of this would be a company, well known in its own field, which decides to diversify its business and enter other markets where its name is not known.

Sometimes a whole industry has traditionally maintained a policy of anonymity. For the progressive companies that wish to rise up out of this anonymous obscurity, corporate-identity advertising confers potent benefits. The classic example of this situation is found in the apparel industry.

Originally a melange of small, specialized, and frequently unstable units, this industry's operations leaned heavily on personal contacts. As it was also difficult to find an economic basis for advertising, the industry remained anonymous.

Growth of business, however, has forced changes in traditional practices. Small units have coalesced into much larger ones, with a hunger for broader markets. At the same time, the big chemical companies, introducing new synthetic fibers, have revolutionized many technical and business procedures. The need for advertising, and especially, the need for break-through corporate *name-identity*, became acute.

This identity became even more desirable when it was noticed that it could produce speedy and tangible rewards—that the best-known names had the best chance to snag the big sales.

Corporate Identity in the Apparel Business

Previously, the apparel industry had had difficulty in applying *sales* advertising to a product that could, unpredictably, be an instant hit or an instant flop and that would, even if successful, have a limited market life—a season, or the duration of a style. The need for nameplate identity now pushed the industry in the direction of *institutional* advertising.

This, in turn, led to a way in which the industry could publicize its products. If a proper showcase medium could be found, advertising for name-identity could be combined with a display of products currently up for sale.

A media showcase for apparel advertising   Such a media showcase *was* found—in the Sunday magazine section of the *New York Times*. Odd though this selection may seem to the layman, it offered a number of advantages to apparel-industry advertisers. It provided full color, with better than average attention to reproduction. And it involved no commitment to high fashion, or any other specialized point of view.

What appears to be the key motivation for selecting this medium, however, was the belief, expressed by members of the industry, that the top influentials who control large-scale apparel buying are readers of the *Times* magazine section. Whether or not this was true originally, it has probably become true, for all segments of the apparel industry now use this section as a super trade paper to advertise to each other.

The makers of the fibers, usually the big chemical companies, advertise to the mills, the mills to the garment makers, and the garment makers to the retail outlets. And all of them use the same ads to advertise to the consumer.

Structure of an apparel advertisement   Though ostensibly addressed to the consumer, these advertisements most certainly are *not* directed solely at the consumer. This is given away by their very structure. They do not look like consumer advertisements. There is no carefree Lord & Taylor swish to the portrayal of the garments, there are no glamorous, but distracting, backgrounds, and the models look like models, not like visiting duchesses. On the other hand, against a limbo background, the garments are worn, arranged, and photographed with meticulous attention to details.

The clincher give-away is the thin strip of text copy at the bottom of the ads. Here one finds no consumer words at all. This is pure catalog data. It tells what cloth the garment is made of, of what kind of fiber, what colors and sizes are available, what stores sell it, and it names an approximate price. It gives the advertiser's name *and address.*

Triple-objective Apparel Advertisements

As has been suggested earlier, display of a garment for sale is not the only objective of typical apparel advertisements appearing in the *Times* magazine section showcase. Actually, there are three objectives:

1. To attract attention
2. To build name-identity
3. To display a garment currently on sale

Attracting attention became important to the apparel advertiser because he found the rest of his industry doing the same thing he was. He needed an attention-getting device to make his ads stand out from the others.

To build name-remembrance, it was desirable that the attention-getting idea be a repetitive *campaign* idea, rather than a disconnected series of individual ad ideas. At the same time, the mechanics of the idea should not interfere with the display of the garment.

A number of repetitive campaign ideas of this type were developed. Some of them were unusually clever and effective. Some others tried too hard to be clever—obscuring the effectiveness of the ads.

Advertising for Russ Togs Perhaps the most incisive name-building campaign idea was that of Russ Togs, a manufacturer of coordinated apparel and sportswear for pre-teens, teen-age girls, and young women.

In these ads, the model, wearing colorful sportswear, stands in an appropriately active pose in what might be called a charging position. Her head is thrust forward in mock belligerency. From her clenched teeth hisses the one-word headline:

rrrrrrrrrrrr*russ*

The last four letters, "russ," are in black. The other "r's" are in red. In every ad, the pose and the headline are the same. Only the garment changes.

Repeated many times, with its simplicity and directness, this one-word headline and uncomplicated ad format has done a tremendous name-identity job for Russ Togs, and is proving highly memorable. The sales growth of this company has been spectacular.

Advertising for Klopman Mills   Another segment of the apparel industry is represented in the advertising of Klopman Mills, Inc., a division of
Burlington Industries, which sells fabrics.

Again, a model wears a showpiece garment, made out of a Klopman fabric.
In this series, the models and types of apparel differ from ad to ad. Models can
be children or men, as well as young women. For the fabrics can be made into
many types of garments.

What is startling about the Klopman illustrations is that, in every ad, the
standing model is leaning backward as if supported by a backrest. But no backrest is visible and it appears as if the model is supported by magic or by some
invisible force. Needless to say, this strange effect has surefire attention-getting
value—and continues to have, even after the ads have been seen many times.[1]

The headline, near the figure and always the same in every ad, reads:

> A MAN
> YOU CAN
> LEAN ON
> THAT'S
> KLOPMAN!

The phrase, *a man you can lean on,* is not without meaning in the apparel
industry. But the phrase's greatest value, combined with the leaning figure, lies
in its memorability and the powerful way it establishes name-identity.

Advertising for Foxwood   A third   right-to-the-point name-identity
campaign has been that of the Foxwood division of Grey-Wood Knitwear
Industries, makers of sweaters. In this format, behind a girl wearing a sweater
is a man who is pulling back the sweater collar in an effort to read the label.
Near the man's head is the headline:

> It says: Foxwood

In a similar, earlier campaign, the man said:

> What was that name again?

And the girl replied:

> Foxwood

The visual effect of this campaign has been enlivened by a small amount of
amusing, but not overdone, mugging on the part of the girl model. The simplicity of this campaign, plus the pointed suggestion to look for the label, makes
it a strong name-identity builder.

---

[1] When photographed, the model *is* supported by a backrest, which is later removed from the
picture.

Other apparel advertisers   Still another campaign of the repeated-pose type has been the Pantino series, showing a pert, amusing, rear-view pose of a model wearing Pantino pants.

The advertising for Cos Cob differs from other apparel campaigns in the *Times* magazine section. Ads are only two columns wide, in black and white instead of color, pen-and-ink drawings instead of photography, and have no headline. Yet, with this low-cost advertising, Cos Cob achieves high and memorable name-identity.

The illustrations, drawn in a nostalgic, old-fashioned-looking pen technique, depict a young man and a young woman in various sentimental situations. These situations are explained in romantic story copy that suddenly switches around to call attention to the dress worn by the girl.

For example, in one advertisement, the young couple are standing on steps before what looks like the stately columns of an old Southern mansion. The copy reads:

> "Everything is just as you left it," she said, indicating the mansion grounds. He leaned closer. "But *you've* changed, Nancy Jane. You're a woman now—and a beautiful one." Her cheeks went scarlet and she clasped her hands tightly against the folds of her Cos Cob shirtwaist, an enduring classic in a delicately flowered cotton print. Sizes 8–18. Look for Cos Cob at fine stores.   COS COB

In this deftly written series, one intriguing little romantic story follows another, in colorful locales from the Taj Mahal to Oxford to the Isles of Greece. Soon the reader gets to look for these ads and reads the text to find out what is happening to the girl in the Cos Cob dress.

Attention-getting Devices Can Be Over-emphasized

The real secret of success in the aforementioned advertisements lies in their simplicity and directness. They are clever, but the cleverness does not get in the way of the message of the ad.

Not all apparel-industry advertising has achieved this simplicity. Some advertisers have gone to frantically excessive lengths to get attention. There has been a craze, on the part of not one, but several advertisers, for picturing people upside down. Another device has been a youngster making "kid" funny faces. In still another instance, trick art director layouts seem to dismember people and put them together again the wrong way.

The ads certainly get attention. But the attention is so concentrated on the stunt device, it is diverted from everything else. The message is lost and the product scarcely seen. And the name of the advertiser can soon be forgotten.

A MAN YOU CAN LEAN ON THAT'S KLOPMAN!

Abby Kent wanted a great fabric for this dress, so they came to Klopman. We gave them the best—Klopman's "Milk 'n Honey"™ 65% Dacron® polyester and 35% combed cotton broadcloth print. It stays cool and collected from one end of the day to the other. That's the sort of virtue you can take for granted in every Klopman fabric. You can discover the difference. Solid trim on print dress in gold, blue or pink combinations. Sizes 10 to 18. About $18. At Gimbel's, N.Y. and branches

John Wanamaker, Philadelphia; The Hecht Co., Baltimore; The Hecht Co., Washington, D.C.; Thalhimer's, Richmond; Jordan Marsh, Miami. Fabric by Klopman Mills, Inc., 450 Seventh Ave., New York 1. A Division of Burlington Industries, Inc.

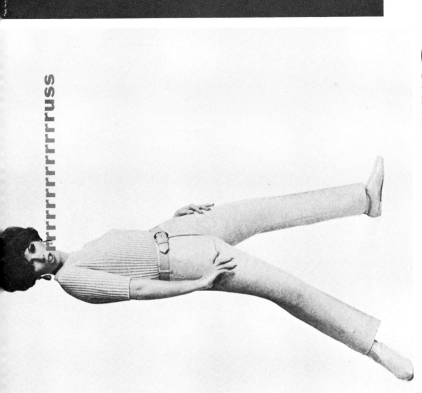

rrrrrrrrrrruss

From the celebrated Russ Corner of country clothes: the rich little poor girl look, made up of heatherspun stovepipe pants, garrison belted in sizes 8-18 at about $8; poor boy ribbed sweater of Orlon® acrylic, S-M-L, about $7. Outfit in gold, blue, pink, or green. At MACY'S, New York City & branches; G. FOX & CO., Hartford; BAMBERGER'S, Newark & branches; LIT BROTHERS, Philadelphia; LANSBURGH'S, Washington, D. C. Russ Togs, 1372 Broadway, New York, N. Y. 10018.

Each of these advertisements is representative of a campaign in which poses and headlines are repeated. Only the garment displayed is changed from ad to ad. Objective of both campaigns is corporate name identity, plus display of a current product. (AGENCY, both campaigns: *Altman, Stoller, Chalk*)

Name-identity Advertising in Other Industries

The apparel industry offers a good demonstration of name-identity advertising in action. Such advertising, however, can also have potency for other industries.

Nicholson files sell well in hardware stores. Yet Nicholson advertising has consisted of one-column cartoon advertisements, showing a file being used in a comic, completely humorous way. These ads made no attempt at all to do any selling for the file. They said:

A NICHOLSON FILE
FOR EVERY PURPOSE

The long-continued series impinged on the viewer's subconscious, linking "Nicholson" and "file" together in a single thought: "Nicholson file." The link suggested that Nicholson was the company that specialized in files—hence, must be good at making them. When the time came to purchase a file—a relatively infrequent purchase—there was a strong psychological urge to select Nicholson, even over the most famous names in hardware.

The Power of Name-publicity

Advertising men, who have talked themselves into believing that only *argument* can make a sale, continually underestimate the strange power of name-publicity. It *can* sell, and it *has* sold many times. It works because it bores into the mind's subconscious regions, gathers emotional strength there, and pops out again at a critical moment, when the buyer's logic guard is down.

By mere association and suggestion, the familiarity of a remembered name instills buyer *confidence*. Actually, name-identity and name-publicity make thousands of sales every day in the supermarkets and department stores. And, the advertising that gave our greatest companies their start was often name-identity advertising. It is still a powerful advertising force—whether for product-selling or the selling of institutional ideas—and is not to be overlooked.

One of the older forms of institutional advertising is corporate-*prestige* advertising. To many advertising men in the past and to some still, this is what institutional advertising is supposed to have meant. It is advertising that concentrates on building the *prestige* of a company's reputation as a means of selling the company's products.

Of course, as we have seen, the present-day use of the word *institutional* includes many other objectives besides corporate-prestige building. Corporate-prestige building is only *one* kind of institutional advertising. And, we have noted that the marketers of competitive packaged goods would consider corporate name-prestige building a rather weak selling force.

Nevertheless, in special areas of advertising corporate prestige continues to have validity and usefulness for some advertisers. For them it not only has a sales-building function, but also offers desired public relations values with certain auxiliary publics.

Chapter 15

CORPORATE-

PRESTIGE

ADVERTISING

The Place for Corporate-prestige Advertising

Corporate-prestige advertising is most effective when:

1. The nature of the product is such that the consumer cannot evaluate it himself and must rely on the reputation of the manufacturer.

2. The nature of the business is such that the seller cannot advertise his products in the usual unrestricted way. (This would apply to ethical drugs.)

3. The company has already built an overwhelmingly dominant reputation in its field and seeks to protect its position.

Combination Uses of Corporate-prestige Advertising

Justification for corporate-prestige advertising is increased when the advertising can accomplish multiple objectives at the same time. That is, while the advertising builds prestige among consumers, it might also be favorably impressing the financial community, or it might present a good image to the government, etc.

In certain circumstances, and if budgets are adequate, corporation-prestige advertising can be run *in addition* to product-selling advertising.

Frequent Weaknesses of Corporate-prestige Building

An inherent weakness of corporate prestige today is the danger that it may not be permanent. With present-day technological advances and with effervescent competition, it becomes increasingly difficult to maintain a strong reputation of superiority. Established leaders can be toppled by up-and-coming competition.

Corporate prestige is good only as long as one possesses it and only as long as it works. Hence, if possessed, it should be protected and fought for as a valuable property. On the other hand, when it slips away, an immediate change in advertising approach is called for. And this should be energetic. Serious corporate declines have been preceded by an attempt to coast along on yesterday's reputation.

For the company that does not really enjoy a true prestige reputation, but merely desires it, corporate-prestige advertising should be approached with utmost caution. It may not be worth its cost. In fact, high among the causes of ineffective corporate advertising are the many ill-considered efforts to buy prestige for its own sake.

And certainly, for the familiar marketplace branded product, straight product-selling advertising normally should be vastly preferred over the doubtful sales effect of mere company name prestige.

Corporate-prestige advertising, then, properly belongs in those special areas where corporate prestige has selling weight, where other selling methods cannot be applied, and where, apparently, it *does* work.

Some Famous Corporate-prestige Advertisements

Corporate-prestige advertising was looked upon with much more favor in the first two decades of the twentieth century than it ever has been since. It was in tune with the times, was highly respected as a way of advertising, and was practiced by leading corporations. Some of the advertisements of this era achieved a lasting fame among advertising men. For example, a 1915 advertisement contained, within a simple ruled border and a fair expanse of white space, the words:

TIFFANY & CO.
PEARLS
PEARL NECKLACES

That was all. There was no address. Everybody was supposed to know where Tiffany was—and everybody did in those days.

The conservatism and the touch of snobbery implicit in the ad appealed to those who could afford to do business with Tiffany's. This type of advertising seemed to work well for a long time. It was not until new generations and new competition came along that Tiffany was forced to include first an address and then pictures of the product.

Also in 1915 appeared Cadillac's famous "Penalty of Leadership" advertisement, a long, all-text essay on the pleasures and pains of leadership. It made a tremendous impression on advertising men, many of whom venerate it to this day as one of the great ads of all time. While other advertising men are somewhat less impressed by the wordy text, the fact remains that the image of leadership projected by this ad is little different from the image borne by Cadillac today.

A few years later, in 1921, E. R. Squibb & Sons published an advertisement entitled "The Priceless Ingredient." The key section of this advertisement was an "oriental fable" in which Hakeem, the Wise One, advises a young man to "look for the priceless ingredient of every product," which turns out to be "the honor and integrity of its maker."

This advertisement received considerable acclaim and was repeated, in various forms, a number of times. But more important, its priceless-ingredient theme became the basis of Squibb advertising for many years afterward. This advertising adhered to an unchanging format: a black-and-white photograph, an abstract headline such as, "From experience comes faith," and brief, but philosophic copy leading to the priceless-ingredient slogan.

The advertising could be described as low pressure, low yield. It was oversubtle, devious, and indirect and often quite dull. Its accomplishment, per ad, was small and hence costly. Yet its relentless continuity over the years did an enviable job for Squibb. It conferred a mantle of industry leadership for Squibb ethical drugs—made it the most "trustworthy" name.

It also included an image of respectability. This was needed by Squibb to counteract a negative image once induced by its own over-enthusiastic toothpaste advertising.

When Squibb was absorbed by Olin Mathieson, the Squibb image remained so strong that Olin has needed special advertising to link the two names together.

Steinway   Corporate-prestige advertising is obviously a correct approach

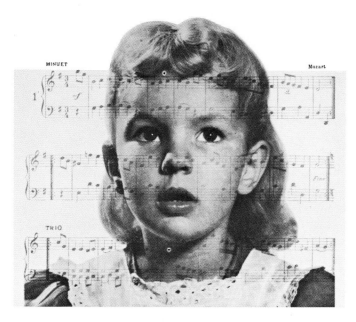

MINUET   Mozart

Beyond range of sight

ARTUR RUBINSTEIN uses the Steinway exclusively, as does virtually every great artist today. Brailowsky, Casadesus, Firkusny, Freccia, Horowitz, Kapell, Levant, Magaloff, Mildner, Milstein, Novaes, Ormandy, Pressler, Serkin, Toscanini, Uninsky, and many more. . . . Over 1000 music schools and music departments of leading colleges use the Steinway. . . . Illustrated is the beautifully proportioned Regency design. . . . For name of nearest Steinway representative, see your classified telephone directory.

Through eager eyes, your child explores a world that grows as she grows. But there is also — beyond range of sight — an inner realm where character is formed. Here music is a profound influence, which leads foresighted parents to help their children look at life through music.

This is the value of a Steinway in the home. The Steinway, whether regal Grand or exquisite Vertical, is both companion and mentor to your child. No other piano equals its depth and brilliance of tone, its power, its incredibly fluent action. And since the Steinway will serve your children, and your children's children, it is both a wise investment and the most economical of pianos! See your Steinway representative about prices, terms, date of delivery. Steinway & Sons, Steinway Hall, 109 W. 57th Street, New York 19.

STEINWAY
THE INSTRUMENT OF THE IMMORTALS

Name prestige is an important element in the selling advertising of Steinway, "The Instrument of the Immortals." This advertising performs both a protective and a selling function. (AGENCY: *N. W. Ayer & Son*)

for a company whose reputation is overwhelmingly dominant in its field. Such a company has been Steinway. Its industry stature has been colossal.

Steinway pianos have been used by almost every great pianist and most great composers since Richard Wagner. It has been standard equipment for the concert stage and in music schools. The objectives of this company's advertising, therefore, were (1) to protect its name reputation and (2) to sell pianos for use in the home.

Steinway constructed its advertising around the phrase "The Instrument of the Immortals." Somewhere, in every ad, at least one of these immortals was pictured, either large or small.

Sentimental themes, woven around an appealing picture of a child learning to play the piano, were used to promote use of a Steinway in the home. These advertisements were characterized by imaginative artwork and well-written copy and were notable for their creative excellence. In them, sentiment and prestige were combined most effectively.

Hamilton Watches   In its earlier advertising years, Hamilton Watches built up a strong prestige image as "The Watch of Railroad Accuracy." Later, to expand its markets, and capitalizing on its reputation for accuracy, Hamilton advertised the watch as an especially fine gift at Christmas, graduation, etc.

Two ads of the later series became famous for their excellent text copy. The copy was in the form of a note. In one ad, the note was written from a husband to a wife. In the other, it was from the wife to the husband. The first note:

To Peggy—for marrying me in the first place . . .
   for bringing up our children—while I mostly sat back and gave advice.
   for the 2,008 pairs of socks you've darned.
   for finding my umbrella and my rubbers Heaven knows how often!
   for tying innumerable dress ties.
   for being the family chauffeur, years on end.
   for never getting sore at my always getting sore at your bridge playing.
   for planning a thousand meals a year—and having them taken for granted.
   for a constant tenderness I rarely notice but am sure I couldn't live without.
   for wanting a *good* watch ever so long . . . and letting your slow-moving husband think he'd hit on it all by himself.
   for just being you . . . *Darling, here's your Hamilton with all my love!*
                                                                          Jim

And the second note:

To Jim—for holding my hand tight the day we were married . . .
   for seldom remarking, "That's what I had for lunch."
   for sparing me those chilly trips to heat the 6 a.m. bottle.
   for never opening my mail (though I sometimes do yours!).
   for the things you didn't say the time I ripped off the fender.
   for balancing my checkbook without grumbling or pitying.
   for not having to be defrosted when I forgot to send your suit to be pressed.
   for treating my women friends as though you liked them.
   for the way your eyes light up when our glances happen to meet at a party.
   for being so eternally *there* for me to lean on!
   for wanting a *good* watch for years and years, but being too unselfish to go and spend the money on yourself.
                              Dearest, here's your Hamilton with all my love!
                                                                          Peggy

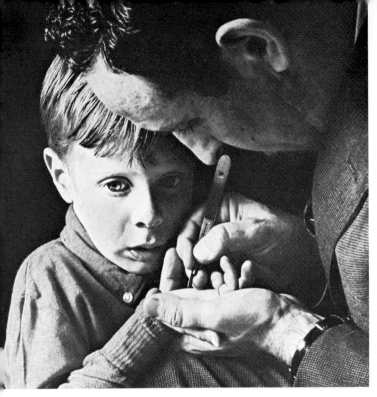

How to take a big risk out of a little injury

Most wounds, regardless of size, carry some risk of infection. But a seemingly trivial puncture wound—from a splinter or a rusty nail that pierces the skin—should always be regarded with suspicion. It may harbor germs of tetanus, or lockjaw.

Fortunately, children can be protected from this dangerous disease with injections of tetanus toxoid. Or, with use of a "triple vaccine," they may be immunized against tetanus and also diphtheria, and whooping cough. Injections should be started in infancy. Thereafter, booster doses are needed every few years to maintain immunity.

If you are uncertain about the status of your child's immunity to tetanus, it's always wise to consult a physician about any penetrating wound.

Medical science has made striking progress in treating wounds of all types—accidental and surgical. Today, the lives of patients are rarely endangered by "blood poisoning" from massive wound infections. This is but one of many advances achieved with newer chemical and antibiotic drugs.

Improving existing medicines and creating new ones for the betterment of your health is the continuing objective of Parke-Davis.

PARKE-DAVIS
BETTER MEDICINES FOR A BETTER WORLD

Dramatic advertisements featuring the beneficial uses of modern medicines provide corporate prestige for Parke-Davis. This, in turn, confers benefits for the company with several publics at the same time. (AGENCY: *Young & Rubicam*)

Parke-Davis & Company Parke-Davis is a manufacturer of ethical drugs.[1] Its sales contacts are with physicians, pharmacists, and hospitals.

This company has used institutional advertising for thirty-six years, the longest continuous series of its kind in the pharmaceutical field.

The most recent campaign is basically a corporate-prestige campaign with public service overtones, but it also acts as an umbrella to encompass a variety of objectives and purposes. It aims, first of all, "to add luster" to Parke-Davis's reputation among physicians and pharmacists, i.e., its customers. It wants to point up the image of Parke-Davis as a leader in medical research. It tries to interest more young people to seek careers in medicine and medical research.

[1] Those drugs prescribed by a physician.

Addressing itself to the consumer public, it seeks both to be remembered and looked upon favorably by that public. And it would like that public to understand that a great deal of talent, time, and money goes into the research, development, manufacture, and distribution of new medicines.

Parke-Davis hopes, overall, that the total effect of the advertising will be to increase business over the years.

And reading between the lines of the stated objectives, one might also suspect that the company hoped, too, that the advertising might have a protective image-building effect in government circles.

On the surface, it would seem that the Parke-Davis umbrella is an exceedingly broad one and that it could be attempting to cover too many subjects at once. In reality, however, many of the multiple objectives overlap and relate closely to each other, thereby making the advertising task less formidable than it might seem at first glance.

It is being accomplished by an informative campaign describing the curative uses of various drugs and medicines. In its dissemination of health knowledge, the campaign has public service values. At the same time, by pointing to Parke-Davis's role in researching, developing, manufacturing, and distributing these medicines, the copy fulfills other objectives. Dramatic color photographs and interesting headlines assure attention-value.

Earlier informative Parke-Davis campaigns rendered a service in publicizing the history of medicine and the history of pharmacy.

Five

THE CREATIVE APPROACH

The word *idea* has a great many shades of meaning, so many, in fact, that its numerous sub-definitions occupy nearly 6 inches of small type in the big Webster dictionary.

Ideas come in all sizes and shapes. Some ideas are small and transient; some are so big that they have dominated the history of the world for thousands of years. They appear in all areas of man's activity.

In all fields, what most aptly characterizes a true idea is its freshness and originality. It is not just merely a thought. It is a *creation of something new—* something that did not exist in the world before.

Curiously, this shining new concept is most often created by the recombination of *old* concepts in a new and different way.

A Picasso abstraction is made up of ideas. So are comedian Bob Hope's jokes. Inventions are ideas. In marketing and advertising, the merchandising gimmick is one kind of idea. Another is the explosive mixture of headline and picture that makes an advertisement a stopper; i.e., it *stops* the reader and plunges him into reading the advertisement's copy message. This last is the type of idea that concerns us specifically.

Such an idea is not just a picture *and* a headline, but the two *combined* together—chemically—in a way to jolt the reader's consciousness and arouse his immediate curiosity.

This *visual-verbal* idea is a vital, basic instrument of technique for institutional advertising. An ability to create exciting ideas is a major key to success in this kind of advertising. For it is the indispensable first step toward the fulfillment of institutional advertising's obligation to be interesting. Attractive artwork and well-written copy can help, but they are only fully effective as contributing factors to the power of the idea. The idea comes first.

Characteristics of a Good Idea

Sometimes, visual-verbal ideas may have *dual-interest* characteristics. That is, if we cover up the

Chapter **16**

THE

VISUAL-VERBAL

IDEA

headline, the picture will be interesting enough to stop the reader by itself. And, if we cover up the picture, the headline will be interesting enough by itself to act as a stopper and a compellent to draw the reader into the copy.

This is highly desirable and a goal to be sought by art directors and copywriters. But much more important is that the picture and headline mesh together as a *combined* visual-verbal idea. As long as this teamwork is complete, it becomes relatively unimportant whether the picture dominates, or whether the words of the headline deliver the punch of the idea.

Another basic characteristic of a *good* idea is that it be germane to the objective of the advertisement, be completely on the track toward the idea-selling message developed in the text copy.

The idea that is only an attention-getter and requires a sharp turn to get into the message is a failure, no matter how startling it might be. Because the sharp turn is where the reader is likely to fall out of the ad. This has been verified many times by readership research.

A good idea starts its selling job at the same time it ensnares the prospect's interest, and the selling should proceed in a straight line to the end of the copy. There is no special advantage in deliberately concealing what the ad is about until the reader gets down into the copy. He may not get that far. Nor is there anything wrong with the advertisement that succeeds in getting across *most* of its objective-selling message in the picture and headline at the same time they are arousing interest, thereby leaving little work left for the copy to do.

When this happens, the advertiser can consider himself fortunate. He is getting ten times as much audience, ten times as much value for his money as when the objective-fulfillment is delayed. His idea-selling message is being delivered in the exciting upstairs part of the ad, the part seen by 40 or 50 or more per cent of the readers, instead of, as so often occurs, far *down* in the copy, a region generally reached by 5 or 7 per cent.

A good idea should have startle, or stopper, quality. This was once called "What-the-hell?" quality. It should make the viewer say mentally, "What the hell?" and then rush to the copy to find out what's going on.

Examples of Visual-verbal Ideas

One example of a visual-verbal idea is provided by the picture and headline of the Better Vision Institute advertisement on page 113. The illustration is a seashore photograph of two shapely young ladies striding by in bathing suits. The picture, however, is blurred and out of focus, much as it might be seen by a near-sighted person. The headline:

YOU CAN GO THROUGH LIFE MISSING A LOT

This advertisement had an important story to tell, namely the need for frequent eye examinations, and it did it very successfully with a dramatic demonstration.

Some years ago, Young & Rubicam created a long and brilliant series of advertisements for the Travelers Insurance Company, based on picture-headline ideas. One of these advertisements revealed a view of a very uncomfortable man sitting in the witness chair at a trial. The picture was entirely black and white, except for the man's face, which had a fiery-red tint on it. The headline read:

THE MAN IN THE SOUP

The copy naturally pointed to the value of the Travelers Company at such an embarrassing moment. The Starch Ratings for this ad, both for observation and for readership, reached record highs. It was not an ad that could be easily passed by without seeing, looking, and reading.

Great Ideas from Simple Ingredients

In many idea ads, unusual artwork or clever layout provides the major punch. In others, the excitement is supplied by colorful words in a brilliant headline. But there is still another type of ad where the visual and verbal elements are relatively simple. The stopper quality comes from the wallop of the idea itself.

An excellent example is a famous advertisement of the Maryland Casualty Company. The illustration was a photograph of a twisted and broken child's tricycle overturned on the curb of a street. Nearby lay a boy's cap and toy policeman's badge. The headline read:

THEY GOT THE "G-MAN"

The text copy that followed drove home the message. It started:

He won't be home for supper tonight. There will be no solemn explaining to Dad that G-men haven't time to scrub dirty hands . . . no imaginative tale of 'desprit' criminals run to earth . . . no drowsy admission that perhaps an ace sleuth can submit to a mother's good night kiss without loss of dignity.

Not tonight . . . nor for all the nights to come . . . because today a heedless driver didn't see a little boy on his tricycle.

The Maryland has been very near to tragedies like this. . . . (The copy then goes on to explain Maryland's role in the highway safety movement).

A black-and-white advertisement for Kennecott Copper showed a close-up photograph of fingers putting a penny in a home fuse. The headline:

EASY, LOW COST WAY TO SET FIRE TO YOUR HOUSE!

After warning against the danger of fire incurred by doing this trick, the copy linked the burned-out fuse to inadequate wiring and urged the reader to call on his electrician for more wiring circuits.

These advertisements exemplify idea in its purest form. What they are, in fact, are powerful dramatizations of the copy story.

Ideas with Visual Impact

Probably the greater part of all ad ideas derive their major excitement from the *visual* presentation. Perhaps the visual predominates over the verbal because the visual, generally speaking, offers the easiest, most natural approach to the development of an idea. The art director's coup, however, must immediately be followed up by the cooperation of the copywriter.

In an almost unbelievable photograph, an Ohrbach's newspaper advertisement featured a cat wearing a woman's hat and holding a long cigarette holder in its mouth. The headline:

I FOUND OUT ABOUT JOAN

The text copy:

> The way she talks you'd think she was in Who's Who. Well! I found out what's with *her*. Her husband own a bank? Sweetie, not even a bank *account*. Why that palace of hers has wall-to-wall mortgages! And that car, Darling, that's horsepower, *not* earning power. They won it in a fifty-cent raffle! Can you imagine? And those clothes! Of course she *does* dress divinely. But really . . . a mink stole and Paris suits and all those dresses . . . on *his* income? Well darling, I found out about that, too. I just happened to be going her way and *I saw Joan come out of Ohrbach's!*

This ad is *all* idea, from beginning to end. But it couldn't have gotten started without the amazing photograph.

Another Travelers Insurance ad showed a cat falling from above, somersaulting, and landing on its feet at the bottom of the page. The words followed each other in a single column down the left side of the ad, from top to bottom. They said: "Cats seldom stumble, tumble, slip or topple. When they do they always seem to land on their feet. Not so with humans. Hence, accident insurance. You need the best."

This is a *layout* tour de force. It gives an effect of actual motion on the page.

A full-color advertisement for Wheeling Steel portrays a table setting, but instead of plates, each item of food, from soup to nuts, is shown in an opened, shining tinned-steel can. Headline:

THE CANS THAT CAME TO DINNER

Text copy reminds that practically any meal at all can be dished up in a jiffy from cans. Steel and tin protect health and the quality of the cans' contents. Wheeling makes the steel.

Ideas with Verbal Dominance

Ideas that draw their major strength from the *words* of the headline are relatively few. This may be because the literary approach to advertising was frightened away by the clamor of the hard-sellers many, many years ago. Or it may be that, in too many agencies today, the art director has been depended upon too heavily to supply the really creative flare for the ads. Recently, however, there has been an improvement in the writing of text copy, and there is hope that this may lead to a renaissance in headline writing.

Of those ideas that are outstanding mostly because of their headline, perhaps the greatest is that British Travel advertisement showing a view of King Henry VII's Chapel at Westminster Abbey, with the magnificent headline:

TREAD SOFTLY PAST THE LONG, LONG SLEEP OF KINGS

The picture is interesting, but it is not in itself a stopper. In this ad, it is the headline that stops the reader.

In an advertisement for National Library Week, there is no illustration at all, just a large area of white space in the center of which are the letters of the alphabet, as follows:

abcdefghijklmnopqrstuvwxyz

The headline is:

Your public library has these arranged in ways that make you cry, giggle, love, hate, wonder, ponder, and understand.

Some other verbally exciting headlines:

Nobody ever comes here. Only artists and poets.   (*French Tourist Office*)

Come to JAMAICA—it's no place like home!   (*Jamaica Tourist Board*)

Why TUESDAY couldn't marry THURSDAY (*General Electric Air Conditioning*)

Special Types of Idea-ads

There are some special types of ads that are worthy of passing notice. The Ogilvy agency has a liking for advertisements that provide useful information in the form of a guide. These advertisements have picture-caption-type layouts (ads made up entirely of a number of small pictures with captions, rather than the conventional large single picture and copy block). The more current guides seem to be descendants of the celebrated 1950 Ogilvy ad "Guinness Guide to Oysters."

This gustatory ad displayed nine different kinds of oysters (all of which went well with Guinness). The captions under each oyster supplied much erudite information. Another ad (1962) in this category bore the headline:

TOURIST'S GUIDE TO BRITISH MONEY
(*Take it with you when you go*)

This agency has also provided guides to British food, British poets, Oxford, and "Britain's castles—their lords, heroes, sorcerers, and scoundrels."

The Idea and Layout

Because the visual so often predominates in advertisement ideas, it may be well to consider the factor of *layout* in relation to idea. Layout is the arrangement of elements on an advertising page and is the natural province of the agency art director. However, since an idea involves *both* art and copy, their interrelation in layout can be of general interest.

Basic Layouts

At present, and for some years past, there have been three basic layouts for magazine advertisements: (1) squared-up solid picture, (2) white space, and (3) picture caption. There are, of course, endless variations. But practically all advertisements fall into one or another of these categories, or of a related variation.

In the 1920s, there was a very popular rat-tail layout that started with a fairly large picture near the top of the ad, then led down to smaller and smaller pictures (usually vignetted), which was supposed to lead the eye along a sinuous "S" path down to the logo signature. Today, this layout seems to be totally extinct.

Layout with squared-up picture The squared-up picture layout, in its purest form, consists of a large rectangular picture, a headline, and a copy block ending with a signature. It is sometimes called "N. W. Ayer No. 1," because that agency made use of it frequently far back in the early days of modern advertising. In its earlier versions, the picture occupied approximately half of

You can go through life missing a lot.
(and never know it)

Odd thing about our eyes.

Just let us see well enough to get along without too much trouble and it never occurs to us we might be seeing a good deal better.

Unless, of course, we've had a professional eye examination.

Then, as a result, many of us suddenly discover what the world actually looks like. See, perhaps for the first time, the bright, beautiful shape of things.

And like what we see.*

This being so, how come we never realized how much we were missing?

Simple. Seeing is subjective. The way we see is the way we think *everybody* sees. So we may well go through life missing a lot.

Unless, as was said, we have discovered otherwise—through the help of a qualified eye-care practitioner.

And when, by the way, was the last time you had your eyes examined? **Better Vision Institute.**

Don't forget, there are prescription sunglasses, too. Most practical, for example, for reading on the beach. And things like that.

The blurred effect of the illustration catches attention. It also helps demonstrate the theme of this Better Vision Institute advertisement.
(AGENCY: *Doyle Dane Bernbach*)

the advertisement (never *exactly* half; there was an art directors' taboo against that). The picture was almost always a painting or other artwork.

Later, as photography gradually superseded artwork, the picture area grew in size and the copy area shrank. An even more recent trend has been to bleed the photograph to the edges of the page to achieve more size and impact. Copy became restricted to a narrow strip along the bottom of the page. Excellent examples are the Olin and Better Vision Institute advertisements pictured above and elsewhere in this book.

113

Finally, following a style at one time much favored by *McCall's* magazine, the photograph covers the entire page, with the text surprinted over lighter areas of the picture.

The squared-up picture layout is simple and practical. It is for that reason that it has lasted so many years and may continue for many more. It has become the fundamental form of the print advertisement.

White-space layout In the white-space layout, silhouetted objects or persons float in a background of white space. Type is printed in the white space. This layout gives the art director unlimited opportunities for design and visual

The picture and headline ingredients of this Maryland Casualty Company ad are relatively simple. The impact comes from the power of the idea itself. (AGENCY: *J. M. Mathes*)

"Unforeseen events . . .
need not so often change and shape the course of man's affairs"

THEY GOT THE "G-MAN"

He won't come home for supper tonight. There will be no solemn explaining to dad that G-men haven't time to scrub dirty hands . . . no imaginative tale of "desprit" criminals run to earth . . . no drowsy admission that perhaps an ace sleuth can submit to a mother's good-night kiss without loss of dignity.

Not tonight . . . nor for all the nights to come . . . because today a heedless driver didn't see a little boy on his tricycle.

The Maryland has been very near to tragedies like this. Close to the automobile industry from the first, it realized that as the speed of travel increased, there would come an increase in traffic hazards,

especially among children. Faced with this problem, The Maryland early became a pioneer leader in the highway safety movement.

• • •

In this 40th anniversary year of The Maryland, we feel that the effort has been worthwhile, that hundreds of young lives have been saved. The educational work will continue . . . posters, pamphlets, lecturers will carry the safety message to motorists, into the schools and the home. You can do *your* part. When at the wheel, remember that children are impulsive, do unpredictable things in the excitement of play, at any moment may dart in front of *your* car. *Drive carefully.*

THE MARYLAND
MARYLAND CASUALTY COMPANY · BALTIMORE

Easy, low cost way to set fire to your house!

Did you ever try to keep an electric fuse from blowing by placing a penny or piece of foil behind it?

That's a trick practiced by too many home-owners whose fuses seem to have a regular habit of blowing-out.

It's a quick and easy way to trouble!

Without a fuse or circuit-breaker guarding them, wires overheat, burn through their insulation...cause short-circuits, sparks, *fire!*

Yes, a penny behind a fuse certainly spells danger. It's usually a sign of something else. too...a sick *electrical system.* Because frequently-blown fuses, tripped circuit-breakers,

indicate wiring too small, too weak to keep up with the demands for power placed upon it.

Does *your* electrical equipment fail to live up to your expectations? Do your lights dim when you turn on appliances? Do your toaster and your iron heat up slowly? Does your TV set show pictures often smaller than they should be? Do you have too few outlets and switches around the house?

If so, you're a victim of *inadequate wiring.* You're not only suffering inconvenience and risking danger. You're losing good money on wasted current!

Why put up with it? Ask your local electrician for an electrical check-up!

LOOK TO YOUR WIRING!

Electricity is today's greatest bargain. But it takes adequate wiring to bring it to you. So...

If you own a house, see your electrician. He will gladly study your wiring, tell you what work may be needed, and its cost.

If you plan to buy a house, check the age and capacity of its wiring. Or have an electrician do it for you.

If you are going to build, be sure to plan for the *future* as well as for today. Remember, your electrical needs will average a 10% increase *every year!*

Kennecott Copper Corporation
161 E. 42nd St., New York 17, N. Y.

Published for your information by

Kennecott
COPPER CORPORATION
Fabricating Subsidiaries: CHASE BRASS & COPPER CO., KENNECOTT WIRE & CABLE CO.

The idea of this ad derives from simple verbal and visual ingredients.
The idea dramatizes the copy theme. (AGENCY: *Cunningham & Walsh*)

effects, which he can control. The versatile white-space form permits more opportunities for idea-development and cleverness.

In the squared-off layout, in contrast, everything is restricted to what can happen *within* the rectangular picture. However, the squared-off picture, due to its massive size, can usually deliver more *impact* than can the smaller pictures floating in white space.

An example of the white-space layout is the General Electric air conditioning ad (page 121) with the headline:

IT WILL OPEN ... *of course!*

Picture-caption layout   The picture-caption layout is exemplified by the British Travel ad "Tourist's Guide to British Money," which also exempli-

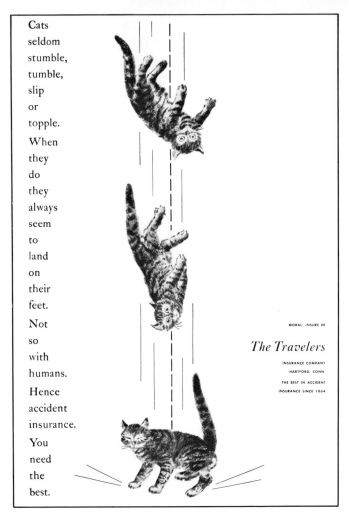

Cats seldom stumble, tumble, slip or topple. When they do they always seem to land on their feet. Not so with humans. Hence accident insurance. You need the best.

MORAL: INSURE IN

The Travelers

INSURANCE COMPANY
HARTFORD, CONN.

THE BEST IN ACCIDENT
INSURANCE SINCE 1864

Layout and illustration provide major interest in this Travelers Insurance advertisement. An effect of motion is achieved with a white-space layout. (AGENCY: *Young & Rubicam*)

fies, quite well, how this layout adapts itself to an *idea*. An advantage of picture-caption layouts is that Starch Ratings indicate that captions are usually somewhat better read than a solid block of copy.

Special Uses of the White-space Layout

The Travelers "falling cat" ad (above) and the General Electric "parachute" ad (page 121) indicate a special usefulness of the white-space layout. It can be used, quite effectively, to depict *motion,* or rather, more accurately, to suggest motion. Unhampered by a fixing background, objects can seem to move with greater freedom in the "air" of white space.

The white-space layout lends itself to a useful idea-device, that of the inanimate *or* animate objects which "talk" to each other. Though not a new idea, this device has been recently revitalized in product-selling advertising by the cleverness and the layout eclat of the ads for Wolfschmidt Vodka, especially the ad in which the orange says to the vodka bottle: "Who was that tomato I saw you with last week?"

In the non-product area, an excellent example of the technique is afforded by the Qantas advertisement picturing two antique porcelain mugs shaped in the forms of jolly tavern characters. The conversation:

This advertisement is loaded with **idea** *from beginning to end. Its amazing photograph triggers the stream of interest on into headline and copy.* (AGENCY: *Doyle Dane Bernbach*)

I found out
about
Joan

The way she talks, you'd think she was in Who's Who. Well! I found out what's what with *her*. Her husband own a bank? Sweetie, not even a bank *account*. Why that palace of theirs has wall-to-wall *mortgages!* And that car? Darling, that's horsepower, *not* earning power. They won it in a fifty-cent raffle! Can you imagine? And those clothes! Of course she *does* dress divinely. But really…a mink stole, and Paris suits, and all those dresses…on *his* income? Well darling, I found out about that too. I just happened to be going her way and *I saw Joan come out of Ohrbach's!*

Ohrbach's

34TH **ST.** OPP. EMPIRE STATE BLDG. · **NEWARK** MARKET & HALSEY · "A BUSINESS IN MILLIONS, A PROFIT IN PENNIES"®

The cans that came to dinner

Swish! And a tinned-steel can is open to solve any one of the housewife's many different meal problems. In fact, entire meals — from rare delicacies to everyday staples — can be dished up in a jiffy from the amazing variety of readily available canned foods.

Yes, today's canned foods solve countless meal problems. Thanks in a large part to Wheeling Steel's *Ductillite.* You see "tin cans" are actually 99% steel, with a coating of tin. These metals are combined because steel is the strongest packaging material known ... and

tin further safeguards your family's health by protecting the fresh-packed quality of the can's contents.

When it was introduced three decades ago, Wheeling's *Ductillite* revolutionized the canning industry—making possible tough, more reliable cans that are so inexpensive they can be discarded once they're used. And Wheeling's *Ductillite* is even better today because of our recently completed $35 million improvement program. *You can always rely on steel ... Wheeling steel!* Wheeling Steel Corporation, Wheeling, West Virginia. **IT'S WHEELING STEEL**

Both illustration and headline are interesting in themselves. A dual-interest, picture-headline idea. (AGENCY: *Cunningham & Walsh*)

FIRST CHARACTER: Have you heard, old boy? I'm off to England via Qantas 707 jet!

SECOND CHARACTER: You lucky mug.

Importance of the Idea

With that kind of advertising which, of necessity, has an obligation to be interesting, the role of the *ad idea* is all-important. In the interest-creating process, the idea must act as both spark and explosion. It must catch the prospect's eye, then explode him forcefully into the copy. The rest of the job is up to the copy.

Ads with powerful ideas work many times as hard as dull ads. Numerous readership surveys have indicated that powerful idea-ads, as a class, are seen by many more people—and are more completely read—than are dull ads. And other things being equal, numerous experiences suggest that the bright, strong ads are much more likely to achieve their final objectives than are dull ones. And a powerful, high-yield ad costs the advertiser no more than does a dull, lazy ad, yet the good one may give him twenty times as much value as the poor one.

Strong idea-ads with high attention-value are especially valuable to the smaller or new advertiser. Because they give him a chance to be seen among the more numerous but often less-interesting advertisements of a big advertiser. Very large advertisers *are* often addicted to the disease of dullness for various

The major interest element in this British Travel advertisement is its magnificent headline: "Tread softly past the long, long sleep of kings." (AGENCY: *Ogilvy, Benson & Mather*)

Henry VII, Elizabeth I and Mary Queen of Scots are buried in this chapel.

Tread softly past the long, long sleep of kings

THIS IS Henry VII's chapel in Westminster Abbey. These windows have filtered the sunlight of five centuries. They have also seen the crowning of twenty-two kings.

Three monarchs rest here now. Henry, Elizabeth and Mary. Such are their names in sleep. No titles. No trumpets. The banners hang battle-heavy and becalmed. But still the royal crown remains. *Honi soit qui mal y pense.*

When you go to Britain, make yourself this promise. Visit at least *one* of the thirty great cathedrals. Their famous names thunder! Durham and Armagh. Or they chime! Lincoln and Canterbury. And sometimes they *whisper*. Winchester, Norwich, Salisbury and Wells. Get a map and make your choice.

Each cathedral transcends the noblest single work of art. It is a pinnacle of faith and an act of centuries. It is an offering of human hands as close to Abraham as it is to Bach. Listen to the soaring choirs at evensong. And, if you can, go at Christmas or Easter.

You will rejoice that you did.

For free illustrated literature, see your travel agent or write Box 700, British Travel Association.
In New York—680 Fifth Ave.; In Los Angeles—612 So. Flower St.; In Chicago—39 So. LaSalle St.; In Canada—151 Bloor St. West, Toronto.

reasons—one being that the advertisements have to be approved by too many people. Another is that reliance on heavy schedules—showing the ad numerous times—makes the attention-getting characteristics of an individual ad seem relatively unimportant. Hence, with a comparatively small expenditure, eye-catching idea-ads help the small advertiser thrive and grow amid the attention-competition of advertising giants.

Finally, the explosive picture-headline idea supplies needed interest to penetrate apathy surrounding an abstract or unpalatable proposition, such as the

An idea based on the concept of supplying useful information. This ad has a picture-caption layout. (AGENCY: *Ogilvy, Benson & Mather*)

Tourist's Guide to British Money

(Take it with you when you go)

A PENNY is worth about one cent in U.S. currency, but is about twice as big. Twelve English pennies make a shilling. The rate of exchange is highly favorable today. You can actually spend two grand weeks in Britain for under $200.

SIXPENCE. The silver sixpence is the equivalent of 7¢, and a delightful little coin it is. The slang word for sixpence is "tanner." Traveling by rail in Britain can cost less than 3¢ a mile. And bus travel works out at about 2¢ a mile.

SHILLING. Equal to 14¢. (Slang: a "bob.") Twenty-one shillings make a "guinea," which is so aristocratic that there isn't a coin or banknote for it at all. You can do a lot with one shilling—see the Crown Jewels, or visit Hampton Court.

FLORIN. A two-shilling piece—28¢. The first florins were minted in Queen Victoria's reign and were known as "Godless florins," due to the omission of the usual Latin initials signifying "by the Grace of God" after the Queen's name.

HALF-CROWN. Two shillings and sixpence—or 35¢. Today, for only a half-crown, you can visit almost any of 450 castles and mansions now open to the public. Stately homes like Blenheim Palace, Luton Hoo and Glamis Castle.

20 SHILLINGS equal £1 (ONE POUND)

ONE POUND. Equivalent of $2.80. There's a bill for this—also for ten shillings. But U.S. law won't let us show either. The British slang for a pound is "quid." Call it what you like, it buys you a fine seat at the theater. *Note:* There's a Scottish shilling in our picture. It has only one lion on its crest. Can you spot it?

For free "Travellers Guide to Britain," see a travel agent or write to Box 440, British Travel Assn. In New York—680 Fifth Ave.; In Los Angeles—606 S. Hill St.; In Chicago—39 So. LaSalle St.; In Canada—90 Adelaide St. West, Toronto.

It will open ... *of* <u>course!</u>

Because it has been folded properly. Because it has been made with care. Because it has been inspected with even greater care.

And because it has been stored in a special air conditioned room—with exact temperature and humidity control—to protect the silk fabric against mildew or other climatic damage.

Ordinary air conditioning . . . the kind of air conditioning you've known in the past . . . wouldn't do for a job like this. *More precise* . . . and *more flexible* equipment . . . the air condi-

tioning of the future . . . had to be developed.

General Electric has been specializing in meeting the difficult air conditioning problems created by America's war effort. Air conditioning to preserve materials . . . to improve the operation of machinery . . . to make it easier for men to work better!

When final Victory is won, many valuable lessons learned in fighting the Battle of Production will be turned to the uses of peace. More people will be able to enjoy air con-

ditioning in homes, offices and other places . . . because it will be less expensive, more compact. And it will be vastly improved air conditioning . . . with accurate control of *humidity* as well as temperature. *Required climates* will be reproduced at will.

When the time comes to supply the air conditioning needs of the post-war world, General Electric will be ready. General Electric Co., Air Conditioning and Commercial Refrigeration Department, Bloomfield, New Jersey.

Air Conditioning by
GENERAL ⊛ ELECTRIC

Example of white-space layout, indicating motion. The aviator and parachute are silhouetted against white space. (AGENCY: *Newell-Emmett Company*)

selling of insurance, selling the idea of getting a medical examination, changing an ideology or a political attitude toward business, or making one department store seem a better place to shop in than another. And so on.

Ads built around a creative ad idea are a necessity for non-product advertising. Such ad ideas can also be invaluable to many categories of product-selling advertising—a point that was underlined by William Bernbach when he insisted that a "selling proposition" was not enough, but what was addi-

Have you heard, old boy?
I'm off to England
via Qantas 707 jet!

You lucky mug.

QANTAS 707 JETS TO LONDON every Thursday, every Sunday. Time of flight: from New York, less than 7 daylight hours; from San Francisco, less than 12. Type of flight: no less than fabulous! And you can fly now, pay later, too. Call any travel agent or Qantas in New York, San Francisco, Los Angeles, Vancouver, Honolulu—and your cup runneth over! (Also BOAC, general sales agent, in all major American cities.)
QANTAS Australia's Round-the-World Jet Airline

Inanimate objects that talk. A device that can be used effectively with a white-space layout. (AGENCY: *Cunningham & Walsh*)

tionally needed were "imaginative, original craftsmen who can take that selling proposition and, with the magic of their artistry, get people to see it, get people to remember it." [1]

How to Get an Idea

Ad ideas are not easy to get. They do not fall out of the sky, or grow on bushes. Somebody has to think them up. And not very many people know how to do that—or even how to start to do it.

Yet there are some who seem to have developed a facility for turning out ideas. They have found that getting an idea is not all sheer inspiration, but can come from a series of little tricks of thinking that can be developed—at least by a person who is reasonably imaginative to begin with. Such a person can *learn* to get ideas.

Most happily, there even exists an excellent *textbook* teaching one how to get ideas. It was written by James Webb Young of J. Walter Thompson and is called *A Technique for Producing Ideas.*[2] It is a small book, but is written in a terse, pithy style that packs a lot of information into a few pages.

Mr. Young starts by describing an idea as "nothing more nor less than a *new combination* of old elements." He then lays down five steps for developing an idea, the steps to be taken consecutively, in the order given.

[1] From a speech at White Sulphur Springs, as reported by *Advertising Age,* Apr. 24, 1961.

[2] Ninth ed., Advertising Publications, Inc., Chicago, 1956.

The five steps for getting ideas   The *first* step is for the mind to gather its raw material. Every single bit of information about the subject should be zealously gathered and poured into the mind.

The *second* step Mr. Young calls "the process of masticating these materials." Think about them, take the bits of material and "feel them all over, as it were, with the tentacles of the mind. You take one fact, turn it this way and that, look at it in different lights, and feel for the meaning of it. Do this until the mind tires itself, and ceases to make progress with the problem."

The *third* step is to stop working. Throw the mind out of gear. Forget the problem. Sleep on it. Turn your attention to something else. Let the subconscious machinery of the mind go to work.

The *fourth* step is the birth of the idea. It will come unexpectedly at odd times, out of nowhere. It is most likely to come, as Mr. Young suggests, when one is half awake in the morning. This is the Eureka! stage.

The *fifth* and final step is the stage of criticism—the time to step back and view the new-born idea with a cold and critical eye. Then hammer it into shape to make sure it *works*. This is a good time to try the idea out on someone else, get criticisms. Perhaps the addition of a single word may make the whole idea "sing."

Developing the Idea-making Facility

While creative people have always followed a procedure roughly similar to that propounded by Mr. Young, he must be credited with being the first to analyze and explain it so tersely and explicitly in a written text. Each person who follows such a procedure usually adds a twist or two of his own to the formula. Creative people in agencies, who are regularly called upon for ideas, become quite adept at the idea-making process.

These people develop a faculty of throwing the mind in and out of gear at will. They know how to let the half-subconscious take over, to let crazy combinations of thoughts toss around at the back of the mind, to be weighed, discarded, and replaced with some other combination. When a fruitful juxtaposition approaches, this dreamy back section of the mind can suddenly go to work at lightning speed, short-circuiting intermediate steps.

At a proper moment, the practiced, creative person can switch from uninhibited synthesis to the front part of the mind for cold, negative criticism, to assay the value of the half-created idea. He brings it to the surface for a good hard look at it. If it is not right, he mentally resets his dials and starts the back of the mind working again.

Getting the Mental Machinery Started

Every good creative man has his own way of getting started. A frequent practice is to try and think of what would make the most absolutely shocking stopper scene if put in an ad. One person thinks of a man standing on his head, juggling plates with his feet. Another thinks of the naked woman going shopping on Fifth Avenue. Another regularly starts by imagining a taxi driver scolding a policeman for not enforcing the law.

None of these work, of course. It's like getting a checker game started. One tries another crazy situation. By this time, the wheels of the imagination are turning.

In trying for an idea, one does *not* start with a statement of the proposition and try to reason his way to a headline or picture. In all probability, he will find himself repeating the proposition statement over and over again. This simply does not work.

Instead, the experienced idea-creator thinks of what picture or what words —*any* picture or *any* words—would be exciting, then works his way *back* to the proposition. Somewhere along the line, he will find a stopper combination that *will* work, will convey the meaning of the proposition *exactly*—and with fireworks! Eureka—the idea! This approach *does* work.

The trick of sleeping on the problem can be put to work effectively. Some copywriters make a practice of saturating themselves with a problem before going to bed, sleeping on it, and then quite regularly coming up with an idea on waking the next morning.

If It's Not Original, It's Not Really an Idea

By our definition, earlier in the chapter, a creative idea is something *new*— something never seen in the world before.

Hence, if one tries to achieve an idea by trying to *imitate* someone else's successful idea (as many uncreative people attempt to do) the result will be unsatisfactory, uncreative, and lacking in the sparkle of the original version. If the process of imitation is continued, more and more lustre is lost.

This does not mean that one is prohibited from using a *device* or *format* that may have been seen before. But what one does with the device should be new and different. We have mentioned the device of two inanimate objects talking to each other in an ad. This is only a device, not an idea in itself. The true idea comes from the words spoken, and their relationship to the objects pictured. Similarly, cartoonists have shown people on a one-tree desert island, perhaps thousands of times. But every joke is different. The island is only a stage setting.

Information Is Inspiration

In his book, James Webb Young bears down hard on the need of getting full information before starting to create. He could not stress this need too much if he continued on for 1,000 pages. Information is the lifeblood, not only of the idea, but of the whole advertisement.

Ample information does two things for the creative operation:

1. It *speeds up* the idea-creating process, because it gives the creative man firm ground to work from and adequate tools to do his thinking job.

2. It improves the *quality* of the idea. In fact, one can confidently say that the quality of the idea—or the advertisement—will be directly proportional to the amount of information that has gone into it.

Most good copywriters, as they become more experienced, learn the value of full information as a vital ingredient for the making of successful advertisements. They eagerly do everything in their power to gather such information.

And it will be worth the trouble for others concerned to do their utmost to assist the copywriter in getting the information he needs. For the time and cost will be repaid in the improved quality of the finished advertisement.

Be Daring

A characteristic of nearly all the greatest idea-advertisements, whether product or non-product-selling, is their *daring*.

The startling impact of the famous "Man in the Hathaway Shirt" advertisement was quite clearly due to the black eye patch worn by the model. To show such a thing in a selling advertisement was a daring thing to do.

"Who was that tomato I saw you with last week?" was a daring phrase to find on an advertising page. The exuberant Ohrbach's ideas and the stark, simple Volkswagen layouts have been daring in their way. So are the advertisements of the Better Vision Institute.

By daring is meant advertisements that dare to do something, or think something, that the essentially timid advertising business would normally hesitate to do or think. The reward for daring in an idea may be lasting memorability.

Ideas Must Be Sold

There is a very important, but usually unnoticed aspect of all the great advertisement ideas that ever appeared in public. Somebody *sold* them.

An idea is not really completed, does not really exist, until it appears in print or on the air. There are many more imaginative, talented people in advertising agencies than one would ever suspect from what is seen or published. In fact, there is a vast graveyard full of wonderful advertisement ideas, excellent in every respect, that never saw the light of day. Because, though created, *they were not sold.*

A surprising number of these advertisements were killed, ostensibly, for rather trivial reasons. Which gives one cause to suspect that an underlying reason for the lack of approval was the timidity of the non-creative buyer, his fear of the unconventional, and his lack of understanding of the rewards a brilliant idea could win for him. And at that moment, there was no one on the spot *able* to sell the excellent advertisement that should have been approved.

Top creative men are rare, but they are not nearly as rare as the men who can *sell* highly creative advertisements—who know how to sell them, and who succeed in selling them again and again. In fact, there are so few of such salesmen that the whole advertising business knows them by name. Without the Bernbachs, the Ogilvys, and one or two others, their talented creative staffs would scarcely be known today. The same might have been said of Young & Rubicam in years gone by.

Therefore, selling an idea can be as important as creating it. And the final selling must be considered an integral part of the total completion of any successful *idea*-advertisement.

Brainstorming

A number of years back, there was quite a fad on Madison Avenue for a game called *brainstorming*. A number of people, not necessarily or usually creative, gathered around a big table to create ideas. The players were encouraged to offer anything that came into their minds, say anything they wanted, but were not allowed to be critical in any way.

They could "hitchhike," that is, latch on to someone else's offering and add their own suggestions. The game was played with as much spirit and action as possible. Meanwhile the suggestions were taken down. The game was played until the participants ran out of steam.

Later, the multitudinous scraps of thought were collected and conscientiously combed through by experienced, creative supervisors to see if any nuggets had turned up. But, alas, this rarely happened. In fact, it was rare that anything of value could be salvaged.

In reality, brainstorming was a form of group boondoggling. It seemed to be an expression of the infatuation for "group-think" prevalent among agencies at the time. It provided fun for the uncreative, because it allowed a momentary, but rather thrilling release from inhibitions. It wasted a lot of expensive time. But it produced very few usable ideas.

Two things were wrong with brainstorming:

1. It was performed, mostly, by uncreative people.

2. By outlawing criticism, it prevented any coming to grips with the problem and forestalled any real progress toward the formation of a useful, real idea.

As noted previously, trained creative people have the faculty of throwing their minds in and out of gear, of alternating uninhibited imagination and corrective criticism, thus working their way toward the desired idea. The untrained, uncreative brainstormers lacked both the imagination and the discipline to guide it. So nothing useful happened, in spite of all the elaborate folderol.

There is one tiny germ of value in the brainstorm concept. If two or three experienced, imaginative, genuinely creative people get together after wrestling with a problem for some time, they *can*, by kicking the problem around among themselves, interact on each other, reinspire each other, begin to compete with each other, and suddenly spout forth not one, but a whole stream of ideas, with one idea, in fact, often hitchhiking on another. But in their procedure, they have wisely criticized and corrected, keeping the creative process on a fruitful track.

This *has* worked. In one instance, it produced, in a few minutes, a topnotch campaign for an entire year. But this is a game for professionals. It is *not* the brainstorming game played by the amateurs during the fad period.

Chapter 17

THE ROLE

OF ART

Today, as much as 90 per cent or more of a print advertisement may be devoted to illustration. Over a long period of time, the role of art, of the *visual* presentation, has been steadily increasing in importance among the ad-makers. In some present-day agencies, it would seem as if the art director has at last come to overshadow the copywriter as top man in the creative operation.

Artwork has always had outstanding importance in non-product advertising. In the selling of *products,* the task of illustration is usually fairly simple—to display the product, to show it in use, and to demonstrate its benefits. But where there are *no* products and ideas are being peddled, the visual presentation finds itself burdened with a greater and more complex responsibility. On its quality depends, very often, the success or failure of the ad.

Traditionally, institutional advertisements have placed special emphasis on interesting, attractive art. In fact, in some instances, this has been carried to a fault; the glamour of the artwork has become a substitute for sound thinking, and a beautiful looking page delivers a vague, weak, or inconsequential message, not worth the money spent on it. The fault, as noted earlier, usually can be traced to the lack of clarity in the objective.

The Visual Evolution of Modern Advertising

The visual appearance of modern advertising has evolved through four rather well-defined periods of time.

The first period, dating back before World War I, might be thought of, in visual terms at least, as the Dark Ages of advertising. Layouts were chaotically cluttered and disorganized. Illustrations were crude, ideas included grisly humor, and the universal means of getting attention was with heavy, black type. The overall effect was primitive and heavy handed.

In the second period, from 1919 through the ebullient 1920s to the Great Depression, advertising art leaped forward. This period marked the rise of the art director, the development of layout, vast improvement in the quality of finished art, and a new aesthetic attitude toward typography.

Art directors sought guidance from the rules of composition laid down by academic fine art and made endless experimental variations of layouts to find the right one. This was a time of formal and informal balance, of eye-leading devices, decorative borders, and elegant hand lettering. Visual thinking had become organized.

The grim, heavy-handed look of prewar years vanished in favor of a clean, light, airy appearance, which exuded a certain gay bounciness which was not at all incompatible with the bubbling spirit of the 1920s. White space had been discovered. High-priced illustrations featured glamorous technical skill in oil painting and watercolor. Black-and-white artwork was enlivened by brisk dry-brush strokes, or dignified by the formality of scratchboard.

But the most significant note was the complexity of the layouts, whose multiple elements were carefully weighed and balanced and organized according to a mystical abracadabra dictated by the art director's taste.

The third evolutionary period, ushered in by the Depression and lasting until the end of World War II, was a time of reaction and transition. In the Depression years, layouts became simpler and lost their lightness and gaiety. Hand lettering was ruled an expensive luxury, and disappeared. Readership surveys made the picture-caption layout very popular. Research also indicated the authenticity-value of photographs, but these puzzled the art directors, and they were used sparingly and not with great skill. Drawn or painted artwork seemed much easier to work with.

During this time, artists and art directors, one by one, began to discover modern art. But, as with photographs, they had difficulty in figuring out how to make it work. It did not seem to fit in with the needs of advertising, which demanded realistic illustration. It did, however, begin to affect layout thinking rather profoundly, and was probably a major cause of layouts becoming simpler and stronger.

The fourth period of visual development started slowly about 1945 and proceeded at an accelerating pace up to the present. It brought revolutionary changes, the greatest of which were (1) the almost total replacement of artwork by photography and (2) the impact of modern art on layout and illustration. Also important was another disturbing new influence, that of television. As a result, print advertising today has a vastly different look from what it had in the 1920s. What is more important, the visual revolution is affecting the *advertising* functioning of the ads.

The Rise of Photography

What caused the delay in the extensive use of photography, which had been shown to be obviously desirable for advertising, was that art directors for a long time simply did not know how to make photography work. Two errors of approach acted as persistent stumbling blocks, namely, (1) the art directors tried to fit photographs into the old, complex "compositional" layouts, which yielded disappointing results, and (2) they viewed photographs somewhat as an amateur does when he stands back and takes a snapshot of a friend—in other words, as a documentary depiction of a person, product, or scene.

The photographic revolution came when art directors, guided by certain talented photographers, learned how to "get inside" a photograph. The easiest move in this direction was to get the camera closer and closer to the subject, i.e., make a close-up shot. This removed the clutter of objects *around* the subject usually seen in a more distant shot. It concentrated *on* the subject, giving it more importance. It also simplified and enlarged the shapes and forms *within* the subject, permitting the art director to make use of them as part of his layout design.

Working more seriously with the photographic medium, it became apparent that to get the most out of a photograph, it should be made big on the page and be presented in the simplest possible shape, which turned out to be a squared-off rectangle. The photograph was seen to be ineffective as a small element in a larger layout; to work forcefully it had to dominate the layout and be the sole and entire illustration.

It was quickly noticed that as the photograph increased in size, it gained in impact. To gain size, the first step was to push the copy down into a small strip at the bottom of the layout. The next step was to use a bleed page, using the paper from edge to edge. Finally, for still more impact, this king-size bleed photograph was spread over both pages of a double spread.

As the dimensions of the photograph were made larger, so also was the close-up of the subject, until life-size faces peered out from the advertising pages with shattering impact.

Getting into the picture meant more than merely increasing size. It was an attitude of mind, a seeking of visual excitement. It meant using all the tricks of the trade and inventing new ones—finding unusual camera angles, startling contrasts, offbeat ways to crop, etc. Sometimes, ideas were borrowed from television.

A second major development in the use of photography was its more intelligent application to white-space layouts, with subjects silhouetted in white space. The silhouetted subject, for example, did not need to be a still life or an inactive figure. It could be a person running or leaping. This could be blown up, diminished, or repeated in various sizes. And so on.

Finally, during the period after World War II, *color* photography became developed to the point where it could be used with complete facility. It could now compete with artists' paintings and promptly proceeded to do so. Because of its realism and authenticity, photography has become the triumphant visual vehicle of advertising. The old-fashioned painted artwork has become the increasingly rare exception.

The campaigns of Olin Mathieson, Better Vision Institute, and Glass Container Manufacturers Institute mentioned elsewhere in this book offer good examples of the use of modern photographic technique.

Modern Art

Modern art, used as an *illustration,* has had little to offer to product-selling advertisers. One cannot display a product very effectively with an abstraction. Nor can one present a practical selling story of uses, which properly needs realistic illustration. Consequently, modern art has been used only rarely for product-selling.

It has, however, found considerable favor for corporate advertising. This is partly due to its fairly reliable attention-getting qualities. And also, at times, modern art's very abstractness has proved to be advantageous to corporate advertisers.

For *all* types of advertising, regardless of whether or not it is used for illustration, modern art has had an enormous influence in another way—its impact on *layout* thinking. Practically all layouts today are either based upon or heavily influenced by the *design* concepts of modern art.[1]

Design is a fundamental ingredient, perhaps *the* most fundamental ingredient, of modern art. All modern pictures are designs. Furthermore, a modern design has an independent visual interest of its own. As such, it becomes a useful tool for progressive-minded art directors. It offers a fruitful approach to layout-making, leading to stronger and more exciting layouts.

Modern art in World War II   Semi-abstract, designy modern art found a growing number of users during World War II when normal marketing conditions were upset by the needs of the war effort. Many products were off the market, or in such short supply they could not be advertised, and many manu-

[1] At one time there was a very popular "Mondrian" layout that borrowed Piet Mondrian's black lines and rectangles.

facturers turned to corporate advertising to keep their corporate or brand names alive in the public consciousness.

At the same time, some companies, particularly chemical companies, were developing exciting new products as part of their war effort. They could not develop them for peacetime uses or promote them at the time. But they did want to publicize the new products as much as permissible and especially, to identify them with the corporate name.

Modern art, in the form of a symbolic abstraction and designed for utmost attention-value, proved very helpful. For example, the Dow Chemical Company wanted to establish knowledge of its new plastic, Styron. All it could say, or cared to say, was that the plastic could come in a crystal-clear tube, could be fabricated in many ways, had efficient electrical properties, made precision moldings with high-dimensional stability, was resistant to alcohol, acids, and alkalies, and would be available from Dow after the war.

Dow published an advertisement with the headline:

STYRON (DOW POLYSTYRENE)

Above the headline was a symbolic semi-abstraction, lively in shape and color. In the design could be recognized a crystal cube, calipers making a precision measurement, a plastic funnel, a flash of lightning, an electrical insulator, plastic jewelry, and an automobile tire. Because of its arresting design and color, and the huge eye peering through the plastic cube, the illustration had surprising stopper quality. Yet, symbolically, it told a story that was easily made clear by the text copy.

There were other such ads in the series. In these, in effect, Dow was using an abstract visual form to present an abstract proposition. After the war, when Dow *could* offer specific products for sale, it switched, significantly, to color photographs of the products in use.

Surrealism   A moden art approach that had value at a time when a connected sales story could not be told and only isolated bits of corporate information could be presented, was *surrealism*. In surrealism, objects were depicted with precise and painstaking realism. But where the objects were placed, or what was happening to them, did not have to make logical sense, in fact, seldom did.

If effects were equivocal, that is, if it were not quite clear whether a battleship was steaming through the ocean or through a wheat field with a factory in the middle of it, so much the better.

Surrealism was intended to startle and to lure the curiosity. Its exaggerated perspectives leading to an infinitely distant horizon, its strangeness and loneliness, its spookiness and "craziness" gave it high attention-value. And its free-

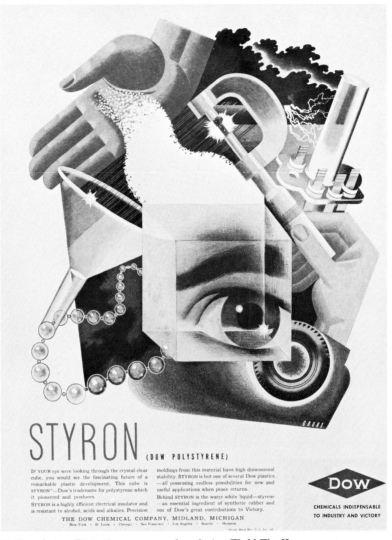

Modern design illustration, type prevalent during World War II.
This Dow Chemical Company advertisement used symbolism to
tell the story of a product that was not yet available to the public.
(AGENCY: *Mac Manus, John & Adams*)

dom from logical visual discipline permitted its use for messages about products that might or might not be available in the future. Such a surrealist technique was used in the wartime campaign of the Koppers Company. In 1942, an ad of Johnson's Wax was built around an illustration painted by Salvador Dali.

Artzybasheff Although the amusing pictures of the late Boris Artzybasheff were not really modern art, except in a very liberal interpretation of the term, they performed during the war period much as did the surrealist and abstract modern illustrations. Actually very imaginative cartoons, with a "crazy," mildly comic quality, they were attention-getting, could be useful symbolically, and didn't have to make sense. The Casco Products Company used these cartoons, in Martian scenes, to display a product that couldn't be sold until after the war.

Container Corporation of America

Container Corporation of America regards itself primarily as a packaging company, even though its operations are integrated from the forest to the printed package. Its products are paperboard shipping containers, folding cartons, fiber cans, and plastic containers. It is the largest paperboard-package manufacturer in the business. It has benefited particularly from the packaging explosion of the past two decades.

A feature of that period has been the great increase in *new* products put on the market. These new products needed new packages. Because of intensified marketing competition, these packages had to be *designed* for utmost effectiveness, not only functionally and economically, but for up-to-date visual attractiveness as well.

Emphasis on design Emphasis on design early became a guiding light in Container Corporation thinking. The corporation instituted an extensive design program, including both marketing research and graphic-design assistance for its customers. It sought also to establish a liaison with customer package-and-product designers who might, perhaps, influence the purchase of the company's products.

Accentuating the modern Everything in this program pointed, necessarily, in the direction of newness and up-to-dateness. The products were new; the packages were new. Appearance and the thinking behind it must be as modern as possible.

The manufacturer who was himself pushing forward with a new product naturally sought the assistance of a packaging company he could be sure would be imaginative and creative in *its* thinking. He looked for the packager with a reputation for being in the forefront of new ideas.

The graphic designers were thoroughly art-minded and lived in an atmosphere of the most advanced art thinking. They were already professionally committed to the new and modern, to the daring, the exciting, and the pioneering in visual concepts.

There was only one form of expression that could be put on paper that could uniquely satisfy all of these considerations and give the company the image it needed. That was *modern art.*

The look of modern art connoted newness as nothing else could at the time the campaign started. Modern art symbolized imagination and up-to-dateness. And it was the type of art revered by designers. In these circumstances, it offered a natural basis for an advertising campaign.

The advertising audience There were other considerations, too. Container Corporation did not sell its products to consumers. It sold to industry.

It did not expect to sell even to industry through advertising. It did, of course, use advertisements in industrial media, but it depended for sales primarily on the personal visits of salesmen. The advertising might help him in his job, but *he* was expected to make the sale.

Actually, Container Corporation's needs were more corporate than product-selling. There were reasons to sell Container Corporation to businessmen in general, investors, prospective employees, and leaders of public opinion. There was value in impressing on unknown influentials that Container Corporation was a company of imagination and original thinking. The time might come when such imagination might be in demand.

Approach to the advertising At the time when the advertising was projected, the company was almost unknown to most of its desired audience. It wanted, most of all, as a primary objective, corporate identity and corporate prestige to be purchased as fast as possible at low cost. In the words of its chairman, the late Walter P. Paepcke, Container Corporation "desired recognition as a leader in the paperboard packaging industry."

This obviously required a highly visible campaign. The company's management felt that the product was unglamorous, served only auxiliary purposes, and was of little concern to the full audience to be reached. The budget was low. An ordinary selling campaign would not have the excitement necessary to make the advertisements stand out from the forest of other advertising pages.

The company's identification with modern design provided a clue and led naturally to the campaign adopted. Modern design, combined with very short copy—fifteen words or less—could be the common denominator for a continuing series of advertisements. The shock value of unabashed modern art would make the advertisements stand out from all other advertisements.

The Container Corporation Advertising Campaign

Container Corporation's advertising campaign started in 1937, with a series of 12 black-and-white design pictures by the famous French poster artist, A. M.

Cassandre. With each picture went a few words about the company or the container industry. For example:

> Pine tree to package—one organization.   CONTAINER CORPORATION OF AMERICA

or:

> First in research, first in laboratory control, and first in the manufacture of paperboard products.   CONTAINER CORPORATION OF AMERICA

The picture illustrated the words, but in very much of a modern design manner. To the reader, the effect was that of seeing an interesting, semi-abstract modern picture and then looking down and finding a few words which partially explained the picture and left the mental message, "This is an ad for the Container Corporation."

On the page somewhere, often small and worked into the design, was a formalized picture of a carton.

The first advertisements were general in approach, but soon switched (1942) to wartime themes. The ads appeared in *Time* and *Fortune* magazines. Among the artists used at the time, besides Cassandre, were Jean Carlu, Herbert Bayer, Fernand Leger, Man Ray and Herbert Matter.

At the end of the war, the company's packaging was distributing materials all over the world. This suggested a new series, saluting the nations of the United Nations, one by one. These advertisements were in full color, and each picture was painted by an artist who was a native of the country featured. Typical captions were:

> U.S. supplies, packed in paper, speed the liberation of The Netherlands and colonies.   CONTAINER CORPORATION OF AMERICA

> ICELAND—island republic of the United Nations—trades for goods in paper packages.

This international series was followed by a series honoring the states of the Union, with the artists selected from the respective states. A typical caption:

> PENNSYLVANIA—annual purchase: $5½ billion—mostly packaged.   CONTAINER CORPORATION OF AMERICA

By 1950, Container Corporation found itself running out of states and territories. So it changed to a new series: "Great Ideas of Western Man." Each ad was built around a famous quotation, expressing ideas of a moral, philosophical, or political nature. Such as:

When truth is buried underground
it grows, it chokes, it gathers
such an explosive force
that on the day it bursts out,
it blows up everything with it.
EMILE ZOLA, "J'Accuse!"
L'Aurore, January 13, 1898.

In this series, as in the preceding ones, the artists' names are displayed prominently. With this series, which is still running, all pretense of selling has been dropped. Even the signature, *Container Corporation of America,* became small and unobtrusive.

Reaction to the campaign Among some businessmen and some professional advertising people, the reaction to this unorthodox campaign was immediate, violent, and negative. To them, this seemed more than *non*-advertising; it seemed almost *anti*-advertising. It violated every rule in the hard-sell catechism.

On the other hand, the campaign also received a great deal of commendation, applause which has continued and grown over the years. The letters received by the corporation have been 90 per cent commendatory.

Inasmuch as many advertising men have been puzzled by this advertising and have wondered whether it could possibly do any good, it would be instructive to look closer at the results.

Results . . . attention-value and recognition Modern art seems to have a certain amount of built-in attention-value of its own. Container Corporation's Starch Ratings held up consistently and clearly indicated that these semi-abstract, modern art ads were generally strong in attention-value, and provided excellent name-recognition. They made the Container Corporation name known and remembered.

The degree of abstractness of the art did not seem to have an effect on Starch Ratings. But strong designs, especially those using red, white, and blue, always rated higher than others in observation.

Text readership was extremely high, but this, of course, would not be entirely surprising in view of the shortness of the copy. Nevertheless, it does suggest, to a degree, that the reader, after looking at the modern picture, eagerly went on to read the words.

Results . . . fulfillment of objectives It will be recalled that one of the first objectives of the campaign was corporate identity and corporate prestige, that the company "desired recognition as a leader in the paperboard packaging industry."

This desired result was conferred speedily and in abundance. The other desired images, of *imagination,* of *up-to-dateness,* of *design-mindedness,* were provided almost automatically by the excellent and well-chosen modern art illustrations. Art-minded audiences, including the designers, were delighted.

The breadth and penetration of the public relations benefits were revealed in the flood of letters received. There were many requests for complete sets of reprints to be used in school and college classrooms. In 1945, the Art Institute of Chicago for eleven weeks exhibited the originals of the United Nations series and earlier ads. This has been described as the first one-company show in the Institute's history.

The advertising had direct recruiting values. It attracted a number of young people who later rose to positions of executive authority in the company and a stream of inventors, artists, writers, and other creative people coming with ideas.

Results . . . public service aspects of the campaign   The campaign pleased a much larger audience than the packaging-industry designer group. Everywhere, artists, art directors, and students collected the ads and studied them. From the ads, many other people learned more about modern art than they had ever known before.

At the same time, the makers of the illustrations, many artists, benefited from their lucrative and exciting assignments.

Whether it originally intended to do so or not, the Container Corporation was performing a public service. It was providing pleasure and education for visual-minded people in a manner quite analogous to Texaco's bringing the Metropolitan Opera to music lovers. The lack of selling copy in the Container Corporation ads accentuated this public service characteristic.

As with Texaco, the goodwill engendered by such public service activities has brought far-reaching image and public relations benefits.

Results . . . sales   Nobody would describe this as a selling campaign. Nobody at Container Corporation expected this campaign, in itself, to make sales. After the few prestige statements of the earlier insertions, the ads did not even attempt to make a sale.

Yet, during the period of the advertising, the Container Corporation has enjoyed a magnificent record of steadily increasing sales. In the ten years from 1954 to 1964, sales rose from $186,595,000 to $352,208,000.[2] In that decade, there was a sales increase every year but one. Today, the Container Corporation of America is the world's largest producer of paperboard packaging. It is also the world's largest industrial printer.

The Container Corporation's policy of depending on the personal calls of

[2] *Annual Report,* 1963.

its salesmen to make sales was noted earlier. But this supposedly non-selling advertising has proven that it takes a part in the operation—by setting the stage for the salesman. According to a high officer of the company: "It helps to 'break the ice' when our salesman calls on his prospect. He does not need to explain who we are and what we do. Indeed, the prospect's interest in our advertising often prompts discussion which introduces a note of welcome informality to a business interview."

To this can be added the observation that, in 1966, essentially the same campaign format, with increasing budgets, had been running for twenty-nine years.

General Dynamics Corporation

Another company, with special-case problems, which called on modern art to help solve them was General Dynamics Corporation—a company made up of a number of other large companies, now reorganized as divisions. Some of these divisions had little to do with each other. Among them were Canadair Limited, Electric Boat, General Atomic, Electro Dynamic, Convair, Stromberg-Carlson, and Liquid Carbonic. This diversity made a corporate-unity advertising campaign obviously desirable.

The products of General Dynamic were highly scientific; in fact, this company was recognized as a leader in a number of fields on the utmost frontiers of science. Much of the company's work consisted of defense projects for the government.

The nature of the company's work led to a recruiting problem, the need to acquire topnotch scientific brains in the face of increasing competition from other scientific-oriented companies.

Objectives and requirements   These were:

1. To illustrate in a highly graphic way the many fields in which General Dynamics was a leader—fields like nuclear power, space, aviation, communications, electronics, and the like

2. To tell the company's story without actually resorting to literal illustrations or copy, for several reasons, not the least of which was the fact that so many of the projects (nuclear submarines, missiles, etc.) were of a classified nature

3. To be part of a company-wide effort at standardizing and unifying what had gotten to be a complex and diverse organization

The General Dynamics Corporate-Advertising Campaign

The company chose, as the vehicle for presenting its story, abstract modern design illustrations occupying most of the space in the ads. The ad structure included a headline and short text copy. The campaign ran for about four years, ending in 1960.

One artist (Erik Nitsche) was engaged for the campaign and the quite abstract design pictures were all of a similar type—of a geometric style and spirit appropriate to the company's scientific attitude.

In a typical advertisement, a double spread in color in the *New York Times Magazine* section, the design picture was captioned, on one page: "Exploring the universe."

Modern art, strong in design, constitutes the illustrations for advertisements of the Container Corporation of America. Aimed at a number of specialized publics, these advertisements have effectively fulfilled their corporate objectives. (AGENCY: *N. W. Ayer & Son*)

The art of progress is to preserve order amid change and to preserve change amid order

Alfred North Whitehead, 1861-1947   artist: herbert bayer

Great Ideas of Western Man   one of a series   CCA Container Corporation of America

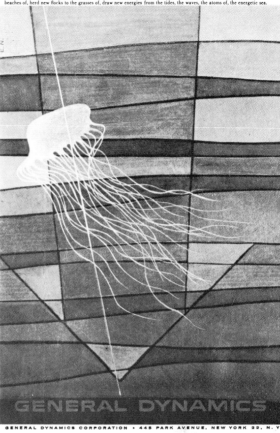

Exploring the Universe: The Energetic Sea .... In vessels powered by the airless "burning" of nuclear fuels, men may soon make voyages of discovery to unknown continents that lie beneath the ocean's surface; and, so, prospect for new metals in the waters of, extract new minerals from the mountains of, seek new elements on the shelves and beaches of, herd new flocks to the grasses of, draw new energies from the tides, the waves, the atoms of, the energetic sea.

GENERAL DYNAMICS

GENERAL DYNAMICS CORPORATION · 445 PARK AVENUE, NEW YORK 22, N. Y.

The geometric abstractions of the General Dynamics Corporation advertising symbolized the scientific spirit of the company. These advertisements were directed, for recognition and recruiting purposes, to sophisticated scientific and educational publics. (AGENCY: *D'Arcy Advertising Company*)

And on the next page, there was the following headline and copy:

THE 4TH STATE OF MATTER

Earth is composed
of three states of matter,
liquid, solid, gaseous.
Yet most of the universe exists as
a fourth state of matter, the *plasma* state.
The bright suns and stars are plasmas,
roving, unattached, electrified particles of matter
that fuse into new particles on collision,
releasing enormous energy.
We seek now to *control* this fusion,
to create here on earth
the plasmas of suns and stars,
to light for all men and all nations
fires of boundless energy
and endless age.

At the bottom of the ad was a short footnote, pointing out that the company's General Atomic Division was taking part in a new program "leading to the utilization of the fourth state of matter—controlled nuclear fusion."

Results   The company considered the campaign a successful one, reporting that "it attracted attention, provided instant recognition for General Dynamics, and served to project an image, somewhat with the general public, and especially with the scientific and educational publics in which we were vitally interested for recruiting purposes, of the kind of company we are." Recognition rating figures were high throughout.

Action-painting techniques contrasted against a background of graph paper have symbolic meaning in Celanese Corporation ads. "Creative ideas work best when they occur within the framework of a disciplined system." (AGENCY: *Ellington & Company*)

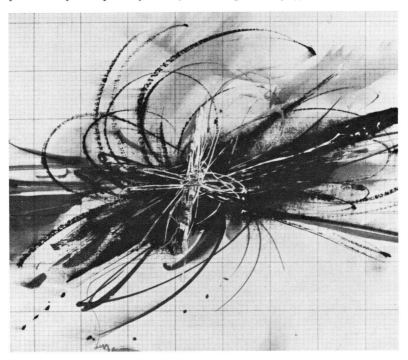

Ideas are fissionable material

It's true. Ideas can explode.

A mathematical formula by a dreamer named Einstein has already devastated two cities and is now contributing to the electric power for Pittsburgh. The author of *Alice in Wonderland* played parlor games that now form the basis of modern computer mathematics. Mendeleeff re-arranged the elements and in so doing re-arranged the world.

Celanese was founded on a boldly imaginative chemical process which made a synthetic polymer for textiles. Scientific discipline has since helped it grow a thousandfold.

The power of a creative idea is beyond measurement. But creative ideas work best when they occur within the framework of a disciplined system.

Celanese®

Celanese

CHEMICALS FIBERS PLASTICS POLYMERS

Celanese

In a somewhat similar corporate campaign, addressed to a limited, intellectually oriented audience, Celanese Corporation also used interesting modern art illustrations. In technique, these simulated the violent visual activity of abstract expressionism—"action painting." This dynamic brushwork was usually foiled against geometric background shapes having to do with science or mathematics, such as graph paper, charts, basic geometric forms, etc. The juxtaposition was intended to symbolize a theme of *discipline behind creativity*.

Chapter 18

WRITING

THE

COPY

Borrowing some terms from baseball and applying them to the making of an institutional advertisement, we might say that the objective is first base, the picture-headline idea is second base, and the attractive artwork is third base. Then *text copy* becomes home plate in the sequence needed for scoring a success.

The text copy is the clincher in attaining the advertisement's objective. Thus, it is no less important than any other part of the advertisement.

In its general characteristics, institutional copy does not differ fundamentally from product-selling copy. But the institutional copy carries a greater burden in that it must sell a more or less abstract idea. And it gets no support from inherent product interest. Therefore, because its job is more difficult, institutional advertising has a greater responsibility to be *good* copy. If something goes wrong between third base and home, the game is lost.

Successful institutional ads are notably characterized by excellent text copy. Unfortunately, one sees too many *other* institutional ads that, although endowed with striking pictures and headlines, nevertheless collapse because of ineffective and pedestrian text copy.

Sometimes this may be caused by the agency concentrating its efforts on a showy picture and headline and then treating the copy as an afterthought. Or, the copy simply may be too selfish. It may be so anxious to sell the company's point of view that it has no time to be interesting to the reader.

Again, on the other hand, the fault may be due to someone who feels he must *always* make changes in the copy—apparently for the mere sake of making changes. This deplorable, but very common practice, not only ruins a really good piece of copy when it comes along, but also discourages agency creative people from continuing to put forth their best efforts in future ads.

To obtain superior copy, one must recognize it when it appears and then leave it alone.

How to Keep a Reader Interested

There are two ways to make institutional copy palatable to a reader. One is to appeal to his self-interest. The other is to write the copy in such an interesting manner that he cannot turn away.

The power of a self-interest appeal was demonstrated by the A&P antitrust-case advertising. Unhappily, institutional advertisers do not often find such clear-cut opportunities to appeal to self-interest. And when benefits can be offered, they are often too dilute, remote, or abstract to be effective.

For example, the Weyerhaeuser Company could offer a benefit in its promise of renewing timberlands for posterity. But this appeal, in itself, was not strong enough to carry the campaign. Wisely, this company added other *interest* factors, such as the visual glamour of the forest, emotional involvement through love of animals, and the attractiveness of informative, educational copy.

Good advertising men will certainly use and will know how to use, a self-interest appeal in planning an institutional campaign, providing the basis for such an appeal really exists. Working with something as tenuous as ideas, however, it cannot be concocted out of nothing. Here, a benefit has no value merely because it is a benefit. It must have weight and pull. It must be tangible. But tangibles of the kind needed are scarce indeed with a form of advertising that deals primarily with *intangibles.*

Therefore, most often, the institutional advertiser must seek interest by other devices. He must fall back on trying to make his copy interesting. This throws a formidable challenge at his agency's copywriters.

Higher Writing Standards Are Required

Truly interesting copy is not easily come by. It requires considerable effort on the part of the copywriter to achieve. It usually requires that the copywriter improve his standards of writing in general.

Most copywriters attain a level of professional writing competence suitable for producing most product-selling advertisements. After he has mastered the somewhat specialized technique of producing such an advertisement, the average copywriter tends to discontinue his self-education in the art of writing.

This complacent level of competence may do for everyday advertisements that concentrate more on selling than on writing. But it is inadequate for advertisements that, *in addition to selling,* must also be written in such a way that the *writing* itself holds the reader's interest.

Thus, to write more *interestingly,* the copywriter must "go back to school" to learn to write *better.* This will involve plenty of hard work and long-continued application. But the effort is usually worthwhile. It has been known to pay off well—in dollars.

Three Steps to Writing More Interesting Copy

Actually, basically good writing is only the first of three steps toward creating more interesting copy. These steps are:

1. Basically good writing to start with; good usage; writing that is smooth and readable; writing that is simple, clear, precise, and strong

2. Writing made more interesting by word color and word-expressiveness; the use of picture words and sound words and writing devices that add interest

3. The doing of something to the structure of the piece of copy that lifts it out of the ordinary and gives it freshness

Good Writing

Good writing is a large subject. It is not easily explained, in a how-to-do-it fashion, in one short chapter. An endeavor to do such a thing would be clearly beyond the scope of this book.

There are a considerable number of books on this subject, a good many of them published quite recently. They contain many useful ideas that can contribute to improvement in writing. A study of this literature is recommended.

A few of the ways that have seemed most effective in making writing better might, however, be briefly noted here.

One of the best of these is the use of *short words*. Rudolf Flesch, the apostle of "plain talk," has proved that words with their affixes removed become much easier to read. There are other benefits, too. Short words clarify language, speed it up, give it a sprightly bounce. Arthur Kudner's famous advice to his son pays eloquent tribute to the power of the little word:[1]

> Never fear big long words
> Big long words name little things
> All big things have little names
> Such as life and death, peace and war
> Or dawn, day, night, hope, love, home
> Learn to use little words in a big way
> It is hard to do
> But they say what you mean
> When you don't know what you mean—
> Use big words
> That often fools little people

[1] Arthur Kudner Foundation.

There is another potent way to improve writing. Use *active verbs,* instead of passive ones, whenever possible. Active verbs bristle with power. They pick up color. They propel the reader through the copy.

As a corollary to this, try to write without using any adverbs at all. Adverbs do not—or hardly ever—strengthen verbs. They are natural verb-weakeners. Their values are largely negative. They *are* useful for weasel wording, for toning down, or as an escape hatch to back away from a too belligerent or a too positive statement.

Some writers on usage decry the meaningless "junk" phrases that muddy the language—phrases such as *the fact that, a subject that, along the lines of,* etc. These, together with clichés, may well be a menace in the long memo a copy-writer writes to his boss. But they are less to be worried about, however, in actual advertising copy. Advertising copy must say a lot in little space. Conse-quently, such needless words are usually edited out long before the copy gets into print.

The approaches to improved writing just indicated are only a beginning. There are many more. But these few have probably been the most fruitful.

Nor are these suggestions new or original. They have been stated often before. Yet, on the evidence of many advertisements, they appear not to have reached, or have simply been ignored by, all too many copywriters. On the other hand, in those instances where these approaches have been followed, they have helped create superlative copy. The A&P antitrust-case campaign (page 26) provides an excellent example of plain talk, short-word copy. The British Travel Association advertisement (page 151) demonstrates, magnifi-cently, the effectiveness of active verbs.

Writing Colorfully

Writing *colorfully* can act more directly than anything else to make institu-tional copy *interesting.* Beatrice Adams, vice-president of the Gardner Adver-tising Agency, once said: "Concentrate on pictures that talk and words that paint pictures." [2]

Color puts blood into writing. When a writer uses picture-painting words, his copy comes to life. It not only makes its points with greater vividness, but also intrigues and delights the reader.

The copy of the British Travel Association advertisement "Tread softly past the long, long sleep of kings" (page 151) is full of pictures, as is the Erwin, Wasey text on "Beer" (page 152). The British Travel ad, with its exciting third paragraph, includes not only picture words, but also *sound* words—the cathe-dral names that *thunder,* and *chime,* and *whisper.*

[2] New York *World-Telegram,* Dec. 7, 1962.

Sound words are also evident in the Esso institutional copy (page 186). Such as, "the leathery slap of a pigeon's wing." And, "they . . . embroider their silences with bells."

Use of picture words is one way to make writing colorful. There is an even more effective, more dramatic way—sometimes used to excess by other types of writers, but badly neglected by advertising copywriters. Namely, the use of two little figures of speech. *Simile* and *metaphor!*

A simile is like a picture inserted after a word to show what the word looks like. A metaphor is a picture substituted for the word.

The point is that readers enjoy these figures of speech, which seem to give pleasure and make the copy remembered. When apt and fresh, they illuminate the language and heighten its *interest.*

Turn again to the British Travel and the Erwin, Wasey advertisements. Note how, in both cases, the *color* in the text copy is provided by *verbs* and *nouns.* Note that there is scarcely an adjective or an adverb to be found anywhere.

A New Twist for Copy Structure

Structurally, most text copy tends to be very much alike. Out of a dozen advertisements, chances are every one will go to work in just about the same way. After the headline, some one will start to sell us something—like a lawyer reading a brief.

There is nothing necessarily wrong with this. It happens in the vast majority of advertisements. But when a rare ad comes along that departs from this norm, it stands out immediately. Its very freshness makes it interesting.

It also tends to compound interest in another way. By breaking himself out of old habits, the copywriter is likely to treat his subject with more freedom and imagination than he would otherwise.

There are many ways to re-structure the writing of copy to get it out of the commonplace groove:

In the famous Ohrbach's "cat" advertisement (page 110), the cat chattered like a gossipy woman.

In the Travelers ad, "Thoughts at Thirty-nine," (page 151), a middle-aged man soliloquized to himself.

Hamilton Watches (page 101) cast its copy in the form of notes from husband to wife, and wife to husband.

The Erwin, Wasey *Beer* ad had the form of a condensed essay. In it, beer was semi-personalized. That is, it "goes with the crowd," "follows the races," "attends prize fights," etc.

A cruise advertisement for the United States Lines told its story in the form of a day-by-day diary of what would happen on the cruise.

Les Pearl, a master of offbeat copy presentation, wrote a piece of copy that suffered from a bad headcold (page 153).

Dialogue conversations have often been used. The California Wine Advisory Board developed this into a debate, presenting two opposing points of view (page 238).

Many ads have been written as memos or letters. Too many. Many ads have been written in verse, particularly in the early days of advertising.

Copy can be presented as a little story. Though not institutional, a strikingly successful example is George Gribbin's amusing Arrow Shirt advertisement, "My friend Joe Holmes is now a horse." And so on.

The Selling Job

While institutional copy has an obligation to be interesting, it also has an objective to fulfill. It has a selling job to do. With skillful writing, institutional copy can accomplish both—be interesting from beginning to end and sell from beginning to end.

The advertisements cited in this chapter demonstrate how deft, persuasive idea-selling can be woven in with the maintaining of interest.

Strengthening the Copy. Know What You Are Talking About

Information is the elixir that makes copy good. An invaluable preliminary step for writing *any* good copy, product-selling or institutional, is to know everything possible about the subject of your writing. Final copy quality is usually directly proportional to preliminary copywriter information.

Know the Person You Are Talking To

Institutional messages *tend* to be beamed at specialized groups of readers. Therefore, the writer should know as much as possible about who the reader is, about his interests, and his likes and dislikes. Research, or client information, should provide this knowledge. Copy should talk to the reader in terms of what interests *him*.

And, of course, as every copywriter should be taught early, he should address himself to an individual, not to an auditorium full of people. Every advertisement is read individually.

Write More Than One Version

Important copy deserves to be written more than once, that is, in more than one version. This is especially so if the copy is short.

In writing copy more than once, the copywriter gets rid of his pet phrases, his half-formed thoughts, his imitative leanings, and other mental debris—and gets down to write the copy. Each time, he writes more simply, more fluently, more directly. The copy progressively improves. Doing this is a highly recommended way to arrive at better copy.

Writing Faults to Avoid

In writing institutional copy, some copywriting faults seem to crop up more often than others. For instance:

1. The use of that form of hard-sell ad language (sometimes alleged to be "telegraphic") that tries to jam as much pressure into every word and sentence as possible—and comes out gobbledygook. Hard sell defeats itself in this area.

2. The use of *any* formula or set of rules for writing copy. Institutional advertising is by nature a *dissenting*, individualistic kind of advertising. It does not want to conform to what others have done, for it achieves its greatest successes by being different and original.

3. Failure to maintain flow of thought. Thought should flow smoothly from the beginning of the copy to the end. It should travel in an untroubled stream —*not* like a wheelbarrow bumping from boulder to boulder.

4. Vagueness and indirection, usually caused, as stated earlier, by an unclear objective. However, it may also be caused by the writer or client trying to employ subtlety and insinuation to sneak over a claim that can't be made openly. It doesn't work. Nobody gets it. And the rest of the copy is undermined.

5. "Writing down." Never write down to a reader. The old idea of the masses being mentally equivalent to a twelve-year-old child has been exploded. Much more useful is the advice attributed to a number of persons, but at least once, publicly, by Reuben Maury, editorial writer of the New York *Daily News,* to the late Raymond Clapper:[3] "Never overestimate the public's information, and never underestimate its intelligence."

6. "Writing up." Even sillier than writing down to a reader is writing up to a reader—such as a banker or an executive. Institutional copywriters have attempted to do this. The result was an oddly stilted style that probably puzzled, more than it appealed to, the audience to whom it was addressed. And most insanely fruitless of all is trying to imitate the style of a magazine—such as "*Time* style." This leads only to suffering.

Examples of Outstanding Copy

Advertisements with outstanding visual-verbal ideas are likely to be the ones with the most outstanding text copy. We can see this exemplified in the adver-

[3] In a *Daily News* editorial, Apr. 20, 1952.

tising for Ohrbach's (pages 88 and 110), for the Maryland Casualty Company (page 109), and for the Better Vision Institute (pages 235 and 237).

The copy for the British Travel Association ad mentioned earlier also does justice to its magnificent headline:

TREAD SOFTLY PAST THE LONG, LONG SLEEP OF KINGS

THIS IS Henry VII's chapel in Westminster Abbey. These windows have filtered the sunlight of five centuries. They have also seen the crowning of twenty-two kings.

Three monarchs rest here now. Henry, Elizabeth and Mary. Such are their names in sleep. No titles. No trumpets. The banners hang battle-heavy and becalmed. But still the royal crown remains. *Honi soit qui mal y pense.*

When you go to Britain, make yourself this promise. Visit at least *one* of the thirty great cathedrals. Their famous names thunder! Durham and Armagh. Or they chime! Lincoln and Canterbury. And sometimes they *whisper.* Winchester, Norwich, Salisbury and Wells. Get a map and make your choice.

Each cathedral transcends the noblest single work of art. It is a pinnacle of faith and an act of centuries. It is an offering of human hands as close to Abraham as it is to Bach. Listen to the soaring choirs at evensong. And, if you can, go at Easter.

You will rejoice that you did.

What many think was the greatest advertisement of the distinguished Travelers Insurance series pictured a man alone in the country, in a pensive mood, leaning against a rail fence. The ad read:

THOUGHTS AT THIRTY-NINE

I'm 39 today.

Not old, as somebody once said, for a cathedral. But well past the starry-eyed stage for a man.

And I've gotten rid of some of my starry-eyed ideas.

Does that mean I'm worn out and disillusioned? No—I don't think it does. Not when I remember the kick I got out of landing that 3½ pound brook on the Tenabeck last spring.

But I'm beginning to see some things as they really are.

That dream every kid has of being rich some day. I don't think it's coming true, as far as I'm concerned.

The securities I bought in '29—well, why go into *that* again? This house . . . it will be mine some day, but there is that boom price to write off. The job . . . good even at cut pay . . . but after all, how many people get rich on jobs?

No, I'll probably never be rich. But I'm losing no sleep over it . . . for I've fixed things so I'm even surer that I'll never be poor.

I've seen to it that I'll have money when I need it. I've done it the only way I know of for the man who hasn't an estate behind him . . . by taking full advantage of insurance.

If anything happens to me, my life insurance policies cover the rest of my mortgage, take care of Mary, and send the boys to college. If I live, there will be an income that will let us have a mighty comfortable time.

My accident insurance takes up where my life insurance leaves off. My house is covered by fire insurance. Automobile insurance protects me when I drive.

I've looked ahead, calculated the hazards of life and guarded against them.

And at 39 I've greater peace of mind than I've ever had before.

Moral: Insure in The Travelers.

This ad won much acclaim from the advertising fraternity. Also acclaimed for copy quality were the Hamilton Watch ads, "To Jim" and "To Peggy," already noted on page 101.

One advertisement has the distinction of being very near to pure literature. It was an advertisement of the agency, Erwin, Wasey & Company and was written by the late O. B. Winters. It read:

BEER

CHAMPAGNE of the poor, bitter nectar of the rich, beer is the beverage of the people.

A great commoner, intimate of men and women in every walk of life, it wears overalls or "tails" with equal ease.

Earthy, Rabelaisian; in its company go song and laughter. Never sorrow.

Friend of the people, it refreshes them in their weariness, slakes their thirst, dulls the edge of their despair, brings gayety to their holiday and helps to bind the bonds of friendship.

Beer goes with the crowd to Coney Island, lodge picnics and clam bakes. It follows the races, attends prize fights and ball games. It accompanies the fisherman to the brook and awaits him in the coolness of the spring. It rides the Twentieth Century, lives at the Ritz and greets the dusty traveller at the hot dog stand. The furtive maid opens it on the kitchen table for her sweetheart while the butler serves it to his master on a silver tray. It christens the freshman, returns the alumnus and presides at the midnight feast.

Beer—the very word brings memories trooping through the mind. A whole kaleidoscope of pictures.

Strange that in advertising, beer has had no real interpreter since repeal.

In addition to its literary qualities, this ad also was successful. It won for Erwin, Wasey the Rheingold beer account.

No discussion of institutional text copy would be quite satisfactory without mention of the long-continued series of small-space, all-text newspaper advertisements written by Leslie Pearl for Wallachs stores. These ads consist of little stories or anecdotes, on all sorts of subjects, but always calling attention to Wallachs and occasionally, in an offhand way, to some of its products.

Although some rather fantastic sales of these products have sometimes followed, the series has been essentially institutional, promoting the store. One rather amusing example of the Les Pearl touch:

BEWARE THE COBBOD CODE

At this tibe of year one cannot be too careful about catching code. It would be bad edough if the weather stayed code. But when it gets warb every few days, it is ody datural that the air is teebig with bugs, viruses ad bicrobes.

You should, by all beans, avoid drafts ad chills. Wear some good wooled or dylod sox on your feet. Wear a warb overcoat and a cashmere scarf. If it rains, put od your rubbers ad carry your umbrella. Ad if you are short of any of these, go to Wallachs where they are havig a sebi-annual clearance sale ad where you bay fide sub real bargains.

It is only by taking the precautions outlide above that we have bid able to escabe a code ourselves.

Dock od wood!

Chapter 19

TELEVISION

AND

RADIO

The largest spending advertisers—the sellers of food, cigarettes, home products, motor cars, etc.— have always been attracted to *mass entertainment* media.

Mass entertainment has advanced through a series of sequential stages, moving from one medium to another. Its first form was *magazine fiction.* Next came *movies,* which, not needing it, rejected advertising support. *Radio* followed. Today, the dominant form of mass entertainment is *television.*

Television is where advertising's big money is going. Television can deliver enormous audiences. Its capacity to present a *demonstration* of the product gives it great selling power. It offers sight, sound, motion, color, and star performance—brought without charge into the living room. And it can also be fantastically expensive. This, however, is not a great deterrent to the big product-selling advertiser who seeks the largest possible audience. To such an advertiser, television's image is very attractive.

The same affluent image, however, can be disconcerting to *institutional* advertisers, who may be searching for selective rather than mass audiences, who have no product to demonstrate, and whose institutional budgets, at least, are limited. They find the *cost* of television particularly frightening.

Yet, the cost of television is quite relative. It can be very great *if* one thinks, as many businessmen do, *only* in terms of television's *big numbers.* If one demands a top-rated national network show in prime time. If one strives for the maximum audience. If one insists on grandiose production. Asks for top stars. Wants the bestest and the mostest—in other words, top *status*—regardless of cost.

But if one disregards status and takes a closer, more realistic view of television, its appearance changes. Its price tag shrinks, and its use becomes more feasible. In addition to the big numbers, television has some *smaller,* less blatantly publicized aspects. And these are precisely the ones that make this medium useful to institutional advertisers.

Television has time to sell that is not prime time, and is purchasable in a wide range of prices. It can offer geographical regions, or individual stations, instead of national networks, small audiences as well as large ones, and programs that are surprisingly inexpensive. And sometimes, a relatively low percentage of viewers, achieved against higher-rating competition, can have hidden values.

The second, third, fourth, fifth, etc., choices are not necessarily bad ones. Nor is local coverage to be despised. For it is here, in what might be called "secondary" television, that the good media man can find selectivity and flexibility and the special kinds of audiences that institutional advertisers so often wish to reach. And when one foregoes big-number prestige, his first reward is usually a tremendous reduction in cost. Furthermore, localized television can be combined with other media—radio or print—to fill gaps or extend coverage.

Special groups or publics are not always as hard to reach with television as it might seem. One institutional advertiser successfully gets to business leaders with an attractive week-end golf program. And it is well-known that many government officials faithfully watch the "Today" show, because visiting celebrities may say something on the show of diplomatic importance.

Cherchez the Program

The key to reaching a selective audience is finding the *program* that such an audience looks at. This is possible. The program preferences of special groups are documented by the rating services.

Such programs may be "small" ones on localized stations. But they can be assembled by a good media man to achieve high results per dollar. If type of *audience,* rather than status, becomes the criterion of choice, television can be bought to fulfill the needs of institutional advertising.

At the same time, thinking in terms of commercials, television delivers its same *quality* of impact, whether on a local station or a national network.

For the Large Advertiser

Sometimes an advertiser's institutional objectives *may* require a mass audience. This faces him with the problems and the high costs of big-numbers television. But there is a simple answer. It is not necessary to devote *all* the commercials to the institutional message. *Most* of the commercials can be given to sales, with an institutional one interjected at suitable intervals. In this way, the cost of the institutional messages can be reduced, at the same time permitting them to reach the desired mass audience.

Creative Aspects of Institutional Television Advertising

In its creative aspects, television offers the institutional advertiser the same opportunities it holds out to the product-selling advertiser. The problems and techniques of creating commercials are quite similar for both types of advertising.

This situation contrasts notably with that of print media. A print advertisement must catch and hold attention long enough to do its allotted job. For the institutional print advertisement, this imposes the special obligation to be interesting.

With television, the catching and holding *attention* is performed automatically by the medium itself. The simple fact of motion fascinates the eye and prevents it from wandering elsewhere. Viewers continue to look at a commercial, even if they know it is going to be a boring one. If they *do* walk out on a commercial—perhaps to get another can of beer during a long program— it is because the commercial minute is the most appropriate time to do so. The act is not necessarily a protest against the commercial. It merely indicates that the commercial is less entertaining than the program.

With the viewer seated before the set and the eye entranced by motion, creative efforts to make the commercial interesting merely to catch and hold attention are redundant. For attention-holding, practically all present-day commercials are adequate. Some are *too* interesting and obscure the message they are supposed to get across.

Hence, unlike in print, product-selling and institutional television advertising start at the same point as far as *attention* is concerned.

Memorability the Key Factor

The true dynamic factor in television creative success is not attention-getting, but *memorability*. This applies to both institutional and product-selling advertising.

A commercial may be very exciting and hardworking. But, on television, it is immediately preceded and followed by other exciting matter, which acts to divert the mind's attention. Before long, perhaps a half dozen other commercials may have been seen and heard, blotting out memory of the original commercial. If no part of the message survives this bombardment and if nothing sticks in the memory, the commercial becomes a total loss.

A normal way to achieve memorability in broadcast advertising is *repetition*. Constant repetition hammers the message into the viewer's brain. There are two drawbacks, however, to the use of repetition. First, it is expensive. Second, if continued too long, it may become boring. As boredom increases, the viewer becomes apathetic to the commercial—and may even get annoyed by it and become hostile to the sponsor and his message.

This reintroduces the need for being *interesting*, but for a different purpose and with a different emphasis from the attention-getting interest of print advertising. What is needed here is that something interesting happen in the commercial that will *continue* to be interesting, even if seen again and again. People must *want* to see it again.

If a commercial contains this nugget of memorable interest, it will need less repetition—do more work at less cost. It will be protected against the dangers of boredom. Such memorability, however, is only attained by a high degree of imagination and creativity.

It occurs, characteristically, in great commercials. It is illustrated by the Hertz aerial dive into the driver's seat, by the Xerox chimpanzee messenger, by the Liberty Mutual auto collision, by the Alcoa litany of "Punch it, cut it, drill it," etc. And others.

The Advertiser's Plant a Television Asset

There is one special area wherein television can be used profitably by the institutional advertiser. Namely, the interior of his own factory.

At first blush, this might seem odd, because print advertisers, long ago, decided that a picture of the factory added little to sales or prestige. And when still pictures were taken of machinery, they turned out to be definitely unexciting.

But television has *motion*. And the interior of a factory has plenty of things that move—some of them in visually intriguing ways. These action pictures of machines making familiar products have genuine values for corporate advertising. Not only the machinery and the workers, but the company itself comes to life.

A particular special value lies in the sector of plant-city, or community-neighbor, advertising. Management forgets, sometimes, that its plant might be an object of considerable curiosity to the thousands of people who pass by it regularly. They constantly wonder what goes on inside, wish they could get a peek at it sometime.

This feeling of curiosity can be capitalized on by taking plant-city neighbors on a guided tour through the factory, via television. During the tour, a variety of institutional objectives can be covered—recruiting, improving employee relations, image-building, humanizing, explaining the company's business, and numerous other public relations goals.

Emphasis can be on the people who work in the plant, or on the machinery, or both. If machinery is shown, a determined effort should be made to depict it dramatically, in a visually exciting manner. The agency creative staff, especially TV art directors and production men, should have ample opportunity to study the factory scene *before* commercials are started. Experimental shots might be tried. And film clips of dramatic operations might be made and kept for future use.

Alcoa has demonstrated, many times, that factory shots can be made intensely interesting. U.S. Steel's signature, the tapping of an open-hearth furnace with a river of molten steel bursting out, has for a long time been one of the most memorable sights on the air.

Use of Long Commercials

Print media has sometimes been preferred over television because of print's ability to deliver a long, and occasionally complex, message. Yet, television can present long messages too. Slightly less than three minutes of commercial time are usually allowed for a half-hour show, slightly less than six minutes for an hour show. It is not necessary to break this time down into short commercials. By using fewer commercials, they can be made longer. And, taking advantage of television's sight, sound, and motion, it is surprising how much can be told in a two- or three-minute commercial.

Areas of Effectiveness and Ineffectiveness

Allied to entertainment, television is an inherently *emotional* medium. Consequently, commercials built on emotional or sentimental themes are likely to prove exceptionally successful. This is why this medium has worked remarkably well for life insurance advertisers such as the Prudential Life Insurance Company.

On the other hand, television loses effectiveness in the presentation of ideas that are overly abstract for a mass audience, such as economic discussions of profits. This reflects the entertainment orientation of the medium.

It has been said that to succeed, a television commercial must identify itself with its viewers, and its viewers must identify themselves with the characters in the commercial. Identification becomes more difficult with abstract subjects.

The Bankers Trust Company used its own employees to sell its services on television (and in print too). These were the same everyday people that the public met at the tellers' windows. Here, the sense of identification was immediate, and worked powerfully to give the bank a friendly, humanized image.

The Worst Way to Do It

The worst way to communicate a corporate message on television is for the company president, or other high officer, to deliver it personally in a "stand-up" presentation.

The audience does not identify itself with a highly successful businessman. He offers poor competition to the great actors, the professional announcers, and the colorful entertainment personalities regularly seen on the family TV set. His business importance, however great, does not come over to his audience, who may know very little about him or his business.

If, in addition to his own ineffectiveness, as often happens, his message also does not communicate, the president's commercial winds up as a flop. Business executives should not attempt to play this role. But some of them keep trying.

Writing the Television Commercial

Although television commercials are spoken of as being written, the word *writing* is a misnomer. *Fabricating, assembling,* or *forging* would be better. The commercial *does* usually start with a "script" written by a copywriter. But, in the next step, when the TV art director makes it into a rough "storyboard," it may come out with little resemblance to the original script. Then the production man will institute other changes, and the client will contribute still more. And still more touches will be added by outside producers and suppliers. The making of a commercial is very much a group effort.

Nevertheless, the script is the starting place. If it is a strong script based on an idea and knowing where it is going, it is likely to wind up as a much better commercial than one which started with a weak and flabby script.

Mechanics of the script   A copywriter's script is divided into two columns, usually with one labeled *video* at the left and *audio* at the right. The audio supplies the words and sounds; the video describes the visual action.

The video is actually a rough blueprint or, rather, a specification (as envisioned by the copywriter) for the filming of the commercial. It tells what is being photographed, where the camera is in relation to the subject, and how the camera moves. It lists, in sequence, the scenes taken by the camera, and tells when to "cut" (or "dissolve," etc.) to another scene. At the same time, the audio column synchronizes the words to the numbered scenes.

It is not necessary, here, to describe the script-writing process in much more detail than this. Such information is usually amply provided in a good book on commercial-writing. What is intended to be indicated is that the mechanics of script-writing are not basically especially complicated. Neither are these mechanics particularly meaningful in themselves—at least, at this early point of development.

To the writer, it is not the camera movement per se that should be important. What is important is what happens *in front of the camera*—not what the camera *does,* but what the camera *sees.* And for dramatic effect, it should see *motion— action.*

A good commercial needs an *idea.* To get the idea, the writer must answer two questions: (1) what is the objective of this commercial, i.e., what am I trying to do? and (2) what is the most exciting, most memorable way to dramatize what I am doing?

In developing his idea, the writer should probe the full possibilities of television. Thinking of motion, he should consider vertical motion as well as horizontal motion, fast as well as slow motion, sudden motion, graceful motion, threatening motion, humorous motion.

He should think of *space.* Television has depth. Close-up is great for demonstrating a small product, but the long shot can have sweeping, dramatic connotations.

And finally, he should never forget that what interests people most is people, then animals. With people, there are times to be serious and times to strive for a laugh. Humor, seldom seen in other advertising media, is popular on television.

Television for Institutional Functions

Television has been used to fulfill a number of institutional functions. Among these are protective image-building, plant-city advertising, public service advertising, association advertising, employee relations, and educational-theme advertising, usually for recruiting objectives.

Localized television permits strong image-building programming along public service, educational, and community-interest lines. Commercials with these programs may be institutional or product-selling. If product-selling, however, they are often curtailed in time allotment.

When Eastern Airlines presented a two-part special on the Bolshoi Ballet, only half of the total eighteen-minute commercial time allotment was used— leaving the other half for the inclusion of an additional ballet.

Standard Oil Company of New Jersey sponsored the Festival of the Performing Arts as a public service, with commercial time limited to four minutes per program. Commercials for the telecast of the Hollywood Bowl concerts, sponsored by the Security First National Bank of Southern California, were low-keyed and stressed only that the program was made available by the bank.

In areas where weather news was not available, Phillips Petroleum presented thirty-second weather reports in place of the company's own commercial messages.

Shell Oil has presented the New York Philharmonic Young People's Concerts for several years. Commercials are institutional, stressing the need for education.

Educational Themes

Educational themes, with their overtones of recruiting benefit, are often favored in the programming of large companies. General Electric's sponsorship of the "College Bowl," a matching of collegiate wits, is said to be "making brains as popular as brawn on campuses across the country." General Electric offers a scholarship to each winning team and obviously improves its own recruiting image.

Sinclair Oil sponsored top intercollegiate debates in Texas, publicizing the colleges of that state.

In the East, Colgate-Palmolive offered an educational series, "Frontiers of Knowledge," in cooperation with the University of Pennsylvania. And Oklahoma Gas and Electric Company sponsored twelve prime-time "Oklahoma Heritage" shows, depicting the state's history. After a preview by history teachers, the program was made "required viewing" for all Oklahoma history students.

Image-building

In New England, Volkswagen encountered strong resistance in that it was offering a product of a former enemy country. To counteract this reaction, Volkswagen used TV to identify itself with the great American pastime—baseball. As a result, public attitudes improved rapidly and so did sales.

The Esso World Theatre underscored the benefits to the United States and to other nations of American private investments abroad.

And television, of course, is an important part of the Bell Telephone System's unceasing image-building effort. One interesting program was that of the Illinois Bell Telephone Company. It sponsored high school basketball tournaments, and the commercials were directed at teen-agers. The commercials showed that the telephone company was a good place to work, but young people were urged to obtain a college degree first. The commercials also asked for consideration in use of the family telephone and suggested that teen-agers use the telephone to inform parents whenever they would be late getting home.

Community-interest Programs

Community-interest programs—documentaries and specials of various kinds—offer excellent programming opportunities for institutional advertisers.

Sears Roebuck has sponsored several major programs of this type in its home city of Chicago. One was called "TUF" Guys (referring to "Tactical Undercover Function") and dealt with a little-known aspect of the police department. Another, "Friday's Children," documented scenes in state institutions for the mentally retarded. Another dealt with the ten-year career of Chicago's mayor. And so on.

Plant-City Television Advertising. Western Electric

The community-interest theme has been used with considerable skill and success by Western Electric in its plant-city television advertising, which supplements and extends its newspaper campaigns described in Chapter 8.

Some typical examples have been (1) a tour of Nebraska's State Capitol, (2) the growth of a medical center, (3) "Destination Everywhere," a program devoted to transportation, and (4) a state's struggle to solve its water shortage problem. Though local in coverage, these programs were in prime time.

This brought them into competition with national-network entertainment and comedy shows, which drew a large percentage of the total audience. On the other hand, Western Electric's smaller percentage undoubtedly included many public-spirited people who could be more interested in a civic-minded subject than in a star performer and his show.

These were often exactly the people Western Electric most wanted to reach, and whose goodwill was the most valuable to the company. It would appear when Western Electric sought an opinion-leader audience that the higher-ranking competition had tended to comb out of the whole audience those viewers *least* desirable to Western Electric and left remaining those *most* desirable. In effect, Western Electric exchanged quantity for quality.

Furthermore, these programs were obtained at exceptionally low cost. In addition to being a good buy, they were tailored both to a desired geographical area and to a desired type of audience.

The interesting ninety-second commercials were, in fact, themselves documentary. They took the viewer through the door of the plant and showed him what was going on inside. He saw telephones and telephone equipment being made. Full advantage was taken of the visually intriguing, busy motion of machinery. At the same time, the commercials explained the relationship of Western Electric to the Bell System, thus fulfilling a major objective of all Western Electric advertising.

Low-cost Public Service Advertising

A commercial that comes close to setting a record both for low cost and high imagination is one produced by Kenyon & Eckhardt for New England Merchants National Bank of Boston. This commercial's objective was to help alleviate the coin shortage and by its public service, build a goodwill image for the bank.

The major prop of the commercial was a large corrugated-paperboard packing box, such as might be used for packaging a refrigerator. Turned upside down, this box moved, propelled by the two small boys inside it. It had cutout windows and portholes and, from the top, there projected a length of stovepipe that looked like a periscope and gave the box a passable resemblance to a landgoing submarine.

In the commercial, two gossiping ladies at a fence are startled by the apparition of the moving box and turn to watch it as it goes down the street. The audio sound is background music.

The strange contraption then stops at a fruit stand and a small arm comes out of one of the portholes, takes an apple, and pays for it. The box continues to the bank and approaches the bank teller in his booth.

The teller opens a drawer and the boys' hands dump coins into it, taking a dollar bill in exchange. Then, as the box walks away, accompanied by a dog, the announcer is heard saying:

> As you know, there's a very real coin shortage these days . . . so why don't you bring in *your* coins too? Round up your change . . .
>
> Take it to the nearest office of New England Merchants Bank . . . or whatever bank you do business with. We're all in the same box on this, and we'd all appreciate your help.

And that is all.

Creatively, this commercial is commendable for the ease with which the viewer can identify with the two small boys in the large box and join with them in their wonderful make-believe world.

The commercial is one of a series on public service themes, which are a continuing part of the bank's total advertising program. These image-building commercials link to the bank, through the teller, "the man" in the bank. He is significant as a symbol illustrating the bank's slogan: "Where the man you talk to *is* the bank."

The Large Institutional Advertiser. U.S. Steel

The television objectives of the U.S. Steel Corporation have been stated as follows:

Public Relations Objectives: To build a more favorable image of U.S. Steel as an employer, as a corporate citizen, as a leader in research and to explain the need for profits to build plants and create jobs

Commercial Objectives: To build new or larger markets for our products and to meet ever-increasing competition of other materials in markets where the general public is, or can be, an important buying influence

In 1964, U.S. Steel sponsored the opening of the World's Fair. More recently, the company's television advertising has leaned toward news and spot commercials, with one-minute spots in thirty markets where steel is sold. These "sell the ideas that sell steel." The advertising is heavily merchandised to the industry.

From 1953 to 1962, U.S. Steel sponsored and "owned" an hour entertainment program known, first, as "The Theater Guild of the Air" and, later, as "The United States Steel Hour." A feature of this program was the striking signature already mentioned—the tapping of the open-hearth furnace.

In the television advertising, U.S. Steel combines product-selling with institutional messages. At one time, as much as 40 per cent of commercial time was devoted to institutional themes. Behind this heavy institutional orientation is the company's continuing need for protective image-building.

It constantly seeks a better image to counteract a negative image, inherited

This dramatic scene of molten steel being jet-tapped from an open-hearth furnace became the memorable television signature of the U.S. Steel Hour. (AGENCY: *Batten, Barton, Durstine & Osborn*)

In a New England Merchants National Bank TV commercial, this packing box moves mysteriously down the street—propelled by two small boys inside. Thus, imagination creates visual excitement, and an effective commercial, at extremely low cost. (AGENCY: *Kenyon & Eckhardt*)

from a now rather distant past, of its being a stodgy old company that makes tremendous profits. Hence, its advertising often emphasizes U.S. Steel *research* and its innovations in developing new products. For educational messages on the economics of profits, it has used easy-to-absorb animation, hoping thereby to overcome the drawback presented by the abstractness of the subject.

The Rebirth of Radio

When television supplanted radio as the major purveyor of mass entertainment in the 1950s, the effect on the older medium was cataclysmic. The loss of big-time advertising billings left radio in a very weakened state.

Nevertheless, radio survived. Within five years after its low point about 1960, it became bigger than ever before. But it is vastly changed, in many ways, from the radio of the "Amos 'n' Andy" times.

Radio's networks had been built up by mass entertainment. With this prop taken away, the importance of the networks began to decline, while that of local stations increased. A characteristic of the new radio is its localized character. Concurrently, the number of stations has increased from 600 in 1948 to nearly 5,000 in 1964.

Unable to compete with television in mass entertainment, the radio networks gave up their comedy, variety, and dramatic shows and concentrated, instead, on news and information.

The local stations found many other things to broadcast, some of which developed entirely new audiences. They not only rediscovered music, but also subdivided it into many types, each of which attracted its own special group of fans. Service features came in—traffic information reported from helicopters, detailed weather information for fishermen, advice to the lovelorn. Religion became a sponsor. But radio's greatest discovery was *conversation* of all kinds.

The revival of radio has been attributed to its new programming, but something else probably had much more to do with it—the development of the portable, small set, a development already well under way.

When the TV picture tube monopolized the living room, radio moved out —into everywhere else. And proliferated. It cuddled into the kitchen, established a place for itself in playrooms and dens. It replaced the alarm clock in bedrooms. In 1965, the national average was four working-order radios in every home.

Transistors and miniaturization made radio sets small enough to be carried anywhere, including the great outdoors. Today, radio walks down the street and goes to the beach, the lake, and the picnic.

The popularity of the battery-operated portables has boosted the total sales of sets to record highs. Nearly 28 million were sold in 1964. As of January 1, 1965, America had 228,279,200 radio sets.

Another important innovation was the car radio. Because the car radio gets much listening, it is helping to change listening habits for significant audiences.

Changed listening times   The network emphasis on news, the preemption of the evening hours by television and the car radio have turned the time pattern of radio listening upside down. Radio's prime time, today, is in the *morning* hours before 9 A.M., when people are getting up and when they are going to work in their cars.

People also listen to the radio when they return home, between 5 and 7 P.M. After dinner, when television takes over, is radio's poor time.

Radio for Institutional Advertisers

Because of its localized and segmented nature, radio today can deliver almost any type of audience desired. It can deliver teen-agers or senior citizens, eggheads or lowbrows, rich or poor. It can talk to ethnic groups in their own languages. By aiming at the morning car-radio audience in suburban areas, it can reach doctors, lawyers, dentists, and businessmen. By beaming at the car-radio audience in an industrial community, it can reach factory employees.

Today's radio is flexible in operation and low in cost. Like television, it offers institutional advertisers many opportunities not yet fully capitalized on. Radio is used extensively by service-selling organizations such as the telephone companies, the airlines, banks, and insurance companies. It is also used, institutionally, by large chemical companies and by many trade associations.

Texaco's sponsorship of the Metropolitan Opera (Chapter 21) is an outstanding example of the use of radio for public service advertising. And Edward P. Morgan's news comment for AFL-CIO offers an instance of labor union image-building (Chapter 9).

The Impact of Radio

Though it communicates by sound alone, radio projects an astonishingly strong impact. It can do this because (1) the listener's *imagination* comes to its aid and (2) by its nature and uses it has been able to identify itself with a sense of *immediacy*.

When telling a story, radio has only voice and sound effects to work with. The listener's imagination fills in, mentally visualizes what is happening in the story. And sometimes, with even greater vividness than real life. When the "Gunsmoke" program switched from radio to television, some loyal fans, who had followed the radio story for years, were so disappointed with the TV version that they ceased to look at it after the second or third time. To them, the actors and scenery on television did not seem as *real* and as appealing as they did when created by the imagination for radio.

The immediacy of radio arises from its effect of nearness. It is a voice right in the room, talking directly to the listener. It deals with matters of urgency such as news. Long ago, it was noted that radio had a special ability to stir listeners to action, and do it immediately. Time and again it out-performed print in getting active response from an audience.

To those institutional advertisers whose objectives are of a type to seek action, radio can be a useful and economical medium.

The Radio Commercial

If the radio-commercial writer remembers that he has the listener's imagination working for him and if he plays to that imagination, he is almost bound to succeed in his job. The well-written commercial will tell a little story, help paint mental pictures, and use sound effects to give the pictures more vivid reality. The stream of thought in the commercial should be continuous and smooth flowing.

Also to be remembered is that the commercial is a voice *talking* to the listener. And it should *talk,* in the normal, natural, loose-jointed way that people do talk to each other. It should avoid the tight, over-condensed, unnatural diction of hard-sell print copy. Arthur Godfrey could always get a laugh by merely mimicking such miswritten commercials.

Rather recently, radio commercials have tended to become brighter and livelier than before, with the occasional injection of "far-out" humor. Some of these commercials have been very effective. And some have failed, usually because the cleverness was so far out that it became incomprehensible.

Like jingles, humorous commercials are devices for selling a product. They are, generally, less well adapted to the needs of institutional advertisers. Though there are exceptions, an institutional objective usually requires a presentation that is sincere, direct, and serious and sometimes, even diplomatic. Commercials for the AFL-CIO, which is well aware that its views are not agreed with by all of its show's listeners, are models of restraint and diplomacy.

Use of radio for bank image-building   One instance of a light touch of humor having value is provided by the Central Valley National Bank. Though this bank had twenty-seven branches in mid-California, it felt itself being submerged by the advertising of its much larger competitors. Its advertising budget was only about 5 per cent of theirs. It sought an identifying image that would keep it in the public mind in spite of the competition.

Its market research (as has similar research by others) indicated that bank "friendliness" could be overdone and that people did not really want the "overpoweringly friendly, smothered-with-love-and-kisses approach." People, it found, "want their banks to be *businesslike, reasonable,* and *courteous.*"

Central Valley National Bank decided it wanted the image of the "almost friendly" bank. It chose radio for its image-building, using eight stations. The first thirty seconds of the commercials were devoted to an image-building humorous situation; the second thirty seconds sold the bank's services.

A typical first section of the commercial:

TELLER: Here he comes into Central Valley, the most friendly bank, our one billionth customer. Come over here, sir.
CUSTOMER: Yeah.
TELLER: As our one billionth customer, it's my pleasure to award you $1,000, a mink coat for your wife and a trip around the world. What have you to say to that?
CUSTOMER: Stick 'em up!
TELLER: Friends, Central Valley is your *almost* friendly bank!

The campaign appeared to have met its objectives. Checking back on results, it was found that awareness of Central Valley was high. When asked to name the major banks of the area, the interview respondents almost always included Central Valley National Bank with its big competitors.

Buick's use of radio to reach employees   Buick uses station WKMF, Flint, Michigan, every workday to reach its 20,000 employees, plus other members of that industrial community. Ninety-five per cent of the workers drive to work. The program is timed to reach their car radios.

The one-hour morning program opens with a blast of a factory whistle at 6 A.M., which serves as an alarm clock for many workers on the 7 A.M. shift. The afternoon shift is similarly alerted at 3:30 P.M. and entertained until 4:30 P.M.

Programming, in typical radio manner, includes:

News, with emphasis on sports

Time

Weather

Lots of music

Traffic advice

Community causes

In-plant safety reminders, pertinent company facts

Personal announcements for employees

Taped on-the-job employee interviews

The last item on the list has special significance. As more and more employee names went on the air, the audience size increased day by day. By the end of a year, 630 factory workers had appeared on or were named on the program.

Replacing regular commercials, some of the employee interviews indicated employee pride in their work and belief in the quality of their product. Most of the interviews, however, were designed to please and entertain the workers.

One employee interviewed claimed to be the eating champion of Buick. He cited his lunch of five sandwiches, a half-ring of bologna, three apples, a banana, and four cookies.

This champion was promptly challenged by another employee, who said he once consumed forty-eight hard-boiled eggs for lunch.

The program was called "Factory Whistle." Its objective was to provide daily communication with employees and to get them to take greater pride in their work. Spillover into the general-public audience was considered desirable, too, as many of the listeners worked for other General Motors divisions.

The cost was estimated to be 40 per cent of the cost of publishing a four-page newspaper once a month. The program has continued since 1960, and by 1964, thirteen other manufacturing companies had instituted similar programs of their own. The radio shows are considered an important part of Buick's over-all employee-relations program.

Six

THE PUBLIC-SERVICE FUNCTION

Public service advertising is simply what its name indicates—advertising that renders a public service. Typical examples are the advertisements of the Advertising Council, such as "Prevent Forest Fires," "Help the College of Your Choice," "Stop Accidents," etc.

Public service advertising is not required to be altruistic in its motivation. In fact, if examined closely, very few, if any, public service campaigns will be found to be 100 per cent altruistic in every respect.

Nor is altruism necessarily a measure of the advertising's value, socially or otherwise. Some campaigns bring tangible commercial benefits to their sponsors and also, at the same time, render genuine and valuable services to the public.

Usually, in return for the public service, the advertiser earns the goodwill of the community, which may translate, to some extent, into increased sales. Sometimes, however, the advertiser may benefit even more directly.

Metropolitan Life Insurance Company's health and safety advertising has been part of that company's unique health-promotion program. When the program started in 1909, Metropolitan stated: "Insurance, not merely as a business proposition, but as a social program, will be the future policy of the company."

The program's advertising campaign, which has continued with little basic change for more than forty years, has been highly beneficial to the company's business. It has also made a massive contribution to America's public health. Few such efforts by any commercial organization have resulted in such a deep and widespread distribution of social benefits.

Health and Life Insurance

The good health of its policyholders and prospective policyholders is a matter of obvious importance to a life insurance company. Healthy people live to

Chapter 20

PUBLIC SERVICE

ADVERTISING...

WITH A

DIVIDEND

pay life insurance premiums longer than unhealthy people. Larger funds become available for investment, eventually making possible the offering of insurance at lower cost. More policies can be sold more easily, aiding the company's growth. Both company and policyholders benefit.

The Special Importance of Health to Metropolitan

With Metropolitan, because of the special nature of its business, the health of its policyholders was a matter of even greater importance than with most other companies. For much of Metropolitan's business in the early years was based on its "industrial" insurance—small policies, with premiums collected weekly at the policyholder's door. These policies were originally designed to bring insurance within reach of the wage-earning masses.

The people who bought these industrial policies were relatively poor and hence subject to greater health hazards than those economically more fortunate. In particular, in the 1890s, when the Metropolitan began to take a greatly increased interest in the health of its policyholders, these industrial policyholders were, typically, laboring men who worked long hours at low pay, under unfavorable conditions, and who often lived in overcrowded slums. These were the people most likely to suffer ill health and to be most subject to the attack of such a disease as tuberculosis.

It very early became clear to Metropolitan Life Insurance Company that any effort it made to improve policyholder health would be good business.

A second factor encouraged Metropolitan. Its industrial business was a mass business, dealing with large numbers of policyholders. This made it feasible for the company to attack health problems on the large scale necessary for success and, later, to use advertising effectively to implement its program.

Beginning of Metropolitan's Health and Welfare Program

Metropolitan Life Insurance Company's Health and Welfare (now Health and Safety) program was started in 1909 on the premise that a great deal of unnecessary sickness and premature death could be prevented by a vigorous campaign of health education.

The education was to be provided by authoritative pamphlets made available not only in English, but also in Swedish, Polish, French, German, Italian, and other languages spoken by immigrants. Next, the (then) 10,000 Metropolitan agents, visiting the homes of policyholders weekly, would be called upon to become an army of health messengers—to distribute the pamphlets.

The first pamphlet, *A War upon Consumption*, giving advice on fighting the greatly feared No. 1 killer of the time, was distributed in this manner in the summer of 1909. Immediately, enthusiastic letters of approval began to pour in and in due time, evidence began to pile up indicating that the idea was working—that health was being improved—that people were being saved from the attack of the dreaded disease.

Expansion of the program   Also a part of the program was the cooperation with existing health officials and welfare organizations. Visiting nurses were paid by Metropolitan to call on sick policyholders, to report cases where a doctor was needed, and to give instructions in sanitation and wholesome living.

This aspect of the program was continuously expanded, year after year. In forty-four years, 20 million policyholders had received more than 100 million nursing visits.

Meanwhile, more and more pamphlets were produced—medically sound, well written, and attractively illustrated—covering all basic health problems likely to affect mortality. In 1921, 25 million of the booklets had been distributed. In 1922, national advertising was called upon to extend the scope of the program and to increase booklet distribution. By 1959, the fiftieth year of the program, 1,750,000,000 booklets on health and safety subjects had been selectively distributed.

Demonstration of effectiveness   In a large-scale, seven-year demonstration, beginning in 1916 at Framingham, Massachusetts, the company marshaled an all-out attack on tuberculosis. The results were highly conclusive. During the demonstration, Framingham's tuberculosis deaths per 100,000 of population dropped from an earlier average of 121 to 38.2 in 1923. After the demonstration, the tuberculosis death rate continued to decrease.

The role of advertising   Metropolitan Life Insurance Company started its Health and Welfare *advertising* campaign in 1922 and has continued it with relatively minor changes in format for more than forty years. It is the longest-continued public service campaign in the history of advertising and probably, too, the most rewarding in terms of social usefulness.

Objectives   The basic objectives of the campaign, essentially unchanged over the years, have been:

1. To give health information to millions more people than the booklets alone could reach, with an ultimate aim of reducing premature mortality among policyholders

2. To build image prestige—specifically to "further enhance the company's good name and reputation built up over the years" and to demonstrate that the company is a "good citizen"

3. To help make life insurance a social program as well as a business enterprise

Media considerations Metropolitan primarily wanted to prolong the lives of *its own policyholders.* It made sense to use mass advertising media to reach them, for the rather special reason that the company had such a huge army of policyholders. One person in five of the whole population of the United States and Canada was a Metropolitan policyholder. The company's 1965 annual report listed more than 45 million persons as insured by Metropolitan.

Those readers and listeners who were not policyholders would be exposed to the health and safety information as well as to the prestige-building effect and selling influence of the public service advertisements.

Magazines, a favorite medium at the time, were chosen for selectivity, long exposure, and the adaptability of their pages to long, informative copy. Soon radio was added. Radio proved superior to magazines in producing booklet requests. On the other hand, magazines permitted longer messages which did part of the selling job for health, making the need for the booklet less imperative. Also, radio reached more people at lower economic levels where health information was less often available.

The campaign originally appeared in black and white only. In 1945, an extra color was added and used very effectively by agency art directors. In 1957, full color was used for the first time in a Christmas ad.

Creative aspects Throughout its long life, this campaign maintained a readily identifiable "look." The neatness and orderliness of the ads, their smartly starched typography, and their deep seriousness of purpose combined, nevertheless, with a reassuring air of friendly cheerfulness, rather strongly suggested the mood of a well-appointed doctor's office. They breathed competence and authority and genuine interest in the reader's health.

Some of the headlines were:

THE LAND OF UNBORN BABIES (1922)

"HOME'S THE PLACE FOR THAT COLD, JIM." (1937)

LIVING A GOOD LIFE WITH A BAD HEART (1942)

THE STRANGE CASE OF THE HIDDEN RABBIT AND THE ALLERGIC PRINCE (1953)

"DO NOT REGRET GROWING OLD,
IT IS A PRIVILEGE DENIED TO MANY." (1959)

CANCER . . . LIKE A SMALL SPREADING FLAME . . .
DEMANDS PROMPT ACTION. (1963)

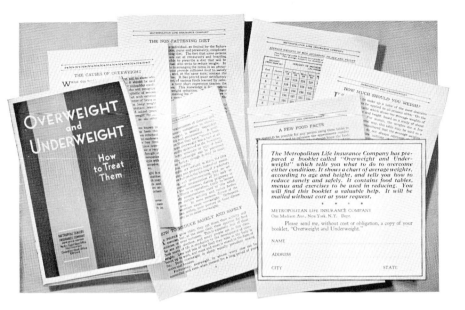

The Metropolitan Life Insurance Company has prepared a booklet called "Overweight and Underweight" which tells you what to do to overcome
either condition. It shows a chart of average weights,
according to age and height, and tells you how to
reduce sanely and safely. It contains food tables,
menus and exercises to be used in reducing. You
will find this booklet a valuable help. It will be
mailed without cost at your request.

* * * * *

METROPOLITAN LIFE INSURANCE COMPANY
One Madison Ave., New York, N.Y. Dept.

Please send me, without cost or obligation, a copy of your
booklet, "Overweight and Underweight."

NAME

ADDRESS

CITY   STATE

Overweight is Dangerous

IT is sometimes extremely difficult to persuade a jolly person who weighs many pounds too much —and who honestly says "I never felt better in my life"—that excess pounds are as dangerous as some of the diseases to which he would give immediate attention, if afflicted.

Consider these figures, especially if you are more than 35: People past 45 who weigh 20% more than the average have a deathrate greater by one half than the average for their age. If they have a persistent 40% overweight, the rate is almost double that of the average.

As a simple cold may lead to pneumonia or to serious bronchial trouble, so excess weight may be a forerunner of high blood pressure, heart disease, diabetes, kidney trouble, hardening of the arteries, or apoplexy. It makes recovery from surgical operations and acute diseases more difficult.

In rare instances, overweight is caused by disease

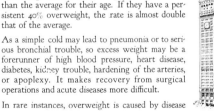

of the glands of internal secretion, but in nearly every case it is brought on by eating too much food and exercising too little.

You will not be uncomfortably hungry if you gradually change to foods which are bulkier and less fattening than the foods which have brought the dangerous extra pounds. With a corrected diet and proper exercise, it is usually possible to reduce excess weight, comfortably, about a pound a week, until a reasonable reduction has been attained.

Do not attempt abrupt or too extensive reduction of weight. Beware of "reducing" medicines. Some of them would wreck a normal person's constitution, to say nothing of a fat person's. Before taking any drug in an attempt to reduce your weight, consult your own physician.

If you weigh too much you should treat your overweight as you would a menacing disease. Give it immediate attention. Fill out and mail above coupon.

METROPOLITAN LIFE INSURANCE COMPANY

FREDERICK H. ECKER, PRESIDENT   ONE MADISON AVE., NEW YORK, N. Y.

THIS ADVERTISEMENT PULLED 104,000 INQUIRIES.

Metropolitan Life Insurance Company's Health and Safety advertisements provided information on health subjects, solicited requests for booklets. Volume of requests has varied primarily according to subject matter, rather than variations in advertising technique. This advertisement, on the ever-popular subject of overweight, drew 104,000 requests. (AGENCY: *Young & Rubicam*)

Subject matter Each advertisement confined itself to one health subject and usually included a coupon offering a free booklet on the subject discussed in the ad.

Subjects were selected on the basis of their importance as a cause of death. Ads on illnesses causing the most deaths appeared most often. For instance, an ad on heart disease or blood pressure appeared in the schedule every year for more than twenty years.

Subjects have changed in relative importance in time. Tuberculosis, which started the campaign, has not been on the schedule since 1954. Pneumonia has become less of a health problem and has been less often featured. On the other hand, *more* attention has been given to emotional tensions and to accident prevention. Also, on occasion, non-health subjects have been included for special reasons.

Coupon returns Coupon returns, i.e., requests for booklets, varied primarily with popular interest in the subjects advertised and did not seem to be much affected by variations in the approach used in the headlines and copy. Subjects of great popular interest regularly pulled the largest volume of requests. The best sellers over the years have been a cook book and a booklet on first aid.

An advertisement on the subject of overweight, an ever-popular subject, pulled the largest volume of requests of any ad in the series—more than 104,000. Arthritis and heart disease also ranked high in returns.

Results of the advertising As so often happens with an advertising enterprise as broad in scope as this, any mathematical tabulation of its results became obviously unattainable.

From all available indications, however, it would appear that Metropolitan achieved practically everything it could possibly ask for, and, particularly as far as the advertising campaign itself was concerned, at gratifyingly low cost.

The formerly dreaded killer diseases of tuberculosis and pneumonia, if not entirely eradicated, have been brought under control.

Early in the program, the mortality rate of Metropolitan's policyholders dropped below the national average and has remained there.

Nearly two billion health booklets have been selectively distributed.

During forty-three years, 12 billions of pages of advertising on health and safety have appeared in national magazines.

A secondary objective of the campaign was creating a character for Metropolitan which, it was hoped, would be an aid to sales.

During the period of the program, the company's life insurance in force increased from 1 or 2 billion dollars in 1909 to more than 113 billion dollars at the end of 1964.

Metropolitan Life Insurance Company tended to gauge the value of the Health and Safety program in terms of fatalities prevented. Judging the program in terms of *public service*, from the viewpoint of the *people* beneficially affected, the value of the undertaking was even greater. Because, in addition to saving lives, the program must have brought improved health and freedom from sickness, with resultant increased happiness, to untold millions of people.

Chapter 21

THE

INVISIBLE

PRODUCT

Gasoline is a product that the consumer rarely sees. He doesn't taste it. He seldom touches it, or hears it. If the attendant puts it in his car carefully, he shouldn't smell it.

He is informed that he is getting it by hearing a little bell ring. Then he can look at a counter on the pump and see how many gallons he has bought.

The consumer knows that gasoline makes his car go. But that's about all he does know about it with any degree of certainty. It is almost impossible for him to judge this product's performance with anything like scientific accuracy.

Can he be sure—is it the gasoline that is responsible for the car's performance, or is it the car's engine? Or is it the weather?

As a matter of fact, the average motorist (who has a psychological love affair with his car) will usually blame the gasoline if the car performs poorly, but if it performs well the credit goes to the car.

Furthermore, most motorists have had the experience of changing from one gasoline to another without any noticeable effect on the operation of their cars. It is not surprising, then, that survey after survey show that the majority of motorists believe that all gasolines are pretty much alike.

Actually, when the motorist buys gasoline, he is in effect not buying a *product* at all. He is buying a form of *service*. The gasoline he pays for is something like scrip, that entitles him to so many miles of *transportation*.

Problems of Advertising an Invisible Product

It is no secret that, for many years, copywriters in advertising agencies have had a baffling time trying to advertise gasoline effectively.

The first and most obvious approach has been to claim that one's brand of gasoline delivers greater *power* than other brands. This has been done in tough hard-sell technique with big black headlines and screaming claims. It has been done gently, with sweet persuasion. It has been done humorously with cartoons and in the folksy manner with lovable, friendly characters. And nothing much has happened. The motorist remains unmoved by claims of power. He doesn't believe them.

The second logical approach is to claim greater *economy*—more miles per gallon—than the other fellow's brand. This is hard to prove. And besides, everybody has made these claims, thus cancelling out everybody else's claims.

The motorist yawns, continues to believe that all gasolines are alike, and continues to get *his* gasoline at the most convenient service station. Or at the one up the street that is cleaner and gives better service. Or at one where he likes the dealer.

Hard-working copywriters have promoted gasoline *as* gasoline—on its ingredients, its atoms and molecules, its refining methods, its octane rating, and numerous other beneficial characteristics—without revolutionary results.

Only once in forty years of gasoline advertising has a *product-oriented* campaign been so successful that it upset the industry and aroused competitors to take retaliatory action. This was the Shell campaign featuring the new additive, TCP. And it is curious, that what was featured in this campaign was not the gasoline itself, but *something added to the gasoline.* And a popular selling point was that this new addition *did* something that gasoline had not been expected to do, i.e., *prolong spark plug life.*

This campaign worked. Its strong and persuasive copy induced people to change over to Shell. Then, one by one, competitor oil companies came out with additives of their own and Shell's advantage was cancelled out.

A Reappraisal of the Gasoline Advertising Problem

Not long ago, one large oil company decided to review its advertising program from the beginning, to see if a better approach might be found. Having noted that the straight product-selling advertisements of the past had not proved especially fruitful, it was then considered whether it would be better to emphasize the service that the motorist received at the company's stations.

But while this service—the convenient locations, the attractiveness of the stations, and the service rendered there—is a matter of top importance in winning customers, this theme did not provide the uniqueness needed for an advertising campaign. *All* oil companies know that service is important. *All* strive constantly to make theirs the best. There was nothing that one company might offer that the others could not instantly match. So this was abandoned as an approach.

Research then offered a clue. Past researches had indicated that while the level of brand loyalty for gasolines was very low, there was, nevertheless, a residue of such loyalty. There *were* some people who clung to the same brand.

Further probing of the attitudes of this group brought out that they bought the same brand of gasoline consistently *because they liked the company*. Somehow, they found the company's image attractive. For them, that was reason enough to buy gasoline, i.e., transportation, regularly from that company.

Impressed by this evidence, the company under discussion reoriented its advertising thinking and henceforth put much more emphasis on its *institutional* advertising.

In doing this, it was not entirely alone. Other companies had had similar experiences. As a result, institutional campaigns appear more often in the oil industry than in other product-selling industries. Behind this respect for an institutional approach appears to be a growing conviction that company image is a definite factor in gasoline sales.

A number of different *types* of institutional advertising have been used by the oil companies. One of these is *public service advertising*.

Oil Industry Public Service Advertising

An outstanding example of public service advertising is Texaco's radio broadcast from the Metropolitan Opera every Saturday during the opera season. With this fine broadcast, Texaco has brought New York's Metropolitan Opera to an audience of as many as 3 million people. This sponsorship has continued more than twenty-five years.

Almost as distinguished as the opera broadcast itself has been Texaco's manner of presenting it. With a program lasting all afternoon, Texaco has been entitled to as much as twenty-eight minutes for commercials. It uses less than two minutes for identification of the company and its products.

During the intermission, commentator Milton Cross conducts an extremely interesting and informative program of opera discussion. The production of this program is brilliantly planned in advance by Geraldine Souvaine.

In 1960, Texaco set up its own Metropolitan Opera Radio Network. It did this to prevent the opera being bumped off the air—locally, by a local high-interest broadcast such as a football game—and then played from tape later at an inappropriate time. With its own network, Texaco could be sure that the opera would be heard "live" and at the right time.

The value of this sponsorship to Texaco, although not measurable in precise terms, is obviously very great. And it is continuous; it does not wear out. The program is deeply appreciated by its audience, who regard Texaco not only with goodwill, but with a feeling of genuine gratitude. The company receives mountains of laudatory mail. Nearly all the listeners who write make a point of mentioning that they are Texaco customers—largely because of their appreciation for the broadcasts.

The Shell Oil Company published a public-service newspaper campaign promoting safe driving. By presenting this theme in the form of a quiz, that is, making a game of it, Shell cleverly avoided the appearance of preaching. Typical headlines were:

CAN YOU FIND 10 TRAFFIC HAZARDS IN THIS PICTURE?

and:

HOW SHARP IS YOUR DRIVING EYE?

This company has also sponsored, on television, the Young People's Concerts of the New York Philharmonic Orchestra. The program's commercials stress the need for education—a viewpoint that Shell backs up by offering scholarships, fellowships, and research grants.

In addition to public service advertising, the oil industry has used other types of institutional image-building advertising.

Campaigns Emphasizing Research

Research is a big word in the oil industry. To the financial community, its connotations are more significant with the oil industry than most others. It is also a vitally important necessity to the industry itself.

Every large oil company has extensive research facilities. These laboratories are used for product improvement to keep in stride with competition, for operations improvement to increase efficiency and lower costs, and for development in the profitable, growing field of petrochemicals.

Institutional advertising featuring research offers multiple benefits. It sends out a desired message to financial, educational, and chemical-buyer publics. Better still, it has a favorable effect on the general consumer public. Surveys have found that a research image attracts consumer customers for oil and gasoline.

A Research Campaign with Lasting Excitement

The remarkable characteristic of a Shell campaign which started during World War II and continued brilliantly for two decades was its ability to sustain a sense of *excitement* over that long period of time.

These were *idea*-ads, interesting in both picture and headline. But the excitement came not so much from technique as from the spirit with which the ads were conceived creatively. These were "magic" ads, full of wonders.

This is an effect often sought on advertising pages, but seldom achieved. The word "magic," for instance, when bandied about by advertisers to make product claims that are really not magical at all, usually flops. But the magic in these advertisements is very different; it is not claimed magic, it is *demonstrated* magic.

In one ad, a magician waves his wand and bolts of bright-colored fabrics *and* a huge demolition bomb swirl through the air about him. In another ad, a man walks across the desert following a mysterious underground sound, the sound of a moving go-devil. In another, a giant plays pat-a-cake with a white-hot steel ingot. A seventeenth century inventor starts an internal-combustion engine that uses gunpowder as a fuel. And so on.

Actually, the ideas in this campaign are imaginative dramatizations of some simple stories concerning Shell research. The headline: "Beauty and The Bomb," and the magician with his colored fabrics, are simply saying *in an exciting way* that the dyes for the fabrics and the TNT in the bomb both come from toluene, which has been made more readily available by Shell research.

This imaginative, long-continued, and well-executed campaign succeeded in building a strong leadership image for Shell research.

A Research Campaign Directed Primarily at Consumers

The discovery that people believed Esso products were good simply because they had been developed by Esso Research led the Esso company to embark on a research campaign directed primarily at the consumer.

In format, the advertisements were deliberately fashioned for a mass audience. Everything was kept simple and understandable and *big*. Picture subjects were simple, familiar, and shown close-up. Copy was brief and the message greatly simplified.

The copy said, in effect, that "something good happens [ski boot-laces stay pliant, roller skates stay bright] because of a product developed by Esso Research. Esso Research works wonders with oil."

The oversized, squared-off photograph illustrations occupying most of the space of the page, the close-up view of the objects, and the brief strip of copy at the bottom of the ad were new and novel at the time this campaign ran. As a result, the layouts of this well-seen campaign may have played an influential part in the art revolution that has made today's ads look very different from those of a generation ago.

BEAUTY AND THE BOMB...

● *What are those brilliant, shimmering scarfs doing in the same picture with that bomb? Odd but true—the viciousness of an American block buster, and the lovely colors in the fabrics, come from the same basic material ...*

Scientists at the "University of Petroleum," Shell's research laboratories, found how to produce nitration grade *toluene*, on a commercial scale, from petroleum. Their discovery was big news in the War and Navy Departments—for toluene is the starting point of TNT.

That's the job now—making enough TNT for our "all out" bombing offensives. Every day, Shell plants are supplying enough toluene to make block busters by the hundreds.

Yet like a good soldier, Shell's toluene will live an enormously important, constructive peacetime life.

After it is demobilized, you will meet it, day by day, in scores of products. The dye manufacturer will use it as the chemical framework on which to hang enduring colors for cotton, rayon, silk, or wool. It will enter the making of low-cost, luxurious artificial leather ... oilcloth and linoleum ... enamels and lacquers ... even the ink on the printed page!

*   *   *

As a result of Shell Research, petroleum molecules reach amazing destinations. Think of the pent-up destruction in toluene as an example of petroleum at war ... Then think of toluene, coming from the same research achievement, appearing as the handmaiden—even the "glamour girl"—of scores of peaceful arts!

SHELL RESEARCH

Sword of Today

Plowshare of Tomorrow

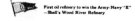

First oil refinery to win the Army-Navy "E"
—Shell's Wood River Refinery

A sense of wonder and excitement permeated this campaign for Shell Research. Imagination, applied to the dramatizing of simple facts, gave this series sparkle for twenty years and helped build up a strong research image for Shell. (AGENCY: *J. Walter Thompson*)

A Strong Informative Campaign

The Pure Oil Company, reported to have a need to "become better known," resorted to an informative campaign about its operations, using black-and-white photographic illustrations.

The campaign was simple, direct, and forthright. It showed the everyday work of the company, its workmen, and its equipment. It told what the workmen were doing, and why, and what the equipment was used for.

Because of its informative nature, the series made interesting reading. And because the public has a hunger for straightforward information and appreciates getting it, Pure Oil probably not only made itself better known, but better liked as well.

Building Goodwill at the Intellectual Level

Probably the most *un*-Madison-Avenue-like series of advertisements one could find anywhere were the twenty-three-bleed color spreads "Published in the interests of international friendship by *Standard Oil Company (New Jersey) —Esso.*"

Each spread was devoted to a separate foreign country, and consisted of a large and striking color photograph of a scene in that country and a rather remarkable piece of copy.

The extremely well-written copy touched on the history, geography, culture, and achievements of the various countries and their peoples. The copy dripped with international goodwill from beginning to end. In the last sentence, there was a brief but polite reference to Esso's affiliate in the country. The signature was about as modest as it could be without becoming totally invisible. The ads had nothing to sell, apparently, but warmhearted goodwill toward the people of the countries described.

But what was unique about the copy was the wit and color with which it was written. It was not afraid to use a metaphor. It was spiced with delightful touches of sly humor. It was fun to read. For example, speaking of flat Denmark:

> This is the town of Odense. Hans Christian Andersen lived at that house on the left. He always carried an escape rope in case of fire. Who wants to jump 4 feet?

and then, of Belgium:

> A cloistered garden so hushed that the leathery slap of a pigeon's wing can seem like a breach of the peace.

Laces and leathers and dozens of things

Ski boots lace easier and faster, stay comfortably tight. They do so because the rawhide leather has been made more pliant with a special treatment perfected by Esso Research. The leather in the skier's boots, the wool in his socks — even the lacquer on his skis — were also made better with the help of other products derived from oil. **ESSO RESEARCH** *works wonders with oil.*

The oversize illustrations and close-up views of subjects of the Esso Research campaign, including this 1957 ad, may have started a trend in art-directing practice. Addressed to a mass audience, the copy pointed to the benefits of Esso Research. (AGENCY: *McCann-Erickson*)

and again, later:

> But just because the Belgians cherish their peace doesn't mean they deplore *sound*. On the contrary, they love to embroider their silences with bells.

Butane storage tanks at a Pure Oil refinery

What Pure Oil keeps in those big white spheres...and why

Butane in these special pressure tanks goes into gasoline for easy starts, smooth warm-ups

As a high-octane gasoline blending component that provides easy starts and smooth, rapid warm-ups, butane is a versatile and valuable product. But it's as tricky to handle as it is useful. In fact, butane is so volatile that, unless it is kept under pressure, it will boil at roughly the same temperature at which water freezes.

That's the reason for the spherical shape of the tanks above. A sphere, with uniform strength at all points, is the best shaped vessel to contain large volumes of butane and keep it in liquid form. These tanks maintain a pressure of 50 to 90 pounds per square inch.

The maze of strange shapes and miles of pipes and tubes in a Pure Oil refinery is complex enough to confuse all but the experts. But the purpose of the whole operation is plenty plain: to keep the *sure* in PURE for our customers—at the nearly 16,000 Pure Oil dealers in 24 states.

THE PURE OIL COMPANY, 35 E. Wacker Dr., Chicago 1, Ill.

BE <u>SURE</u> WITH PURE

By telling interesting facts about its business, Pure Oil not only publicized its name, but built goodwill among a public which appreciates rewardingly informative advertising.
(AGENCY: *Leo Burnett Company*)

England:

England is part of a tight little island, almost entirely surrounded by Scotchmen, Welshmen, and Irishmen.

Iran:

Herodotus tells us that the first Iranian oil well was flowing in 500 B.C.! We take off our hat to the only nation that has been in the oil business for two thousand years.

The ads pleased many people immediately. Though their subject matter had an international flavor, they were really directed at *Americans*—at several intellectual publics, including upper-level educational, financial, editorial, and governmental influentials. This was underscored by the opinion-leader media chosen—*Harper's Magazine, Atlantic, Time, Newsweek, Saturday Review,* and the *New Yorker.*

The campaign appeared to do an excellent, goodwill public relations job for Esso, which was well pleased with it.

There was another possible benefit. If these ads, each highly flattering to a country in which an Esso affiliate operates, should *happen* to fall into the hands of *any* national of those countries, surely no harm could come to Esso.

International goodwill is the theme of this Esso campaign beamed at opinion-leader publics. Its interesting photographs, its theme, and its brilliantly written copy were aimed at building a favorable image for Esso in intellectual circles. (AGENCY: *Ogilvy, Benson & Mather*)

INDIA

Flowers, fireworks and a fellowship of spirit

OUR PHOTOGRAPH captures a moment of togetherness at the Festival of Dasara in Mysore. Note how gently the mother elephant is nudging the apple of her eye to join the parade.

We chose this picture because it evokes our childhood dream of India—of a country entirely inhabited by maharajahs and elephants. The idea is preposterous—and the truth is clear. No dream of India can ever encompass the full reality. Here are some *facts.*

Every seventh person in the world lives in India. The nation harbors seven major religions—and has given birth to three of them. There are fourteen basic languages and countless dialects, one of which is said to be known by only one person. A lonely man.

It is only when you take a closer look at India's blaze of festivals that you begin to sense the spiritual unity that weaves her variety into one nation. At some festivals, you will see your slouch of elephants. At others, you will see flowers and fireworks and even fire-*walking.* But almost every festival seems to celebrate the same thing—the triumph of good over evil. It is probably this fellowship of spirit that explains why India is the biggest democracy in the world today.

Visit modern India and you will be impressed by the way she is facing up to the future. Among other things, she is aiming to provide ten million new jobs, two million new homes and three thousand new health centers by 1961. Quite a task.

Oil is playing an important part in India's development. The firm that is affiliated with Jersey Standard recently built India's first modern refinery on the outskirts of Bombay.

We like to think that their enterprise is benefiting one seventh of the human race.

Published in the interests of international friendship by Standard Oil Company (New Jersey) (ESSO)

Greek terra cotta c. third century B.C., Louvre, Paris

Aphrodite, an ancient Greek potter, and a shell

About 2300 years ago a Greek artisan fashioned this lovely terra cotta celebrating the fabled birth of Aphrodite from a seashell. Intended for use as a votive offering or as an ornament, small figures such as these enlivened the shops and shrines of Athens and Corinth. This anonymous craftsman — like so many artists before and since — turned to the forms and legends of nature for inspiration.

Scientists, too, turn to nature for inspiration, for it is their task to equate the offerings of nature with the things man can use. At Shell, hundreds of scientists — inspired by one of nature's most versatile natural resources, petroleum — create, develop and perfect ideas that result in substances useful to man. This imaginative research yields petroleum and chemical products that perform better, last longer and cost less. Millions know these products by the sign of the familiar shell.

The Shell Companies

Shell Oil Company
Shell Chemical Company
Shell Pipe Line Corporation
Shell Development Company
Shell Oil Company of Canada, Ltd.

In a series featuring fine-art depictions of scallop shells, the Shell Oil Company called attention to its distinctive trademark. In addition, copy talked about Shell research. (AGENCY: *Kenyon & Eckhardt*)

Putting a Trademark to Work

Shell is the only oil company whose trademark, product name, and corporate name are the same. It is one of the few major oil-company names that have not changed. And the shell symbol has historical meaning. This company's founding family were originally importers of seashells.

To draw attention to its trademark and thus create possible name-identity values, Shell developed an institutional campaign around its scallop-shell symbol. Illustrations, making use of depictions of the shell in famous works of art, were very attractive. In addition, by equating the shell symbol with the idea of quest and exploration, the text copy managed to publicize Shell research.

Institutional Advertising with a "Free Enterprise" Twist

Most unorthodox, in its direction of thought, of the oil-industry institutional campaigns has been that of the Union Oil Company of California. With an impressive array of figures and arithmetic, it attacks the high Federal income tax, defends adequate profits, and extols the virtues of free and competitive economy.

This campaign is superior to the "free enterprise" ads of an earlier era in that its arguments are somewhat better directed to people of average income. It also constructs its story on specifics.

In attempting to assay the value of this campaign to the Union Oil Company, it must be remembered that the company's center of operations is in the politically conservative Los Angeles area.

Chapter 22

ADVERTISING

FOR

SOCIAL

CAUSES

An excellent example of public service advertising at its best is provided by the many campaigns of the Advertising Council. The Advertising Council is a mobilization of the advertising industry to produce non-commercial advertising in the public interest. The industry donates its creative services and millions of dollars worth of time and space to promote carefully selected public service projects of nationwide scope.

The projects are usually proposed by a public service organization or a Federal government bureau or agency and are screened to avoid regional, sectarian, and special-interest drives. They are required to be non-partisan and non-political.

In the fiscal year ending June 30, 1964, sixteen major campaigns were produced and assistance given to sixty-six other programs and organizations. In that yearly period, the total volume of this donated advertising was 234 million dollars—a truly impressive expenditure.

Among the 1964 campaign subjects were:

- Retraining (Automation)
- Support for Higher Education
- American Red Cross
- Forest Fire Prevention
- Keep America Beautiful
- Peace Corps
- United Funds and Community Chest
- Challenge to Americans
- Religion in American Life
- Mental Health
- The United Nations
- Radio Free Europe Fund
- United States Savings Bonds
- Operation Goodwill Mexico
- Youth Fitness
- U.S.O. (United Service Organizations)

The Advertising Council

Originally called the *War Advertising Council,* the Advertising Council was organized in January, 1942 to marshal all parts of the advertising industry to help win the war. It has continued ever since, switching to peacetime public service projects at the end of hostilities.

During the war, the Council produced scores of campaigns, including the promotion of war bonds, recruitment, conservation, salvage, rationing, victory gardens, etc. Advertisers and media voluntarily contributed 1 billion dollars worth of time and space to these war campaigns.

The Council is a private, non-profit organization. Although it works closely with the government, it accepts no subsidy from the government and remains completely independent.

Its organization consists of, in addition to a representative *Board of Directors,* a *Public Policy Committee* and an *Industries Advisory Committee.*

The eighty-three-member *Board of Directors* represents all branches of advertising, particularly the trade associations of advertisers (ANA), agencies (AAAA), newspaper publishers (ANPA), magazine publishers (MPA), broadcasters (NAB), and outdoor advertising (OAAA). There is also representation of transit advertising, the business press, and the two committees.

The *Public Policy Committee* of twenty members represents major sections of the national community, including management, labor, public welfare, medicine, education, and the principal religious denominations. This committee is given final approval or veto power on all campaigns proposed to the Council, except those originating with departments of the Federal government, where the public interest is presumed to have been established by an act of Congress.

The *Industries Advisory Committee* is composed of business leaders who assist in raising operating funds for the Council. This committee also gives advice on campaigns of special interest to business and industry.

When a campaign subject has been approved, a *volunteer coordinator* is selected by the Association of National Advertisers. The coordinator acts as advertising manager of the project. He in turn calls on a *volunteer agency,* which contributes its full creative services free of charge.

Out-of-pocket costs such as artwork, engravings, TV films, etc. are paid for by the client organization for which the Council conducts the campaign. The print *space,* or the broadcast *time,* for the campaign are contributed by either the media or the advertisers.

The advertising and its results   From the beginning, this volunteer advertising has been exceptionally high in quality. Some of the major campaigns have continued for ten or twenty years. The agencies seem to vie with each other to make outstanding creative contributions. The coordinators strive for sound and powerful selling themes. Everyone concerned strives to do a top-quality job.

The results have been correspondingly gratifying. The National Safety Council credits the "Stop Accidents" campaign with helping to save more than 550,000 lives on the nation's highways during the past twenty years. The United States Forest Service gives *major* credit to Smokey the Bear for helping to save more than 10 billion dollars in timber resources in about the same period of time. The National Citizens Council for Better Schools said that this advertising helped build 670,000 new classrooms in twelve years. Council campaigns have taken part in the raising of billions of dollars for the Red Cross, Community Chests, Radio Free Europe, etc.

Altruism   In its operation, the Advertising Council presents almost every aspect of altruism. Its own staff is surprisingly small, the bulk of its labors being handled by volunteer advertising professionals. Its accomplishments in the public service are enormous.

The Advertising Council's bear, "Smokey," has become one of the nation's best known advertising symbols. The Council's advertising, on many subjects, provides a demonstration of **public service advertising** *at its* **best.** (AGENCY: *Foote, Cone, & Belding, Los Angeles*)

Yet, as stated previously, even the most altruistic-appearing public service advertising campaigns may not be 100 per cent altruistic in *every* respect. There may be a benefit somewhere. And this can be said of the Advertising Council's public-spirited advertising. Its stated objective[1] has been: "To improve the welfare of American people as a whole, and in so doing to demonstrate to the public that the advertising community is concerned with the public welfare and that advertising is a powerful force for public service."

Or, in other words, to prove, to *demonstrate*—by *deeds*—that the advertising industry is a *good citizen.*

A desirable objective. For the advertising business has been criticized many times for *not* being a good citizen. The demonstration provided by the Advertising Council acts as an effective rebuttal to such criticism.

In this respect, it is very beneficial to the entire advertising industry. Yet, at the same time, its operation is many, many times *more* beneficial to the American public at large. Hence, it can be repeated, total results, rather than total altruism, most truly measure the social value of public service advertising.

Religious Advertising

Most religious advertising has been small in scale and localized, usually consisting of a public notice announcing Sunday services. There is, however, one religious campaign that is both large in size and national in its audience.

This is the magazine, newspaper, and newspaper-supplement campaign of the Knights of Columbus, a campaign that has continued since 1948. Its annual space appropriation is about $600,000.

It is addressed to non-Catholics. In two-column, all-text advertisements, extremely well-written copy presents friendly, easy-to-understand explanations of Catholic doctrine. Each advertisement contains a coupon requesting further literature, but promising, "Nobody will call on you." Since the beginning of the campaign, approximately 5,500,000 coupons have been received.

That copy delving into fundamental and often disputed points of religious belief, yet not offending in its manner, should be written at all is remarkable. That it should be prepared, without loss of dignity or authority, for the Roman Catholic Church—as *advertising*, by an advertising agency—is startling. Its success is a tribute to both the power and the flexibility of advertising as a means of communicating ideas.

Since the establishment of the program on a national basis in 1948, all of the advertisements have been written by Virgil A. Kelly, president of the St. Louis agency of Kelly, Zahrndt & Kelly.

[1] *General Memorandum,* Advertising Council, May, 1965.

Yes, The Bible Has a LIVING Witness

It may sound absurd to say this about a collection of writings prepared so many centuries ago.

For in that space of time every living thing on earth has been repeatedly replaced. Empires and civilizations have run their course and disappeared. Who, then, could possibly be still around to bear living witness to events so remote in human history?

The answer is, of course—the Catholic Church.

The Church had been carrying on its work of salvation for years before the New Testament writings were completed. And from the very beginning the sacred texts were in her custody and were used in her ceremonies. When the time came to decide which writings were to be accepted as divinely inspired, it was the Church which made the official decision.

For more than a thousand years prior to the invention of printing by movable type, all copies of the Scriptures were laboriously hand-made by monks and scholars of the Catholic Church. With the perfection of the printing process in 1440, one of the first and certainly the most famous publication was the Vulgate version of the Catholic Bible—the celebrated Gutenberg.

Not all Christians agree exactly in all their interpretations of the Scriptures. But all can agree that the Bible is the inspired word of God... that the New Testament presents the life and teachings of Jesus Christ. For we have in the Catholic Church, a living witness to prove it.

Being responsible for the formation of the New Testament, and as custodian for the Old, the Catholic Church can provide a great deal of interesting and helpful information about the Bible. We have put some of this into a pocket-size pamphlet which we will be happy to send free to any Bible lover who requests a copy.

It contains a short story of the Bible... explains why the Catholic Bible contains 46 Old Testament books, inherited from the Jews, and 27 New Testament books, which the Church approved as inspired... gives you solid reasons why you can believe the Bible, but why the Scriptures are not easy to understand... tells you what Catholics believe about the Bible and how they use it.

You can get your free copy of this interesting pamphlet by writing your name and address on the accompanying coupon and mailing it today. You can study it in complete privacy and without obligation. If it raises any questions in your mind and you want additional answers, we will be glad to supply them. But nobody will call on you.

Fill in the coupon and mail it today. Just ask for Pamphlet No. PC-3.

Knights of Columbus advertising counteracts anti-Catholic propaganda by presenting correct Catholic doctrine in factual, highly informative text copy. Tone is friendly and persuasive. (AGENCY: *Kelly, Zahrnt & Kelly*)

Objectives of the advertising   The objectives of the campaign were originally entirely defensive and protective. For years, the Catholic Church had been assailed by a huge volume of hostile literature of the Know-Nothing and Ku-Klux Klan type. These attacks influenced many well-meaning people who were not well-informed about Catholicism.

As stated by a proponent of the advertising:

> In the beginning, one of the primary purposes of the program was to refute anti-Catholic propaganda and to combat the tremendous volume of pamphlets, books and tracts which had for so long poisoned the minds of non-Catholics with half-truths, canards and outright misrepresentations. The objective was to achieve understanding which, in turn, would promote good-will and overcome suspicion based on ignorance.

And again:

> Objectives of the program are to explain Catholic doctrine and practices to the millions of people who are not usually exposed to such information—in other words, to give the public generally an accurate understanding of what the Catholic Church teaches and what Catholics believe. Gaining of converts is not necessarily a primary objective, but there are many of them.

Structure of the advertisements   The appearance of the advertisements was simple, with bold-face headlines and highly visible typography, inviting readership.

The headlines were provocative and challenging. Some of them were:

YOU HEAR STRANGE THINGS ABOUT CATHOLICS

THE BIBLE IS A CATHOLIC BOOK

"BUT WHY THE CANDLES, HOLY WATER AND BEADS?"

YES, THE BIBLE HAS A LIVING WITNESS

YES . . . I CONDEMNED THE CATHOLIC CHURCH

THE REAL SECRET OF SUCCESSFUL MARRIAGE

The text copy was informative, factual, and friendly in tone. It makes its points calmly and meticulously avoids any semblance of contentiousness. It then invites the reader to send for a pamphlet describing the subject of the ad in more detail.

The pamphlets were also written in a similar, informative style, but offering much more detail than could be given by the ad. They offered further means of learning more about the Catholic Church.

Approval of the copy   The advertising copy is based upon pamphlets written by priests and theological authorities. Topics were chosen on the basis of the questions most often asked by outsiders.

The copywriter, who has not had any theological background, consults with the Knights of Columbus Religious Information Bureau. Copy is submitted to the top authorities of the Knights of Columbus and to the St. Louis Archdiocese of the Catholic Church. Final approval is given by Joseph Cardinal Ritter, archbishop of St. Louis.

Providing funds for the advertising   Funds for the advertising come from an assessment of 80 cents a year upon the 1,200,000 members of the Knights of Columbus. This provides for the operation of the Religious Information Bureau and other costs, as well as the cost of advertising space.

Success of the advertising   The campaign is considered highly successful by its sponsors. It is given much credit for the improving of relations between Catholics and people of other faiths. It may have done much to make possible the election of the first Catholic president. And, a matter of timely importance, it may have contributed to the widespread acceptance of the spirit of ecumenism.

In terms of advertising technique, the results produced by this campaign demonstrate, notably, the surprising effectiveness of low-pressure, informative copy.

To the typical advertising man, who forever looks forward and never backward at the past, World War II is something that happened a long time ago. He must consider the advertising of that period ancient history indeed.

Yet it would not be entirely wise to forget that advertising completely. For although World War II ended more than a generation ago, the threat of a possible future war has never faded very far into the background. No one can guarantee that some of the experiences of that war period may not be repeated again.

Then, too, were advertising men history-minded, which most of them seem not to be, they might view the wartime effort with respect as the precursor of much present-day advertising. As we have noted in another chapter, the "look" of today's advertisements derives primarily from that period. It was also a time of unprecedented expansion and development of institutional advertising.

Chapter 23

WARTIME

ADVERTISING

The Wartime Problem

Wartime advertising was dominated by one overriding situation—the need to keep corporate names alive during the years when products could not be advertised.

With a great part of industry's production capacity channeled into war work, the manufacture of consumer products was sharply curtailed, and these products became so scarce that to continue to advertise them would and did serve only to arouse customer irritation.

At the same time, the new developments and the diversification fostered by war production indicated, disturbingly, that former great-name advertisers would face new competitors and sharpened competition after the war. To leading corporations, with heavy investments in name-reputation built up by years of advertising, it became imperative to keep those names alive in the public consciousness.

Institutional advertising a solution   The logical way to do this was with institutional advertising. And the most obvious subject for that advertising was the war work being done by the companies. Furthermore, if the advertising struck a patriotic note and supported the war effort, it would appear to be good public relations. Almost immediately, magazines, newspapers, and radio[1] bulged with institutional messages.

But there were complications. Security restrictions limited what a company could say about its war production. Furthermore, everybody was telling approximately the same story at the same time and the repetition became boring. Particularly boring was the selfish and unimaginative type of ad that said, in effect: "The X Corporation is winning the war by making tank treads. Don't forget, after the war, we will again make baby carriages for *you*."

Seasoned advertisers and their agencies realized that they must make their advertisements more interesting than ads of their competitors, to stand out from the crowd. They also appreciated, better than new advertisers, that appeals to patriotism should constructively support the war effort and not be merely boastful.

Agencies were called upon to apply their best talents, were allowed to give imagination free rein, were encouraged to offer fine writing and their newest and freshest visual techniques. What was sought were more exciting advertisements.

The result was most beneficial. Many advertisements rose to heights of creative excellence not seen before in the business. Institutional advertising was revitalized and improved its techniques. Of course, some dull ads continued, but were overshadowed by the good ones. At the same time, the War Advertising Council turned out a great many excellent advertisements promoting *specific* phases of the war effort requested by the government.

Value of the advertising   The advertising succeeded well in attaining its original objective of keeping company names before the public. It also performed a valuable service to the nation.

Some advertisements, notably the selfish and boastful ones, aroused criticism. One critic berated this selfishness while GIs were dying on the battlefields and seemed to hint that all advertising should be stopped. This critic, though justified in a few special instances, totally misread and misunderstood the significance of war advertising as a whole.

Actually, the advertisers fulfilled a massive and extremely important function in keeping the war effort constantly before the public's eyes. The advertisements kept the people *interested* in the war, a vital necessity in a modern total

---

[1] Television had not yet reached its commercial stage.

war. They counteracted *apathy*, which could be a dangerous saboteur of victory.

Also, by supplying reassuring information about our war weapons, the ads acted to improve the public's morale. And finally, through the financial support given to media, the advertisements kept the nation's communications in good health. All in all, advertising's contribution to the war effort was substantial and meaningful.

Preparing for postwar Particularly toward the end of the war, as victory was coming into sight, more and more advertisers turned their attention to what would happen when war production stopped and retooling for peace began. Clearly, things would be very different from prewar days. There would be many product changes and many new products. These would require time for development.

It was necessary, then, to continue institutional advertising until the products were ready. It was desirable to prepare consumers for their coming, but because no one was quite sure what form they would take, the products could not be described specifically. They could only be hinted at.

This brought a wave of crystal ball advertising predicting the future, but in very vague and general terms. An amazing new world of postwar marvels was promised. Concepts and artwork suggesting the things to come were highly imaginative. The campaigns, generally, were colorful and interesting.

When the products finally arrived on the market, they seldom resembled anything promised in the institutional advertising. But the institutional advertising had done its job and could quietly retire in favor of new product-selling campaigns.

Some Famous Wartime Advertisements

Undoubtedly the best remembered of all wartime ads was the one of the New Haven Railroad with the headline:

THE KID IN UPPER 4

The illustration showed a very young-looking soldier lying awake in the upper berth of a railroad sleeping car. The copy began:

> *It is 3:42 a.m.* on a troop train. Men wrapped in blankets are breathing heavily.
> Two in every lower berth. One in every upper.
> This is no ordinary trip. It may be their last in the U.S.A. till the end of the war. Tomorrow they will be on the high seas.
> One is wide awake . . . listening . . . staring into the blackness.
> *It is the kid in Upper 4.*

In the copy, the "kid" thinks of the boyish world he is leaving behind, and of "the pretty girl who writes so often . . . that gray-haired man so proud and awkward at the station." Then it tells of the people, all over the world, waiting for him to come. It finally reminds the reader that if train passengers are inconvenienced by wartime travel difficulties, it is for the benefit of "the kid in Upper 4."

This advertisement, written and rewritten many times by copywriter Nelson Metcalf, seemed to strike a sentimental note that moved people everywhere. No other wartime advertisement was nearly as well or as long remembered.

A somewhat analogous emotional approach was followed by the United States Rubber Company in a series of well-constructed advertisements.

A striking magazine color campaign, written by Walter Weir for American Locomotive, consisted of stopper picture-headline ideas followed by strong copy. One ad pictured a hangman's noose and bodies of people hanging on a gibbet in the background. The headline was:

TRY THIS FOR SIZE

Another ad portrayed a Japanese firing squad pointing their rifles at the reader, as the Japanese flag was glimpsed flying from the national Capitol in the background. The headline:

EVER FACE A FIRING SQUAD?

The text copy, in each ad, vividly described what would happen if we *lost* the war. Relentlessly, it seized the reader and put him on the spot, by showing that what *had* happened to others *could* happen to him. The series delivered a powerful war-effort message.

The wartime institutional color-magazine series for Shell Oil was distinguished by exciting picture-headline ideas and dramatic artwork. In an interesting, readable way, the text copy told how Shell research had produced war products and would produce new peacetime products in the future. After the war, by merely changing to peacetime subjects, the campaign format was continued for many years, colorfully dramatizing the activities of Shell research.

Perhaps the most imaginative of those campaigns predicting the future was the General Electric "electronics" campaign, using color pages in magazines. In this campaign, the strong layouts indicated the influence of modern art on thinking.

One advertisement showed the feet of Icarus ascending into a blue sky. Below was a picture of a small boy walking on stilts. The ad read:

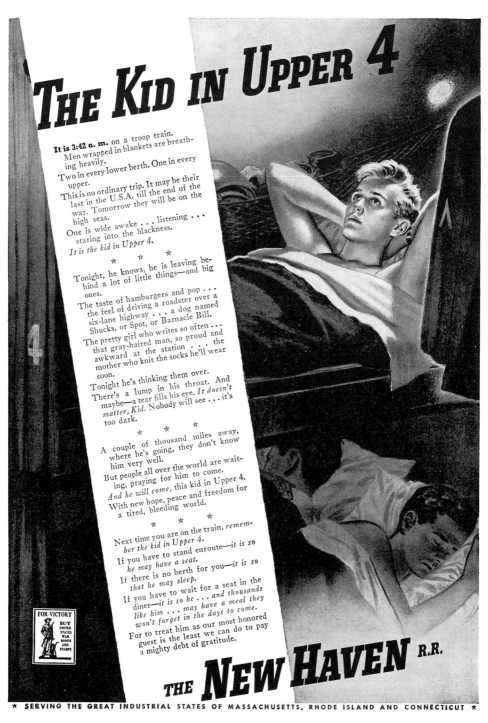

THE KID IN UPPER 4

It is 3:42 a. m. on a troop train. Men wrapped in blankets are breathing heavily.

Two in every lower berth. One in every upper.

This is no ordinary trip. It may be their last in the U.S.A. till the end of the war. Tomorrow they will be on the high seas.

One is wide awake . . . listening . . . staring into the blackness.

It is the kid in Upper 4.

☆   ☆   ☆

Tonight, he knows, he is leaving behind a lot of little things—and big ones.

The taste of hamburgers and pop . . . the feel of driving a roadster over a six-lane highway . . . a dog named Shucks, or Spot, or Barnacle Bill.

The pretty girl who writes so often . . . that gray-haired man, so proud and awkward at the station . . . the mother who knit the socks he'll wear soon.

Tonight he's thinking them over. There's a lump in his throat. And maybe—a tear fills his eye. *It doesn't matter, Kid.* Nobody will see . . . it's too dark.

☆   ☆   ☆

A couple of thousand miles away, where he's going, they don't know him very well.

But people all over the world are waiting, praying for him to come. *And he will come,* this kid in Upper 4. With new hope, peace and freedom for a tired, bleeding world.

☆   ☆   ☆

Next time you are on the train, *remember the kid in Upper 4.*

If you have to stand enroute—*it is so he may have a seat.*

If there is no berth for you—*it is so that he may sleep.*

If you have to wait for a seat in the diner—*it is so he . . . and thousands like him . . . may have a meal they won't forget in the days to come.*

For to treat him as our most honored guest is the least we can do to pay a mighty debt of gratitude.

THE NEW HAVEN R.R.

★ SERVING THE GREAT INDUSTRIAL STATES OF MASSACHUSETTS, RHODE ISLAND AND CONNECTICUT ★

Most famous of all World War II ads, Nelson Metcalf's carefully written copy gives readers a reason not to complain about poor train service in wartime. (AGENCY: *Wendell P. Colton Co.*)

TRY THIS FOR SIZE...

ODDLY enough, this type of collar fits all kinds of people...Czechs and Poles, Frenchmen and Norwegians, Russians and Greeks.

It fits women as well as men, the old as snugly as the young, the strong as firmly as the weak.

It is designed especially for conquered people... and reserved for those among the conquered who dare to stick their necks out. Who presume they have the right to read or circulate forbidden newspapers and magazines, to listen to forbidden radio programs. Who get themselves accused...on no matter how little evidence...of spying or interfering or getting in the way.

Now, in the newspapers and magazines we so freely read, we see pictures of strange people... foreign people...hanging from such nooses. Still

and silent, their arms by their sides, their heads slightly askew as if they did not completely comprehend what had happened.

We have escaped it...so far. So far, these hangings have happened only to far-away people. Have you ever seriously thought that someday *you* might be the mute subject for such photographs?

You *can* be...

The country that we expect to fight this war for us, the country we assume is invincible, the country we look upon as millions of "other people"...that country can *lose* this war.

Can lose it unless *you*...and unless we who sign this advertisement...look upon it as our individual responsibility. Unless we do not wait to be *told* what to do, but go out and *find out for ourselves* what

to do, and *do* it. Unless we realize that each one of us *is* the country.

It's not a minute too soon to get the picture straight...not a minute too soon to pitch in and help turn the tide...not a minute too soon to do everything humanly possible, *now*, to save our necks.

AMERICAN LOCOMOTIVE

30 CHURCH ST., NEW YORK, N.Y. · MANUFACTURERS OF TANKS · GUN CARRIAGES · ARMY AND NAVY ORDNANCE · STEAM AND DIESEL LOCOMOTIVES

In this dramatic wartime series of magazine ads, the copy made its point by stressing what would happen if the enemy did win.
(AGENCY: *Kenyon & Eckhardt*)

FLIGHT TO THE SUN

Icarus puts on feathered wings and rises to the sky. Aladdin rubs a lamp. A young boy walks on stilts.

All are part of one eternal gesture. Man, seeking for powers beyond his own capacity, reaches for the stars!

Today, in the General Electric Electronics Laboratories, science is extending the potentiality of human brain and senses to a degree undreamed of in childhood legend or fantasy.

By the control of an infinitesimal particle of matter—the electron—man can now use eye, ear, and intellect as they have never been used before!

Somewhere in the Pacific a lookout scans the azure sky. His sight is limited.

But new electronic devices come to the aid of human faculties! The watcher can now detect enemy planes one hundred miles away—and chart their speed and direction.

In a thousand other fields, electronic devices work seeming miracles. They "sight" ships through fog, reveal hidden flaws in steel armament, hold color printing presses in register, sort fruits and vegetables, examine candy, guide in the treatment of sinus.

Wartime ads for Shell imaginatively dramatized the uses of products developed by Shell research. After the war, the same format was used for many years, describing peacetime instead of wartime products. (AGENCY: *J. Walter Thompson*)

Helium is a Hellion to Hold

BARRAGE BALLOONS are made of sturdy cotton fabric coated with a rubber-like material which will hold *helium*—and this thin, buoyant gas is a Houdini for getting out of tight places.

Natural rubber won't do—helium seeps through its "pores." A dense, non-porous, *synthetic* rubber was found . . .

But it wouldn't dissolve in an ordinary rubber solvent. *How to apply it?*

Shell scientists came out of their laboratories with *toluene*. They had first produced toluene from petroleum to increase this country's production of TNT. And here

was another use—it would dissolve the synthetic rubber so this could be spread over the fabric of the barrage balloon, making a helium-tight container.

As toluene is precious for explosives, the scientists weren't quite satisfied—yet. More experimenting, and they had a solvent of toluene and another material that is plentiful and low in cost.

Manufacturers of barrage balloons today are working with Shell-suggested formulas, and Shell scientists are continuing their research to conserve toluene. Barrage balloons, buoyed by helium or hydrogen, are

mounting skyward on their vital mission.

This widening knowledge of petroleum molecules—what they will do, how they behave—today is "coming home" to you in dozens of ways. Already it has led to better food, better clothing at lower cost, more effective drugs, "beauty aids," plastics with scores of uses . . .

This scientific knowledge "carries over" to your motoring—in the Shell gasoline and motor oil you buy today.

"Oil is ammunition—use it wisely."

SHELL

General Electric Electronic tubes will <u>lift</u> the fog from sky, sea, and land!

Fog coming in!

Ships crawl. Planes are grounded. Cars hug the side of the road. You can't see for the "pea soup."

But General Electric is "lifting" the fog!

Tomorrow, amazing electronic devices will tell the ship captain the position of reefs . . . permit the pilot to land blind . . . warn the locomotive engineer of danger on fog-drenched tracks, no matter how thick the whiteness.

Ship and plane and train will ride as safely in fog as in sunlight!

The exact nature of these miraculous inventions must remain a war secret. But General Electric research has already developed a thousand other electronic devices that add to your health, comfort and general well-being.

Electronic tubes, basically the same as the ones in your General Electric radio, can distinguish 2,000,000 shades of color — match lipstick, fabrics, stockings, paints. An electronically controlled welder stitches together metal parts of war planes as easily as your sewing-machine stitches cloth. By electronics, you can study the stresses in an airplane wing during a power dive, or make photographs with the correct exposure automatically determined. Your General Electric radio is an electronic instrument.

General Electric electronic equipment will some day be available to every home. Today, it is limited to businesses engaged in war activity. If you believe that electronics can be applied in your factory, write to General Electric — Radio, Television, and Electronics Department, Schenectady, New York.

GENERAL ⊕ ELECTRIC

Leader in radio, television, and electronic research

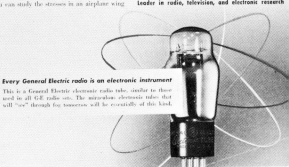

Every General Electric radio is an electronic instrument
This is a General Electric electronic radio tube, similar to those used in all G-E radio sets. The miraculous electronic tubes that will "see" through fog tomorrow will be essentially of this kind.

A type of wartime advertisement, predicting products that might become available after the war. A way of keeping a corporate name alive until the time came when postwar products could be marketed. (AGENCY: *Batten, Barton, Durstine & Osborn*)

The most elemental force in nature, the electron, has been harnessed for your comfort, safety and health!

General Electric leadership in electronics goes back over thirty years. Here, in the tradition of Steinmetz, Alexanderson, Coolidge, Langmuir, Whitney and their associates, research continues steadily.

Tomorrow, because of electronics, we will live in a finer and better world. . . .

Seven

The St. Regis Paper Company is a large and fast-growing company in a fast-growing industry. A considerable part of its expansion has resulted from diversification.

St. Regis makes many kinds of paper bags (plus burlap and cotton bags) and many kinds of shipping containers, boxes, cartons, wrappers, and envelopes. It makes printing papers, fine papers, paperboard, kraft, corrugated board. It sells plywood and lumber, laminated Panelyte, and plastics. It also provides packaging machinery to fill its bags and boxes. It has a subsidiary specializing in food-processing equipment made mostly of stainless steel. And, in addition, St. Regis maintains a New Product Development Department to develop still more products.

This company has tended to expand in a somewhat unusual way. Namely, by the continued and fairly frequent purchase of smaller companies, mills, and other facilities. Perhaps one reason for this procedure may be the delay occasioned by the long time necessary to build a *new* mill—for engineering and construction, sometimes as long as three years.

The company is organized, not geographically, but in thirty-one product divisions.

Chapter 24

CORPORATE-

UNITY

ADVERTISING

Corporate-unity Problems of the St. Regis Paper Company

All this has given rise to problems of *corporate unity*. Major activities have been consolidated; but with smaller and newer undertakings, this may be a slow and difficult process. Meanwhile, the advantages provided by the St. Regis company's size, reputation, and importance are not fully exploited.

For a hypothetical example, suppose the ABC Specialty Bag Company of Pulptown, Georgia has just been acquired by St. Regis. For a long time, both employees and customers of ABC will continue to visualize their business in terms of the ABC mill rather than of the much larger St. Regis Paper Company with its much greater prestige.

In fact, almost all of the small divisions of the company have shown some tendency to go their separate ways, selling separately to separate markets. Thus, no contribution is made to any other division or received from any other division.

Yet, sometimes, some of these small divisions locally face *big* competition from *big* companies, particularly in the timber areas of the West. Such divisions have dire need of all the support they can get from the St. Regis name and reputation.

Swinging around to the customer's point of view, it can readily be seen that the small-division image is weak in selling power. Contractual business wants to do business with *big* companies, not with unknowns (such as the ex-ABC). Indeed, St. Regis learned that one of its big-business customers, buying from one division, did not even know of the *existence* of certain other St. Regis divisions which had much to offer.

The need for corporate-unity advertising   It became apparent to St. Regis management that, in the paper and paperboard industry with its clutter of large and small units, *a big name had big selling force.* This pointed to the need for corporate advertising to associate the *big* name of *big* St. Regis with its individual selling divisions. Such advertising would have selling force with its customers. It would also have *unifying* force within the St. Regis family, educating employees—especially salesmen, about their own company—and inducing them to take a larger viewpoint and to cooperate more wholeheartedly for the welfare of the entire organization.

Primarily, what was needed was an *informative* campaign that would throw light on the various divisional activities, educating both customers and employees on the scope of the St. Regis operation. Such a campaign would also have value in the financial community, but this was not a primary objective.

The St. Regis Corporate Advertising Campaign

Choice of media had an important bearing on the operational success of the campaign. The key medium was *Fortune* magazine, backed up by *Business Week*. *Fortune* provided several special advantages, namely:

1. It was a magazine likely to be found in a board of directors room or a company president's office. It was associated with top management and conferred a prestige of its own.

2. Its large-page size permitted the merchandising of impressive full-color reprints of the advertising.

3. It was relatively inexpensive. Its color-page cost was less than half of that of *Time* and less than one-fifth of that of *Life*.

In other words, this publication was ideally suitable as a showcase for exhibiting a series of good-looking informative advertisements, and one that cost far less than most other high-prestige magazines.

The inclusion of *Business Week* provided a broad business circulation. St. Regis sells to business, not to consumers.

The advertisements The advertisements were double spreads in full color. When occasion demanded, the large rectangular photograph, bleeding to the edge of the page, was used. For most of the ads, however, a silhouetted white-space style was followed. Inasmuch as the white space extended to the edge of the paper, it had the effect of a white bleed page, but the ad cost only as much as the regular page size.

Each advertisement featured an interesting recent product development of one of the St. Regis divisions. The nature of these subjects is indicated by some of the headlines:

BIG BOY . . . THE ST. REGIS CONTAINER THAT CAN
CARRY 1000 POUNDS.

THE WHITEST WHITE YOU'VE EVER SEEN.

HOW TO MAKE A BAG ACT LIKE A BOX.

PACK YOUR PRODUCT IN A FOAM SANDWICH . . . TO GET IT
TO MARKET . . . DRY . . . AND SAFE . . . AND ECONOMICALLY.

One ad in the series served a special dual purpose. It, additionally, helped justify to stockholders a costly purchase of timberland by the company. A magnificent photograph pictured miles and miles of lush green forest land. The headline read:

WE'RE BUYING ROOM TO GROW.

Need for an identifying common denominator This campaign threw beneficial light on St. Regis's divisional activities. In time, however, due to the increasing diversification typical of the fast-growing wood-products industry, St. Regis found a need for renewed corporate-unity efforts on a somewhat different plane.

Its diversification raised questions. Was it a paper company? Or a building-materials company? Or a packaging company? Or a plastic company? It needed a symbolic unifying theme—a common denominator—that could apply to its many activities.

It found this unifying symbol in its basic source of raw material—the tree and the forest.

Second corporate advertising campaign The tree and the forest became the theme of a new corporate advertising campaign appearing initially in

Big Boy...the St. Regis container that can carry 1000 pounds...

It's a corrugated board container ... some people might call it a "carton."

But it's a big one and a strong one, a real giant, able to carry 1000 pounds.

It was perfected for industry, to ship materials in bulk—safely and economically without contamination. So far, it is the Big Boy of the St. Regis line.

You'll hear of more and more unusual containers coming from St. Regis...bags with the strength of boxes and boxes that load like bags ... and many other new developments.

For St. Regis is rapidly establishing itself as the pioneer of new uses in the world of paper and paperboard, of film and plastic. Masters of the art of packaging, we're constantly putting new ideas to work—to help Industry move its goods to market in better condition and at lower cost.

If you have a problem that bothers you—in packaging, shipping, storing, wrapping—let us know about it. You may be surprised how much we can help you. St. Regis Paper Company, Dept. B-1, 150 East 42nd St., New York 17, N. Y.

St.Regis
PAPER COMPANY
150 EAST 42nd STREET NEW YORK 17, N.Y

Each of a series of St. Regis advertisements publicized one division of the company. Note the "white-space" layout, which makes the

Time and *Business Week*. Informative copy presented the tree as an interesting manifestation of nature and also as the source of St. Regis's many activities. Artwork by Jack Kung, an accomplished nature illustrator, gave the campaign both authenticity and dramatic interest.

Olin Mathieson and Its Need for Corporate Unity

The Olin Mathieson Chemical Corporation (which now prefers to be known by its first name, *Olin*) found itself in a situation similar to that of the St. Regis Paper Company. Like St. Regis, Olin had grown rapidly, had grown by acquisition and merger, and consisted of numerous divisions, many of them not particularly related in any way.

Thereupon, Olin decided to run an "advertising campaign which would accurately identify the company and closely associate its many divisional products with the corporate entity."

Olin stated its objectives as:

1. Enhance the reputation of Olin as a progressive company producing quality products with those publics important to the company: current cus-

Another St. Regis campaign identifies the company with its basic source of raw material, the tree and the forest. This approach offers "common-denominator" corporate unity values. (AGENCY: *Cunningham & Walsh*)

tomers, future customers, stockholders, plant communities, employees, suppliers, government, etc.

2. Improve the market position of Olin divisions by helping to sell end products through corporate advertising

3. Create in advance a market acceptance for future new products which bear the Olin name

Olin advertising format   The advertisements were bleed double spreads in full color. Each advertisement publicized products of a separate division of the company.

What particularly characterized the advertisements was their excellent execution. The beautifully designed, yet simple and powerful Doyle Dane Bernbach layouts gave the ads tremendous visual impact. These are idea-ads with *both* picture and headline creating interest. An offbeat layout innovation was the centering and surrounding of the logotype, *Olin,* with the text copy.

Though the subject matter of the ads was sometimes quite technical, the language was always kept extremely simple—"people-talk." It is interesting to note how many of the words in the text were *one* syllable words. This gave the copy a fast, staccato tempo. For example, from the "Oops" ad:

> Frozen food packages are wet. So are milk containers. Load a week's groceries on top of them and OOPS! Grocery clerks sometimes try to solve this problem by doubling up on bags. But two bags cost the grocer twice as much as one bag. Olin has developed Water Buff, a water resistant bag that can carry a load of soaking wet groceries for 45 minutes. That means one bag for the clerk to use. One bag for the grocer to pay for. One bag that carries the groceries *all* the way home. Another creative solution to a problem . . . from the Packaging Division of Olin.

The ads present, in each case, one or more benefits to the public as well as to the intermediate businessman. This is a wise and logical procedure for this particular campaign, because it was *expected* to do some selling in addition to fulfilling its corporate-identity function.

Results   According to a brochure circulated by *Time* magazine, "Results were quickly apparent. Public awareness studies completed 16 months after our campaign began showed a 66 per cent increase in the proportion of people who had heard of Olin. At the same time, substantial sales increases followed ads featuring particular products."

Corporate Unity and Corporate Identity

There is a slight semantic differentiation between the phrases *corporate unity* and *corporate identity,* when applied to advertising. Corporate-unity advertis-

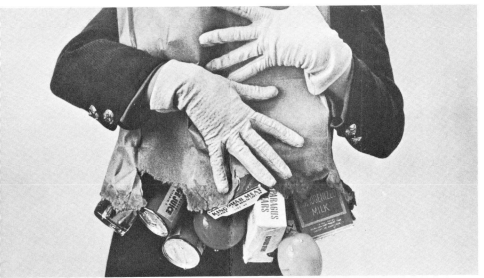

Who took the OOPS out of supermarket shopping?

Frozen food packages are wet. So are milk containers. Load a week's groceries on top of them and OOPS! Grocery clerks sometimes try to solve this problem by doubling up on bags. But two bags cost the grocer twice as much as one bag. ■ Olin has developed WaterBuff,* a water-resistant bag that can carry a load of soaking wet groceries for 45 minutes. That means one bag for the clerk to use. One bag for the grocer to pay for. One bag that carries the groceries all the way home. ■ Another creative solution to a problem . . . from the Packaging Division of Olin.

Olin

OLIN MATHIESON CHEMICAL CORPORATION, 460 PARK AVENUE, NEW YORK · CHEMICALS · INTERNATIONAL · METALS · ORGANICS · PACKAGING · SQUIBB · WINCHESTER-WESTERN

Who let the cat out of the box?

The inside of an ordinary corrugated box is actually abrasive. Millions of tiny claws scratch away at the contents. Refrigerators often arrive scarred, furniture marred, and customers don't like it. • Olin has developed a container that doesn't scratch. Not even when thumped, bumped and joggled in transit. With "Scuffmaster," as it's called, the paint stays on refrigerators. Furniture keeps its finish. Hub caps arrive with their dazzle intact. At last the cat is out of the box. *This* box, anyway. • Another creative solution to a problem . . . from the Packaging Division of Olin.

Olin

OLIN MATHIESON CHEMICAL CORPORATION, 460 PARK AVENUE, NEW YORK 22, N.Y. · CHEMICALS · ENERGY · INTERNATIONAL · METALS · PACKAGING · SQUIBB · WINCHESTER-WESTERN

Powerful layouts characterize the corporate advertising campaign for Olin. Subjects are "blown-up" in size for greator visual impact. Each ad tells the story of a product of one division of the company.
(AGENCY: *Doyle Dane Bernbach*)

ing is intended to *unify* the activities of a multiple-division company. Corporate-identity advertising is intended to *identify* a company, i.e., make its name known (for any purpose).

Sometimes, however, the two terms overlap, in fact, coincide. This happens when the way to achieve corporate unity is to achieve corporate identity. Such a situation has arisen in, of all places, the hard-selling world of package goods.

Corporate Identity and Package Goods

A common practice in package-goods selling is to promote a brand name heavily, but to suppress the corporate name almost entirely—both on packages and in advertising. This is particularly noticeable with soaps and detergents and with such branded drug products as Anacin, Bufferin, etc. On these products, the manufacturer's name is often printed in such small type that it is difficult even to find.

R. G. Rettig, an advertising vice-president of American Home Products, is quoted[1] as saying, in reference to that company's division, Whitehall Pharmacal, "Why spend money on the corporate name? Isn't it wiser to spend it on the brand? That's the thing you're selling. We don't have a bottle of Whitehall to sell. If we did, we'd promote that."

This summarizes, succinctly, an advertising philosophy that is widespread and has been considered sound for a long time. Today, however, due in part to the technological explosion of recent years, it is beginning to reveal some flaws. Two in particular are apparent, namely:

1. With a line of products, some products may be strong and some weak. When the corporate name is suppressed, the reputation of the strong products cannot come to the support of the weak ones.

2. With the corporate name suppressed, when a *new* product is introduced, it can get no support, either from the company's name or from the names of its well-known products.

The supermarket accentuates the effect of these flaws. There is no clerk there to say to the customer: "Now this is a new product. It must be good. It's made by the same people who made Tide and Ivory Soap."

Package-goods marketers (including Whitehall) have begun to see the value of corporate identification as a means of bolstering up weak products in the lines and especially as a catapult for launching *new* products. Alan Jacobson of *Printers' Ink*[2] cited General Foods as one company interested in increasing its corporate identity in connection with its products.

---

[1] Alan J. Jacobson, "The Corporate Image Becomes a Marketing Spearhead," *Printers' Ink,* Sept. 13, 1957.
[2] Sept. 13, 1957.

Thus, when a company reasserts its corporate identity in this way, it is also strengthening its corporate unity.

The strength of a solid corporate identity and image, built up by years of institutionl advertising, is shown in the case of E. R. Squibb & Sons. Nine years after Squibb became a division of Olin Mathieson, most of the consuming public still did not associate Squibb products with the parent company. Hence, increasing that association is an important objective of Olin's corporate-unity campaign.

Corporate Unity Aided by a Visual Symbol

In 1949, Union Carbide and Carbon Corporation started a series of corporate advertisements in which every illustration contained a large hand or pair of hands. In each ad, the hand was seen doing something pertinent to the subject matter of the copy.

The subject matter was one or more of the varied products manufactured by Union Carbide's subsidiary companies (later to become the fourteen divisions of the Union Carbide Corporation). These products were largely in the chemical area, and included alloys, chemicals, carbons, gases, and plastics. Union Carbide marketed a few consumer items, but the greater part of the products were basic materials sold to industry for further fabrication and manufacture.

The picture and headline of each ad, and the beginning of the text copy, featured an interesting aspect of one of the products. The copy then spread out to include a number of other Union Carbide products and also to stress the role of Union Carbide research.

The dominant characteristic of the campaign was the large hand that appeared in each of the well-painted illustrations. This campaign, with its ubiquitous hands, continued for fourteen years.

The Union Carbide Hand

Use of the hands probably started as an advertisement idea. At the time, probably no one suspected that this idea would have such a long life. That it did so can be ascribed to the fact that it turned out to be very useful.

The hands quickly became a highly visible, easily remembered symbol for the Union Carbide Corporation. They also became an effective device for demonstrating, in a general way, the company's multitudinous and diverse products. Each hand "acted out" the function of the product advertised. And because the hand appeared again and again, each time with a different product,

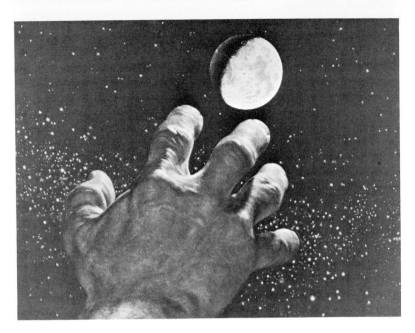

Reaching for the moon

Only a dream yesterday...reality today

Who dares call anything impossible today? Not when scientists have created rockets and missiles that bring the moon itself within our reach.

Union Carbide research in fascinating new materials has helped take the attack on space out of the realm of science fiction. Such research has developed super-alloys to withstand the forces of launching and flight . . . liquid oxygen to fire the mighty thrust into space . . . and components for solid fuels that burn in an airless universe. And research is now leading the way to new plastics for nose cones and new batteries and other energizers for instrumentation.

With the same compelling search for knowledge that has brought us so close to space travel, the scientists of Union Carbide are constantly developing new substances that make possible a host of useful things for our everyday life. Today's work-saving detergents, miracle fibers, and quick-drying paints and lacquers are only the beginning of an endless stream of products that will enrich the world tomorrow.

Learn about the exciting work going on now in carbons, chemicals, gases, metals, plastics, and nuclear energy. Write for "Products and Processes" Booklet C, Union Carbide Corporation, 30 East 42nd St., New York 17, N.Y. In Canada, Union Carbide Canada Limited, Toronto.

...a hand in things to come

For many years, illustrations for Union Carbide advertisements were built around a large hand (or pair of hands), which became a powerful identifying symbol for the company's business. (AGENCY: *J. M. Mathes*)

it served both as a symbolic *unifying* agent for the company's diverse activities and as an *identifying* symbol for the company itself.

The hand as a device Perhaps, in the first ad or two, the hand itself might have been considered as the *idea* of the advertisements. But as the campaign wore on, it became apparent that the hand was only a *device,* only part of the total advertisement idea. The real idea was contained more in what the hand was doing, rather than in the hand itself.

Hands seem to have a peculiar fascination for some advertising practitioners. They are interesting to artists, partly because they can be so aesthetically expressive and partly because they present a challenge in drawing. In an advertisement, however, their attention-value, per se, is not very great. What drew the eye to the Union Carbide advertisements was not the hand, but what was *around* the hand and the glamorous style with which the whole was painted. The hand itself remained a useful *device* and a symbol.

Objective of the campaign   This was primarily a corporate campaign and its objectives were of a corporate nature. It did not pretend to do more than a slight and incidental selling job for specific products. The actual selling job was performed, *as was the case with most of the other corporate advertisers mentioned in this book,* by hard-working product advertisements addressed to specific buyers *in industrial and trade publications.*

The hand campaign was beamed at such corporation publics as the general business community, the financial community, opinion leaders, government officials, and undergraduates in the physical sciences. The benefits to be gained were of a broad public relations type—to help the company *do business,* rather than sell its products. The task of the text copy was to familiarize the various publics with the many-sided operations of a rather complex corporation.

Chapter 25

An interesting area of advertising is that in which an institutional or non-product approach is used, in an oblique manner, to *assist* in selling a product. Sometimes a company, instead of advertising its product directly, devotes its advertising to promoting the interests of its *customers.* Or a company may present one of its own divisions institutionally, but with an ultimate aim of contributing to sales.

The companies which promote their customers' interests are, characteristically, either dominant in their industries or market a product that is unique or dominant. These companies do not sell to the general public. Their products or processes go into the making of other products or services. Typical examples of such advertisers are the Ethyl Corporation, the Sanforized Company, and the Caterpillar Tractor Company.

HELPING

OTHERS

TO HELP

YOURSELF

The Ethyl Corporation

The Ethyl Corporation makes the familiar Ethyl antiknock compound widely used by the gasoline industry as an antiknock component in gasolines. Ethyl's customers are the gasoline companies.

After using its advertising for many years to publicize the name *Ethyl,* this company switched, in the late 1950s, to the promotion of touring by car. The purpose, of course, was to increase the consumption of gasoline. This would naturally increase usage of Ethyl's product, but more important, it could build substantial goodwill among Ethyl's customers, the oil companies. Because, in promoting American motor tourism, Ethyl was doing a needed job for the gasoline industry, a job which presented certain difficulties for the industry itself (companies with wide geographic distribution would be more interested in national advertising than those serving more compact areas).

The Ethyl advertising featured locations attractive to tourists, such as the New Bedford Whaling Museum or Williamsburg, Virginia and told interesting stories about them. An effective device, in each ad, was the "Magic Circle," a small circled section of road indicating a tourist area and how it could be reached.

These Magic Circles were selected, strategically, from all areas of the country. An obvious purpose of the advertising was to get the motorist out of the habit of using his car only for short trips near home and to encourage him to tour to more distant spots, thus increasing his car's annual gasoline consumption.

The Sanforized Company

The Sanforized Company, a Division of Cluett, Peabody & Co., provides a process to keep garments from shrinking. Its customers are the mills which make the fabric. But its advertising is pointedly directed at consumers.

The objective of the advertising is to protect and build business for those mills buying the Sanforized process and to implement this protection by use and promotion of a Sanforized label to be attached to the garments made from the processed fabrics.

Previous advertising, over many years, had sold the name *Sanforized* as a sign of protection against shrinking. The new campaign directed the consumer to *look* for the Sanforized label. Text copy was strongly worded.

A typical illustration, a photograph, shows a customer in a store grimly searching for the label. The text copy:

BE SUSPICIOUS!

Make sure you see it on the label.
If you don't, stomp off.
Or see the manager.
Be a real pain in the neck.
You can't be sure the fabric won't shrink unless
you see *SANFORIZED.*
You can't be sure of the best wash-and-wear performance
unless you see SANFORIZED-*plus.*
Right there. On the label.
Don't fall for a glib "It's the same thing."
If it is, why doesn't it say so?
You're entitled to "Sanforized" and "Sanforized-Plus."
Get them.

The media selection was aimed at consumers, both men and women, but it was intended that the garment industry read the advertising too, including the garment makers. On the schedule were *Life, McCall's, Look,* the *New York Times*

"How could a man kill a whale with a harpoon?"

"Stand up, Tashtego!—give it to him!" The harpoon was hurled. "Stern all!" And off they go on a "Nantucket sleigh ride."

The pages of *Moby Dick* tell the story so vividly a boy almost feels he's there. But drive him to the Whaling Museum at New Bedford and he *is* there, standing on the deck of a half-scale model of a real whaling ship, ready to cast off her lines for a three-year voyage in search of the great sperm whale.

When he stands on the quarter deck of the Bark, Lagoda, gazing at the great incomprehensible jungle of rigging and spars and sails . . . as he stands in a fragile cockle-shell of a whaleboat, surfing in his mind's eye in the wake of a harpooned sperm whale . . . perhaps he gets a glimmering of what it was like to be an American in those times. And what a won-

derful gift to give your children, the realization that learning like this can be *fun*.

This land of ours is filled with places that can bring history alive for a child. Museums, battlefields, historic sites . . . they're all yours, just a pleasant drive away from your home.

Ethyl calls this fascinating world that surrounds you a Magic Circle. Why not start exploring your Magic Circle this week end?

Ethyl Corporation
New York 17, N. Y.

Ethyl Corporation of Canada Limited, Toronto

These Magic Circle advertisements are published to help you get more enjoyment out of your car. Ethyl makes additives used by oil companies to improve their gasolines and your driving pleasure.

This Magic Circle is in New England. Among other points of interest to see in this area are Old Sturbridge Village and the Giant Sand Dunes, Truro, Cape Cod. Or your service station dealer will be glad to help you map out a Magic Circle trip in your own area.

By promoting motor-car tourism, Ethyl Corporation helps its customers, the gasoline companies, sell more gasoline. This leads to increased sales of Ethyl's products, plus goodwill building with customers. (AGENCY: *Young & Rubicam*)

Magazine section—and *Cue* and *Playbill*, "because the industry goes to the theater."

It may be observed that this campaign functions in a somewhat similar manner to the ILGWU Union Label campaign described in Chapter 9.

The Caterpillar Tractor Company

The Caterpillar Tractor Company, maker of tractors, bulldozers, and other earthmoving equipment, is the leader in its industry. The objective of its campaign, which it calls market-development advertising is "To stimulate the nationwide growth of projects involving extensive earthmoving that require public support for their initiation."

Actually, this company is advertising *for* its customers, trying to create more work for them which, in turn, will require more machines.

In the past, Caterpillar had supported road building, snow removal, city-dump removal, forest-fire protection, etc. As a result of a Senate committee's report on natural water resources in 1961, a water-management campaign was started. Insertions were placed in the *Saturday Evening Post, Reader's Digest, Time,* and *Rotarian.*

The campaign stressed the need for better *water management*—conservation of water resources, prevention of waste, flood control, pollution control, recreation, etc. It was realized that although water problems are nationwide, most of the work to be done would be handled locally. The greatest difficulty was lack of public awareness that a nationwide water problem existed.

The copy urged communities to take action. Case-history ads demonstrated what happened to localities which have ignored their water problems, then told how they solved the problems and what benefits were derived. At the end, the reader was asked to appraise his own community.

The ads were black-and-white spreads, with photographic illustrations and fairly long informative copy. Some of the headlines were:

> NOT ENOUGH WATER? IN RAIN-SOAKED SEDRO WOOLLEY?
>
> WATER-RICH BAY COUNTY, FLORIDA . . . WHERE FORESIGHT AVERTED A WATER CRISIS.
>
> WHEN THEY ADDED WATER THEY ADDED 2000 NEW JOBS.
>
> WE NEEDED NEW INDUSTRY, BUT THE LITTLE TALLAPOOSA STOPPED US COLD.

Although this advertising was admittedly commercial in its motivation, it also provided the company with overtone image benefits. Inasmuch as the water problem has become a very serious one, the advertising picks up a strong public service connotation. It can also be said that the company has asserted notable industry leadership.

Helping Others to Help Yourself

Advertising in which a company helps its immediate customers is, in a sense, protective. It acts to protect a franchise which the company, by virtue of its industry position or of the special nature of its product, is privileged to hold. It supports the trade or industrial advertising which does the actual product-selling job. It also supports, importantly, the activities of the company's sales-

Be suspicious!

Make sure you see it on the label.

If you don't, stomp off.

Or see the manager.

Be a real pain in the neck.

You can't be sure the fabric won't shrink unless you see •*SANFORIZED*•

You can't be sure of the best wash-and-wear performance unless you see (*SANFORIZED plus•*)

Right there. On the label.

Don't fall for a glib "It's the same thing."

If it is, why doesn't it say so?

You're entitled to "Sanforized" and "Sanforized-Plus".

Get them.

Ads to consumers, urging them to look for the Sanforized label, support the mills which buy the Sanforized process. Ultimate result is increased sales of the process. (AGENCY: *Young & Rubicam*)

men. Though its approach may be indirect, it is usually a very practical kind of advertising and well worth the expenditure.

Fisher Body

Another version of helping-hand advertising is that of Fisher Body, today a division of General Motors. Originally, Fisher Body was an independent company selling bodies to automotive manufacturers. In 1926, it was absorbed by General Motors, its biggest customer. Since then, as a division of that company, it has continued manufacturing auto bodies exclusively and is staffed by people who are body specialists.

This arrangement has value to General Motors in two ways. First, General Motors is the only American car manufacturer with such a separate and distinct body division. Second, the quality of Fisher workmanship has been so high that it is the constant envy of General Motors' competitors.

Many years ago, General Motors decided that Fisher Body was an institutional asset that could be advertised to help sell General Motors cars.

General Motors advertising for its Fisher Body Division has the semblance of institutional advertising, but works to assist other General Motors ads (and salesmen) to sell specific GM cars. (AGENCY: *Kudner Agency*)

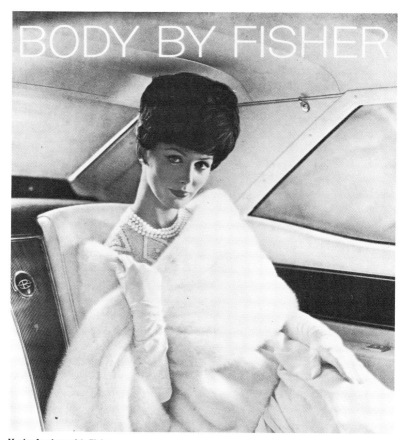

You're fresher with Fisher

You get a car-full of clean, fresh air twice a minute—even with the windows shut! You feel as refreshed as if you were riding on a cloud. Our Snorkel System does it. And it comes only with Body by Fisher—the most carefully crafted, solidly built, longest lasting car body ever. So much of the buy is in the body. And Body by Fisher makes a GM car a <u>better</u> buy: Chevrolet, Pontiac, Oldsmobile, Buick, Cadillac.

Body by Fisher

GENERAL MOTORS SYMBOL OF QUALITY

The advertising has been distinguished since the beginning by its visual look. Fisher was one of the earliest advertisers to use color photography and has used it expertly ever since. Although exterior views appear occasionally, car interiors are usually shown. Although a few men (usually in full evening dress) have been seen in these ads, smartly clothed children are seen more often. But most often of all, the model is a very beautiful, elegantly dressed young woman sitting in the car. The general visual effect is that of regal luxury.

So long has this type of picture, always accompanied by the words, *Body by Fisher,* been used that it has almost become a trademark in itself. Text copy is somewhat more varied, usually pointing to some Fisher body feature and then identifying Fisher with the General Motors cars.

Institutional Selling

The Fisher Body campaign offers an unusual instance of advertising that is both institutional and product-selling at the same time. In General Motors' advertising of one of its own divisions, and in tone and approach, the ads can be called institutional. On the other hand, these ads help *other* General Motors ads sell specific products, by stressing a special benefit common to those products.

Eight

There are more than 11,000 associations of businessmen in the United States. Seventeen hundred of these associations are national in scope. The rest are state, regional, and local. According to Magazine Advertising Bureau, 211 associations placed advertising in 1964, spending more than $75,746,000.

In sizes, types, motives, and operations, these associations are infinite in their variety. As advertisers, their problems and objectives are even more varied than those of individual businesses. Sometimes an association represents a heterogeneous cross section of an industry, sometimes a homogeneous segment of the industry, such as manufacturers, or utilities, or retailers, etc.

Business associations exist, in general, to do things for the benefit of their member companies that the companies cannot do for themselves, or cannot do as well, or as economically. Associations function in two ways—internally and externally.

Some internal functions are the setting of standards for the industry, providing industry statistics, assuming chores such as credit reports, disseminating industry news, providing research facilities, and establishing safety practices.

The most important external functions are to provide advertising, public relations, and promotion (1) to protect the industry against the competition of other industries and (2) to increase usage of the industry's generic products.

Advertising operations are usually vested in an advertising committee, which often reports to a board of directors. Most associations have an advertising manager and staff and an advertising agency.

Chapter **26**

ASSOCIATION

ADVERTISING

The Association's Greatest Problem As an Advertiser

It is more difficult for an association to produce top quality advertising than it is for an individual corporation. The problem can be stated simply—too many cooks.

In his *Confessions of an Advertising Man*,[1] David Ogilvy elaborated on this a bit more: "Too many masters, too many objectives, too little money."

To which might be added, too many committees—a natural proliferation of the original problem, caused by the desire to provide "political" representation for members of the association. Still more cooks.

If there is actual hostility between members of the association—usually arising from intense, direct competition *within* an industry—either very poor advertising, or no advertising at all, may be forthcoming.

Resolving the problem Experience has shown that the best way to resolve the problem of too many cooks is simply to reduce the number of cooks. To replace committees, wherever possible, with competent and responsible individuals.

A workable arrangement is for the committee in charge of the advertising (1) to establish advertising *policy*, (2) to reduce the number of objectives to a minimum, and (3) to *define* the objectives.

From there on, the *operation* of the advertising should be centralized in *one* advertising manager, or in an advertising agency. Ideally, the manager should have complete or near-complete control of the creative aspects of the advertising, including approvals. Multiple committee-member approvals should be avoided.

The most outstanding association advertising campaigns have occurred where operational responsibility has been thus delegated to individuals.

Association against Association

In a world that is rapidly getting smaller, where science and technology are expanding, where many businesses are diversifying, where competition everywhere is intensifying—the struggle of industry against industry is becoming more frequently evident. And more serious to the participants. For while an internal industry competition between brands can lead to loss of share-of-market and slower company expansion, the struggle between competing *industries* can be to the death; if one industry succeeds too completely, its outdistanced competitor may be forced out of business.

The struggle is continuous and everywhere. Glass containers vie with steel cans. Aluminum battles copper for the electric-wiring market. Gas heat muscles in on oil heat in the construction of new houses or vice versa. On the highways, concrete strives against asphalt. Florida citrus fruit challenges California citrus fruit. Commercial banks fight savings banks. Railroads glare at truckers. Plastics steal markets from metal. Wood fights plaster. Ad infinitum.

[1] David Ogilvy, *Confessions of an Advertising Man*, Atheneum Publishers, New York, 1963.

In all of these industry struggles, associations and association advertising play an increasingly important role. Curiously, industry adversity seems to have a beneficial effect on its association. When the struggle gets hot and the inroads of a competing industry begin really to hurt, the association is galvanized into new life. Its organization is unified and its advertising improves. Copy hits harder. The industry that used to squabble internally gets together and starts punching. Competition reactivates a moribund association and also increases the flow of non-product advertising.[2]

Expanding Product Usage

The same technological advances that stir up competition between industries also point up the need for promotion of generic products. Glass, concrete, wood, aluminum, plastics constantly seek new uses, new forms in which to go to market. While it is the manufacturer's job to advertise his own brand against the brand of his competitor, someone is needed to promote generically the product they both sell, lest some new generic product arrive and put them both out of business. The "someone" assigned to expand usage of the brand generically is the association.

Hence, increasing product usage becomes an important part of the work of such associations as the Edison Electric Institute, American Gas Association, American Dairy Association, Portland Cement Association, etc. Large sums of money are spent on research to develop new product forms and usefulness. Usage-building advertising is employed on a continuous basis.

Some Case-history Examples of Association Advertising

So varied are the natures, the objectives, and the techniques of association advertisers, it becomes extremely difficult to hold up any one as a typical example of association advertising. Yet to fully comprehend the role of this advertising, at least a few instances of association-advertising in action should be discussed.

The first example, selected for the soundness of its planning and conception, as well as its excellence of execution, is the advertising of the *Better Vision Institute.*

Better Vision Institute

The Better Vision Institute is the association of the ophthalmic field, including eye doctors, opticians, laboratories, and manufacturers of eyeglasses. Basic

---

[2] The competition between industries is highly beneficial to the consumer, forcing product improvements and the development of useful products.

policy had been established by a seven-man governing committee. An executive secretary (advertising manager) had been given complete latitude and freedom in directing the execution of the advertising. He was the only person to whom the advertising agency, Doyle Dane Bernbach, was obliged to go for approvals.

The objective The long-range objective of this advertising was to expand the market for eye-care services and eyeglasses.

Research revealed a great need for the product—many people with bad eyes, but no glasses. Hence, the immediate objective became *to get as many people as possible to have their eyes examined.* And this was to be the *one* basic theme.

When was the last time you had your eyes examined?

Maybe this print looks okay to you. Believe us, it's blurred.

Even if you can read clear type clearly, don't jump to any hasty conclusions about your eyesight.

The truth is, we can't tell for ourselves how well we actually see.

We just have no standards for comparison. No way we can judge by experience what the other fellow sees that we don't. (How, for example, do you describe the color blue to a color-blind person?)

For another thing, our eyes change so gradually, all through life, we're generally unable to detect any differences from day to day in the way we see.

We don't ordinarily get any warning as you do with a toothache.

Sooner or later, of course, age itself takes over. When we start holding the phone book at arm's length, we begin to realize what has happened.

But long before that time, for many of us, there's a whole wide wonderful world we could be enjoying more every day with better eyesight. In our work, our study, our play.

It took Nature some 2½ billion years to develop the miracle of the human eye.

Wouldn't it be worth an hour, once a year or so, to have a qualified eye-care practitioner find out how well you're seeing.

Or could be. **Better Vision Institute.**

The blurred type of this Better Vision Institute ad is not merely an attention-getting device. It is also a startling demonstration of the campaign's selling message. (AGENCY: *Doyle Dane Bernbach*)

It was decided, right from the beginning, to keep the campaign at a high ethical level. Everything in the advertising must meet the tests of being sound, in the public interest, and devoted to the patient's welfare.

An overall image of public service was sought, and, thanks to the restraint and purity of the copy, almost instantly achieved. Because, though the campaign might have benefited the manufacturers, it *did* render a valuable public service.

The advertisements The advertising appeared in general magazines. Most of the ads were black-and-white bleed pages (with the picture extending to the edge of the paper)—in fact, in most cases the photographic picture occupied all of the page except a small strip of white at the bottom, which carried the text copy. This was not a fixed-layout format; there were variations, but at almost all times the photographic illustration was very large and dominant.

Each advertisement was characterized by a visual-verbal *idea*. These ideas had arresting stopper quality. Yet, at the same time, every one adhered closely to the basic selling theme—*the need for an eye examination.* The text was extremely well written and maintained interest as it completed its selling message. All three major elements of the ads—picture, headline, and copy—were each in themselves interesting and each took part in the selling operation. These are technically excellent advertisements in every respect.

Selling an idea One of these advertisements has already been referred to in Chapter 16 (page 113). The blurred effect used in this advertisement was taken advantage of in several other advertisements—to drive home the basic idea of the campaign. One was an all-type ad, but the type was blurred—out of focus—as it might be seen by a person with bad eyes. The fuzzy letters of the headline read:

WHEN WAS THE LAST TIME YOU HAD YOUR EYES EXAMINED?

With the blurry type, the headline made its point completely. Still another ad displayed a blurred school blackboard. The *un*blurred headline below said:

WHY JOHNNY CAN'T READ.

Then the text copy added another hook to its idea-selling when it pointed out:

So often, when bright children like Johnny have trouble learning to read, the trouble is with their eyes.

Why doesn't Johnny say so?

Because Johnny doesn't know. He thinks the way *he* sees is the way *everyone* sees. That's natural, isn't it?

The blurred out-of-focus effect was by no means the only illustration device used. There was a sharp close-up photograph, very much enlarged, of fingers failing to get a thread into the eye of a needle. The headline:

IT ISN'T THE NEEDLE'S EYE THAT'S CHANGED.

Another advertisement consisted of a completely *black* page, except for the one-inch strip of white at the bottom. On this white strip were printed the words:

Picture, headline, and copy combine to catch the eye, ensnare the curiosity, and arouse interest in this Better Vision Institute ad. At the same time, all three elements take part in the selling job. (AGENCY: *Doyle Dane Bernbach*)

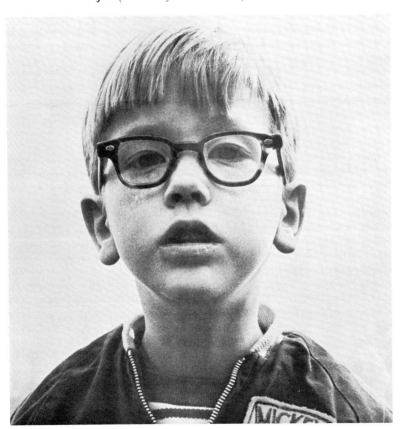

Don't feel sorry for the kid. He can see now.

You see a kid wearing glasses, and your first impulse might be to feel sorry for him.

But actually, if you're going to feel sorry, feel sorry for him *before* he got glasses.

Before he could see the infinitely varied and delicate patterns of a seashell.

Before he could follow the soaring flight of a bird overhead. Or a baseball over the infield.

Before the furry kittens in his picture book looked like kittens. And the ducks like ducks.

If you're going to feel sorry, feel sorry for kids who don't know that there's a far clearer, brighter world to be seen.

And who don't say anything, because they think everybody sees the way they do.

If you're going to feel sorry, feel sorry for kids

who have never had their eyes examined by a qualified eye-care practitioner—the one person who might help them see better. Hence, play better, study better, *live* better.

How about your children? Have they had their eyes examined lately? Now, with the start of a new school year, would be the sensible time to have it done. **Better Vision Institute.**

This is how yellow daisies in a green field against a blue sky look to many Americans. You have only one pair of eyes. Have them examined once a year. (*Better Vision Institute*)

And another advertisement showed a close-up photograph of an extremely appealing youngster peering through his new glasses. The headline read:

DON'T FEEL SORRY FOR THE KID. HE CAN SEE NOW.

The Wine Advisory Board

California is one of the great wine-producing regions of the world. Its wines are excellent and the grape industry represents the state's largest and most important fruit crop. Yet this industry could be much larger, if it could induce more Americans to drink more wine than the small amount they do at present.

The Wine Advisory Board, founded in 1938 under a marketing order issued by the California State Department of Agriculture, is the industry's promotional association. Its basic objective is to increase usage of all California wine.

The wine problem—part 1   Two major problems confront the association in its efforts to increase wine usage. The first is the long-continued American apathy toward the use of wine. There has never been an American tradition of wine usage. In fact, wine is almost unknown in many homes. At the time the association was formed, California-wine sales had been declining.

The per capita consumption of wine in the United States is one gallon per year. California's per capita consumption is two gallons. But France's per capita consumption is thirty-five gallons. If America's national consumption could be increased only up to California's two gallons, it would more than double the state's 700 million dollar wine industry.

The wine problem—part 2   The second problem faced by the association is the fact that California's wines fall into two classifications, best described as *premium-priced* wines and *popular-priced* wines. The premium-priced wines come from a relatively small area in north-central California. The popular-priced wines come from more extensive areas up and down the state.

The premium-priced wines, of course, are higher in quality, but the gallonage of the popular-priced wines is many times greater. The two types of wine appeal to quite different markets.

Inasmuch as the association's objective was to promote *all* California wine, it could not ignore one type in favor of the other. Both large and small wineries contributed to the association according to a per-gallon assessment. It might be said that the lower-priced wines yielded the greatest economic return, while the higher-priced ones provided a higher status reputation for California wines in general.

How to play the Wine Game so both sides win [*Rule for storing*]

The Traditionalists say:
"Wine should always be kept in a cellar where it's cool and dark."

The Non-Conformists say:
"Just keep it handy!"

In the Wine Game, *keeping* wines can be as controversial as serving them.

To the Traditionalist, a cellar is essential for storing an adequate supply. "You can store capped bottles upright," he says, "but always lay corked bottles on their sides to keep the corks moist and airtight. Air is the enemy," he declares, "along with sunlight and heat. Keep your cellar dark and cool and you can't go wrong."

To the Non-Conformist, a cellar is where you find it—the handier the better. "Any cool, dark closet or cupboard will do nicely, thank you," one Non-Conformist told us, "long as it's handy."

Although there's disagreement on *where* to store wines, there's none on what wines to store. Both Traditionalists and Non-Conformists agree on the excellence of *California* wines.   WINE ADVISORY BOARD

No C.O.D., cash or stamps. Allow 3 to 5 weeks for delivery. Quantity limited. Offer good in U.S. except where prohibited, terminates June 30, 1964, may be withdrawn earlier. Make checks payable to "Cookbook." Mail to: Cookbook, P.O. Box 88, San Francisco, California 94101.

SEND ME RULES FOR ENJOYMENT OF CALIFORNIA WINES
☐ I'm a Traditionalist – I'd like the refresher course.
☐ I'm a Non-Conformist – send me the rules to break.
SPECIAL OFFER: FAVORITE RECIPES OF CALIFORNIA WINE MAKERS. Only $2.00, *including tax and postage.* A new wine cookbook. 128 colorful pages. Over 300 recipes. Stand-up cover. Great gift idea–send for several!

Enclosed find $_____ for _____ cookbooks.

NAME_____

ADDRESS_____

CITY_____ STATE_____

The fine wines come from CALIFORNIA where the great grapes grow

Wine Advisory Board advertisements solve a complex problem with a human-interest approach, plus a touch of humor. By making the advertising a "game," the series lets everybody get into the act. (AGENCY: *Foote, Cone & Belding, San Francisco*)

The falling-off in California wine sales before the formation of the Wine Advisory Board was not due to inferior quality of product, but rather to lack of promotion while other wines were stepping up their advertising.

Stated objectives   An advertising campaign was devised to solve the industry's two-part problem. The formal, stated objectives were rather broad and general:

1. To increase acceptance of California wine
2. To encourage occasional users to enjoy wine more often
3. To attract new users of California's wines
4. To complement the various public relations programs of the California wine industry

Approach to the advertising   The best approach to selling wine, it was decided, was to emphasize *simple enjoyment.* It was important to eliminate mystery from the drinking of wine. Then a device would have to be found to talk at the same time to two different markets, to two different types of people, who might be facetiously, but aptly, categorized as "sippers" and "gulpers."

The "wine game"   To avoid any semblance of preaching, the advertising message was presented as a *game.* The advertisements staged a good-natured controversy between two very human, everyday people, one labelled *traditionalist,* and the other, *non-conformist.*

The argument revolved about the rules of wine etiquette. Copy was written, however, to satisfy both sides and to get in a great deal of educational information for both. And, of course, both contestants concluded that the glasses should be filled with *California* wine.

The traditionalist was the sophisticate, the natural prospect for the premium-priced California wines. The non-conformist, who often poured his wine from a large jug, was the prospect for the popular-priced California wines.

Advertising to change a national attitude   It has long been suspected that America's reluctance to drink wine more eagerly may be due to some sort of psychological barrier, such as the fear of transgressing some rule of wine etiquette and thus committing a social error. If so, this advertising, with its kidding manner, was skillfully designed to overcome such a barrier.

The campaign's down-to-earth, clowning characters had the look of real human beings. They did not look like advertising models. (Could they have been agency personnel?) They gave the advertising a feeling of authenticity, and their spirit of having fun reached out and involved the reader. The advertising was *interesting.*

Coupon returns were high. And although this was only part of the total advertising effort over the years, California wine sales rose from 54,979,000 gallons in 1938, when the Wine Advisory Board first went into action, to more than 130,000,000 gallons in 1964.

The Glass Container Manufacturers Institute

The Glass Container Manufacturers Institute, the successor of an earlier association founded in 1919, performs a variety of activities for the glass container industry, including industry-wide labor relations. Its most vital function, however, is the defense of its industry's products against the competitive inroads of other forms of containers—notably, steel cans and paperboard cartons.

Advertising for glass containers   Advertising for the defense of glass containers started in 1955. In the face of newsworthy advances in packaging at the time, members of the glass industry complained that people "took glass for granted." They felt it was time to act.

Utilizing the transparency and natural beauty of glass for attention-interest and its many advantages for a basic copy theme, a simple format was established and was adhered to for many years because of its apparent success.

A very large bleed color photograph of a selected product in glass containers filled almost all of a magazine page. At the bottom, very brief copy, no more than twenty to thirty words, presented one of the advantages of glass. For example: "Shining *glass bottles* keep milk and cream wholesome and farm-fresh. Glass is clean and pure, never alters original flavors. That's why so many foods are packed in glass!"

The color photographs, which showed the subject close-up, were extremely attractive and brought out the sparkle and beauty of the glass jars and bottles,

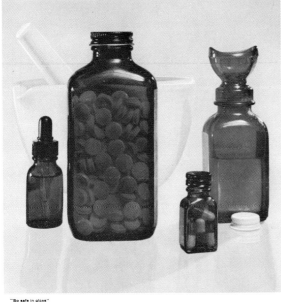

"So safe in glass"

Safely sealed in <u>glass</u> <u>bottles</u>, medicines retain their full effectiveness. Glass itself is so pure— you know medicinal purity is safeguarded.

GLASS CONTAINER MANUFACTURERS INSTITUTE, 99 PARK AVENUE, NEW YORK

Full-color photographs portrayed the beauty and sparkle of glass containers in advertisements of the Glass Container Manufacturers Institute. Brief copy made a single sales point.
(AGENCY: *Kenyon & Eckhardt*)

especially when the contents were colorful. The foods and beverages looked very appetizing. The extra-large, slightly oversize, close-up illustrations created an attention-value that held the reader's gaze long enough for him to glance at the short copy. And because the copy was so brief, it invited readership, thereby succeeding in clinching its sales point (which was closely allied to the picture above).

No one ad tried to tell the whole story. Instead, each ad told a part of it, in an unusually close continuity of as many as twenty-two ads a year in one publication (*Life*). In that time, a regular reader of the magazine could not help but absorb a good deal of the Institute's total selling message.

The subjects selected were keyed to the season. Jarred fruit was shown in the winter when fresh fruit was scarce. Soft drinks were featured in the summer, household products during the spring-cleaning season, and milk during the National Dairy Month in June. The general magazine campaign was supported by trade campaigns in retail food-and-packaging publications.

The Glass Container Manufacturers Institute credits the campaign with changing a negative chain-store attitude toward glass to a positive one and also with contributing importantly toward a rising consumer preference for products in glass.

United States Brewers Association

Formed in 1862, the United States Brewers Association is said to be America's oldest incorporated trade association. It has gone through several name changes, including United Brewers Industrial Foundation, and Brewing Industry Foundation, but returned, in 1961, to its original name.

The association met its greatest challenge in the years immediately preceding World War II. The prohibitionists, though defeated by Repeal in 1933, were staging an impressive comeback by winning local-option elections in many parts of the country. Their success was partly due to unruly taverns whose misbehavior provided fuel for "dry" propaganda.

The Brewers' organization met this challenge with an industry self-regulation program aimed at policing the retailing of beer in taverns and with efforts to counteract the prohibitionist propaganda.

Advertising to sway public opinion   Direct self-regulation pressure in affected localities was accompanied by local-newspaper advertising explaining the program to the public. This, in turn, was supported by a campaign in national magazines.

One of these advertisements showed a flock of white sheep that included, very visibly, one black sheep. The headline and subhead read:

SURE . . . EVERYBODY NOTICES

THE ONE BLACK SHEEP!

That's one of the reasons why the Brewing Industry has adopted a plan to eliminate ALL black sheep from Beer Retailing.

The text copy went on to describe self-regulation and told how it would eliminate the few antisocial beer retailers. It then emphasized the wholesomeness of beer and touched on some of its economic benefits.

Another advertisement displayed a long line of soldiers on dress parade. One soldier had dropped his gun. The headline read:

BUT WHY COURT-MARTIAL THE WHOLE REGIMENT?

At the bottom of all the ads was the following base line: "Beer . . . a Beverage of Moderation for the Nation."

The campaign continued on into the war period and contributed, along with the other self-regulation operations, to successfully blunt and repulse the prohibitionist drive to dry up the country piecemeal.

Later advertising   After the war, the Brewers' advertising changed its format to large paintings by noted illustrators, and a continuing headline:

BEER BELONGS . . . ENJOY IT.

The paintings depicted family groups of people at home, enjoying beer in various nostalgic situations. The campaign, which continued for many years, was intended to maintain and build up existing markets for beer and ale by emphasizing their social acceptance and to suggest even greater use of them in the home.

National Lumber Manufacturers Association

In 1956, the competitive inroads of other building materials made it urgently necessary for the National Lumber Manufacturers Association to institute a protective national-advertising campaign, supported by trade campaigns and by merchandizing and public relations activities.

The consumer advertisements—intended to resell the many advantages of wood—were photographic, full-color double spreads. They exhibited the wooden framework of a house being built, which blended, in the other half of the picture, into a completed interior of the home. The ads were attractive and visible and undoubtedly helped the cause of the wood industry.

Trade advertising   The trade advertising was notable. These trade advertisements were constructed with as much care and creative excellence as the more expensive consumer ads. They stood out from their shabby, pinch-penny competitors. The ads addressed to architects were particularly of high visual quality. Similar well-made campaigns were addressed to builders and to buyers of building materials for schools.

Incidentally, it should be noted that institutional advertising of various types appears and has appeared from time to time in trade and industrial publications.

Sure...everybody notices the *one* black sheep!

BEER WAS BREWED IN ANCIENT EGYPT:

Beer has been brewed for thousands of years. Ancient Egyptian manuscripts mention beer. Perhaps beer helped quench the thirst of workmen who built the Sphinx and Pyramids.

NEEDED: 312,500 FREIGHT CARS.

A freight train, 2485 miles long would be needed to hold the 25,000,000,000 pounds of farm products bought by beer since re-legalization. Every year, the produce of 3,000,000 farm acres is purchased by beer.

TRADITIONAL BEVERAGE OF FRIENDSHIP AND OF MODERATION.

Good beer has always been associated with good manners and good friends. It is also the beverage of moderation . . . a point worth remembering in these busy, fast-moving modern times.

That's one of the reasons why the Brewing Industry has adopted a plan to eliminate ALL black sheep from Beer Retailing

Out of a quarter of a million retail establishments in America selling beer, there are bound to be a few retailers who disobey the law or permit anti-social conditions. Actually, the percentage of these "black sheep" retailers is very low.

Nevertheless . . . to protect the good name of beer . . . the brewing industry wants undesirable, anti-social retailing *eliminated entirely*. We want *all* beer taverns to be what the vast majority of them already are . . . clean, attractive, decent places, *as wholesome as beer itself*.

We are now taking action to do this with a new "clean-up or close-up" program. It is already in operation in a number of states and will be extended to others as rapidly as possible. We want you to know about it. May we send you an interesting *free* booklet? Write—United Brewers Industrial Foundation, Dept. C13, 21 East 40th St., New York.

BEER . . . A BEVERAGE OF MODERATION FOR THE NATION

The brewing industry met the challenge of a resurgence of localized Prohibition with a militant "Self-Regulation" program, publicized by these ads. (AGENCY: *Newell-Emmett Company*)

Only WOOD makes every dining occasion so festive

Wood invites fun to a little girl's birthday party, cheer to a family breakfast, warmth to a formal dinner. It confirms your good taste so many ways . . . in paneled walls that subdue sound for a quiet meal, parquet flooring that cleans up beautifully after the children. Windows of all kinds are shaped by wood; furniture of every period is styled with wood. Structurally, its posts and beams strengthen your area for dining . . . wonderfully, wood's varied grains and tones work into your color scheme of things for any gathering. Whether you build, buy, or remodel . . . *there's nothing in the world like wood.*

NATIONAL LUMBER MANUFACTURERS ASSOCIATION

PLANNING BOOK! "Open House: previewing your new home of WOOD" . . . 28 color pages, 6 home designs. Send 25c to WOOD, P. O. Box 1816, Washington 13, D.C.

Imaginative illustration provides attention value and also displays wood glamorously in this consumer ad for National Lumber Manufacturers Association. Copy sells the advantages of wood. (AGENCY: *VanSant, Dugdale & Co.*)

Marketing Associations—Florida Citrus Commission and Sunkist Growers

Perhaps among the largest advertisers in the association category are the citrus-fruit marketing associations of Florida and California—Florida Citrus Commission and Sunkist growers. The advertising of these associations is essentially product-selling advertising, as they have undertaken a marketing function for their fruit-grower members.

Oddly, these famous rival associations are not nearly as competitive as most people suppose, for their fruit is both different in type and ripens at different times of the year. Thus, their individual advertising campaigns may have the effect of actually helping each other, by keeping citrus fruit in the public mind more continuously throughout the year.

The American Dairy Association

The activities of the American Dairy Association, a food-promoting rather than a food-marketing organization, are characterized by their almost bewildering diversity. This results from the considerable number of milk products, each one with specialized market problems.

A major promotion—using television and radio as well as magazines, newspapers, billboards, and merchandising—is the fluid-milk promotion. There are other promotions for ice cream, non-fat dry milk, butter, evaporated milk, cheese, and cottage cheese. There is also a special June Dairy Month promotion. Most of the advertising is not far removed from product-selling brand advertising.

Edison Electric Institute

Edison Electric Institute is the principal trade association of investor-owned electric-utility companies. Its "Live Better Electrically" Program has been aimed at increasing kilowatt-hour sales in the residential, commercial, industrial, and rural-residential markets.

The Institute's advertising has promoted the total-electric concept through the "Gold Medallion Home," electric home heating, water heating, clothes drying, and cooking advertising.

American Gas Association

The American Gas Association has as its objective "to do everything possible to promote the usage of gas in every possible way." Hence, its promotional activities are broad and complex. The Gas Association cooperates constantly with its members and with gas-appliance manufacturers, in advertising and in other ways.

This differs, in emphasis, from the policy of the Edison Electric Institute. Electricity has very large manufacturers such as General Electric, Westinghouse, etc., well able to tell their own part of the story. Gas-industry manufacturers are much smaller in size.

In its advertising, the American Gas Association has striven to build an image of modernity. It wishes to dispel any idea that gas is more old fashioned than electricity. Feeling that television connotes with modernity, the association has used the TV medium since 1957.

Inter-industry Conflict

The national advertising of the associations of the two great competing industries, gas and electricity, has been characterized by an air of politeness and dignity. Perhaps this is because many important utilities supply both gas and electricity.

But the politeness vanishes in another sector of inter-industry conflict, in certain local areas, in the fierce competition between oil heat and gas heat. Here, in unrestrained newspaper copy, the clamor of claims and charges and counterclaims and countercharges has taken on the aspect of a gang rumble.

When the price of natural gas becomes low enough to be competitive with oil, the simplicity and lower price of gas-burning *equipment* provides gas with a formidable advantage, especially in new-home construction. Oil distributors see their entire business being swept away, and then the donnybrook begins.

Battle of the Banks

Another area of controversy is the once-upon-a-time sedate field of banking. When commercial banks switched emphasis from the old wholesale banking to their new retail banking concept, they found themselves in competition with the savings banks and savings and loan associations.

To provide industry advertising, the Foundation for Commercial Banks was organized in June, 1958. The savings banks and savings and loan organizations had their own protective associations, some of them established for many years. The Savings Bank Association of New York State, for example, was founded in 1894. The battle of the banks is developing an increasing amount of association advertising.

The Portland Cement Association

The Portland Cement Association, organized in 1916, both (1) promotes the interests of Portland cement and concrete externally through advertising and (2) conducts an extensive internal-industry program to improve and extend the uses of cement and concrete.

Cement and concrete are ancient materials which are enjoying an astonishing rebirth of usefulness, thanks to modern technology and design innovations. One function of the association is to help develop *new uses* for its versatile product. Another function is to disseminate *news* about these developments to the industry and to its customers. The association maintains a 10 million dollar research laboratory, offers technical field assistance, education, and supervision of safety practices.

In its advertising, the objective of the association is (1) in all ways, to try to extend the use of concrete and (2) to aid and protect the industry in its "unceasing competition with steel, aluminum, glass, wood, brick, asphalt and other materials too numerous to mention."

In facing this competition, each challenge is met in individual detail in the trade press. In a typical recent year, 392 trade and professional publications were used, plus 158 farm publications. In addition, a twenty-publication consumer program is aimed at a vast unknown audience that includes potential customers and opinion leaders whose influence may be important. This advertising frequently promotes the use of concrete for major highways.

Other Associations

These are only a few of the numerous trade associations employing advertising. Some others that have advertised importantly in national media have been the Copper and Brass Research Association, Association of American Railroads, the Watchmakers of Switzerland, Institute of Life Insurance, Asphalt Institute, the National Paint, Varnish and Lacquer Association, American Wool Council, and Leather Industries of America.

In everyday sales-advertising procedure, individual companies in an industry promote the sale of their own brands in competition with other brands. Once in a while, however, a single company in an industry may take it on itself to promote the industry's products *generically*. When it does this, it acts as if it were the industry's trade association.

Generally, the company that promotes the whole industry's product will most likely be the largest company in the industry. Thus it will stand to gain at least a little more from the generic advertising than its competitors. Conversely, smaller companies in an industry studiously avoid such advertising, fearing that competitors would be helped more than themselves.

By advertising for the whole industry, whether promoting its generic product or speaking for the industry in some other way, a company is said to exert *industry leadership*. This may bring considerable goodwill and public relations benefits, plus a favorable effect on sales. The company gets credit for its selling effort. With a dominant company, the expenditure for an industry-leadership effort has usually turned out to be a good investment.

One motivation for advertising of this type appears to be (1) the need for protective advertising directed against the competitive inroads of other industries and (2) the inability or failure of the industry association to provide this protection. The industry leader then assumes the function individually.

Chapter 27

EXERTING

INDUSTRY

LEADERSHIP

Industry Leadership by U.S. Steel

The United States Steel Corporation, at one time, ran an impressive campaign of double spreads in color that, although it spoke of "USS steels," was in reality an industry campaign. It displayed steel consumer products which U.S. Steel itself did not make in finished form and the steel for which might have been supplied by many other steel companies.

Today's U·S·S steels

✦ lighten your work . . . ✦ brighten your leisure . . ✦ widen your world . . .

Woman at work. Talk about automation! The ladies don't anticipate washdays with dread anymore, thanks to work-lightening automatic laundries styled in durable USS steels. Clothes still get soiled, it's true. But now steel does the work of cleaning them.

Autumn outing. Even the season's last picnic generates tremendous young Indian Summer thirsts. And what better way to quench them than with delicious soft drinks sipped from no-deposit, no-return cans of steel that store and handle easily, and chill quickly.

Wanderlust. Hotels as smart as this one beckon strongly to the eager traveler in you. They are designed almost entirely in steel. Not just the steel girders and beams that you can't see in the finished building. But gay, wonderful things you can see, too—like these modern walls of colorful porcelain-enameled steel.

(US) United States Steel
TRADEMARK

This mark tells you a product is made of steel.
Look for it when you buy.

Lightens
your work
Brightens
your leisure
Widens
your world

U.S. Steel exerted industry leadership in this campaign which promoted products of steel generically. The whole steel industry benefited, but U.S. Steel, of course, most of all. (AGENCY: *Batten, Barton, Durstine & Osborn*)

The campaign really competed against the products of *non-steel* industries. Each ad in the series carried the headline:

TODAY'S USS STEELS . . . LIGHTEN YOUR WORK . . .
BRIGHTEN YOUR LEISURE . . . WIDEN YOUR WORLD . . .

The three-part illustrations were appropriate to each of the three promises of the headline. For example, the pictures of one ad showed (1) colored-steel kitchen cabinets (*competitive with wood*), (2) a child playing with a toy boat in a bathtub in a bathroom with ceramic-fused steel tiles (*competitive with all-ceramic tiles*), and (3) steel desks in a classroom (*competitive with wood or other metals*). The brief captions emphasized the advantages of steel, generically. The steel industry's three-star *steelmark* was prominently displayed.

Other steel products shown in the campaign were pianos, a Ferris wheel, a steamship, cans of food, laboratory equipment, cars, television sets, stainless-steel tableware, and a hotel building.

This series could easily have been signed by the steel industry's association[1] without change, except for the occasional removal of the USS symbol. Not another word need have been changed. The whole steel industry benefited to some degree from this campaign, but U.S. Steel naturally benefited much more than the other companies.

Leadership Campaigns in the Copper Industry

The opportunity to exert industry leadership is not necessarily reserved for any single company in an industry. If the industry has two, or three, or more large companies, *any* of them might advantageously vie for leadership by speaking for the industry. In the copper-mining industry, made up almost entirely of such giant corporations, at least two companies have published industry-leadership advertising campaigns.

Anaconda ran a long series of ads devoted entirely to selling copper generically. Typical headlines were:

COPPER . . .
THE AGELESS METAL

COPPER . . .
SYMBOL OF SECURITY

COPPER . . .
VOICE OF MUSIC

Kennecott's campaign, featuring the humorous Eric Gurney cartoon character, "*Skimpy Wiring*, the 'Dead End Kid of the Electrical Business,' " pro-

[1] American Iron and Steel Institute.

moted the cause of adequate wiring in the home. Another Kennecott generic product campaign dramatized the slogan: "No substitute can do what copper does!"

Industry Leadership with a Public Relations Objective

The liquor industry offers a notable example of industry leadership with a public relations motivation. Once or twice a year, the House of Seagram has run an advertisement urging moderation in drinking. Creatively, these ads have been well executed and well written and, as a result, have gained wide readership.

The most famous of these advertisements pictured a man and his son, with the following headline and copy:

YOU'RE A HERO . . . TO YOUR SON

Most boys worship their Dad as a hero whose standards and ideals they gradually acquire as their own.

Nothing is quite so disillusioning to the clear eyes of a youngster as the sight of a man—his own father—who has used liquor unwisely.

The damage goes far deeper than a momentary shame.

Any man who cannot drink wisely and moderately, owes it to his son . . . his family, not to drink at all.

The coming generation will be less apt to use liquor intemperately if older people will regard it as luxury and treat it as a contribution to gracious living— to be enjoyed in moderation.

Surely, Father's Day is an appropriate occasion for the House of Seagram, as one of America's leading distillers, to say as we said *four* years ago, and have constantly reiterated . . . "Drink Moderately."

Another advertisement had the headline:

WE WHO MAKE WHISKEY SAY:
"DRINKING *and* DRIVING DO NOT MIX"

Interestingly, a question that must have popped into many readers' minds is answered in the first three sentences of the copy for this ad:

This statement may seem to work directly against our self-interest. But actually it does not. It is very much to our self-interest to see that the privilege of drinking is not abused.

The public relations value of this advertising to the liquor industry may go deeper than is apparent on the surface. That such advertisements were written at all is an important point. And that they should be written so well is also sig-

You can obtain a reproduction of the above drawing, suitable for framing, by writing to Seagram-Distillers Corp., Chrysler Building, New York City.

YOU'RE A HERO ·· TO YOUR SON

Most boys worship their Dad as a hero whose standards and ideals they gradually acquire as their own.

Nothing is quite so disillusioning to the clear eyes of a youngster as the sight of a man — his own father — who has used liquor unwisely.

The damage goes far deeper than a momentary shame.

Any man who cannot drink wisely and moderately, owes it to his son . . . his family, not to drink at all.

The coming generation will be less apt to use liquor intemperately if older people will regard it as a luxury and treat it as a contribution to gracious living—to be enjoyed in moderation.

Surely, Father's Day is an appropriate occasion for the House of Seagram, as one of America's leading distillers, to say as we said *four* years ago, and have constantly reiterated . . . "Drink Moderately".

··· THE HOUSE OF SEAGRAM ···
Fine Whiskies Since 1857
Seagram-Distillers Corp., Executive Offices, New York

By showing an interest in what happens after its product has been sold, Seagram has not only helped improve the public relations image of its industry, but has also established itself as a responsible industry leader. (AGENCY: *Warwick & Legler*)

nificant. In view of the fact that traces of the demoniac image of the liquor industry painted by the prohibitionists still linger in the public mind, this industry could use still more public relations expressions of this type.

Of any credit, of any goodwill benefits that may have accrued from this advertising, the lion's share has rightfully gone to Seagram.

Nine

One extensive branch of advertising that is not primarily concerned with selling products is *service* advertising.

This category of advertising covers a broad range of activities and approaches. Sometimes, in its philosophies, its techniques, and its objectives, it is not distinguishable from product-selling advertising. At other times, it can be far removed from product-selling attitudes and methods.

Nearly always, service advertising involves the dissemination of *ideas*.

Also, almost always, the service is closely identified, in the public mind, with the name of the corporation supplying it. Such as *Brooklyn Union* gas, *Metropolitan* life insurance, *Chase Manhattan* banking service, etc.

Utility Advertising

The services most likely to be sold in a product-selling manner are those that have been long established, are well understood by everybody, and generally fulfill fairly basic needs. The most typical examples are gas-and-electric utility services.

Curiously, these utilities *do* sell a product (gas, electricity), but the product is not consumed directly in its primary form by the purchaser. Entering the house, it is distributed by pipes or wire and fed into appliances. By means of the appliances, then the product *performs numerous services* desired by the consumer.

This secondary application of the product has an immediate bearing on utility advertising. Instead of attempting to sell cubic feet of gas or kilowatts of electricity, the utilities concentrate their advertising effort on increasing *usage* at the outlet or burner.

Gas companies, in particular, bear down hard on the advertising and sale of gas appliances, even though they are not in the appliance business. The utility's office building usually has a large showroom where all leading brands of gas appliances are on display. After the customer makes a selection, he can *buy it from the gas company*, which also often installs, guarantees, and services the appliance.

Gas-company advertising is, in fact, product-selling advertising and it is often presented in a robust, hard-sell manner. But it is advertising that sells someone else's product in order to sell one's own.

Electric utilities also seek to increase usage through the promotion of appliances. Their efforts, however, tend to be more generalized, for the reason indicated on page 246, i.e., that electric appliances are already given heavy advertising support by large electrical-appliance manufacturers.

Telephone Service

It has been somewhat facetiously stated that the Bell Telephone System got to be the largest company in the world by giving people an opportunity to *talk*. Certainly, at least in its usage advertising, this company invites its customers to talk—long distance to grandmother on her birthday, when lonely, from college to home, for conducting business, and so on. It suggests extension telephones to save steps and thus make talking easier. Obviously, the public has not been backward in accepting the company's invitation.

The Bell System is the largest seller of service of all. As it deftly sells telephone usage, this System also continues, as skillfully, its public relations image-building discussed in an earlier chapter. Both functions are blended together in the same polite, friendly, people-conscious tone that has now become characteristic of Bell System advertising.

Generic Versus Competitive Advertising . . . Hertz and Avis

When a product or a service is new and unknown, it usually must for a time be advertised *generically*. People have to be informed what the product is, how it works, and what benefits it confers—in a generic way. Later, when the product and its uses become familiar, competitors may enter the field and advertise *competitively*, extolling the special merits of their *brands* over the original brand.

This sequence occurs increasingly in service advertising, as well as in product-advertising. A dramatic instance is the advertising of Hertz and Avis rent-a-car services.

Hertz, well-established and first in the field with advertising, sold the general *idea* of using a rented car. It did this effectively with the startling TV commercial in which the driver sails through the air into the driver's seat,[1] accompanied by the words: "Let Hertz put *you* in the driver's seat!"

---

[1] Accomplished by *lifting* the driver out of the seat by a wire and crane, reversing the film, removing evidence of the wire, and adding the background by using a matte process.

When Avis, which had competed with Hertz for some time, decided to advertise, it chose to employ a *competitive* rather than a generic theme. It assumed that the "you-drive" idea had become sufficiently well known. Its copy, therefore, was devoted to selling the idea that Avis's "you-drive" service was better than its competitor's.

Excellence of Service a Strong Selling Point

The excellence of the service offered can be an important selling point in service advertising. This is because service selling strikes a note of personal involvement. The customer is very much interested in the *quality* of service he pays for.

Avis seized on this theme and exploited it with great forcefulness. It professed a heroic determination to do a super-fine job of providing service, because "Avis is only No. 2 in rent a cars. So we have to try harder."

One advertisement exhibited a crushed cigarette butt. The headline:

IF YOU FIND A CIGARETTE BUTT IN AN AVIS
CAR, COMPLAIN. IT'S FOR OUR OWN GOOD.

The text copy:

We need your help to get ahead.

Avis is only No. 2 in rent a cars. So we have to try harder.

Even if it's only a marked-up map in the glove compartment or you waited longer than you felt you should, please don't shrug it off.

Bug us.

Our people will understand. They've been briefed.

They know we can't afford to hand you anything less than a new car like a lively, super-torque Ford. And it's got to be immaculate, inside and out.

Otherwise, make a noise.

A Mr. Meadow of New York did.

He searched and came up with a gum wrapper.

The value of excellence of service is, of course, thoroughly appreciated by the telephone company. AT&T's chairman, Frederick R. Kappel, said, "It isn't enough that people should merely accept what we do. Our job is to give them service they positively enjoy. And this is no little challenge. It is a great one."

Advertising Travel

Travel is not only a service; it is a whole bundle of services. Because of the multiplicity of details, the once fairly simple travel business has become bewilderingly complex. Travel advertising and some of its problems will be discussed in the next chapter.

Banking Services

A revolution has taken place in American banking. Banks formerly were chiefly interested in the "big" dollar, in lending to business (the bigger the better), financing commercial shipments, serving wealthy individuals, executing international transactions, etc. This type of banking is now designated as "wholesale banking."

The tiny account of the consumer, the man on the street, was then considered something of a nuisance. The bankers didn't trust him. In fact, they feared him, as evidenced by the barred cages that once protected bank tellers.

The revolution came when some bankers discovered that it was both *safe* and *highly profitable* to do business with the small consumer and that banks that did so prospered.

A new concept of "retail banking" emerged. Today, instead of spurning him, the banks rush to court the small consumer. They offer him a growing multitude of services adjusted to the size of his pocketbook—easy-to-handle checking accounts, personal loans, auto loans, boat loans, savings accounts, gift checks, banking-by-mail, and what not.

The retail banking concept has transformed the banking business. Its impact has changed the appearance of banks, affected personnel, and multiplied the number of branches. It has done strange things to the banking image. And it has completely revised banking's approach to advertising.

The Bank's Image—and Bank Advertising

Banks have always been conscious of their image. During the wholesale banking era, many banks sought a "Tiffany" image. Their ads imitated the Tiffany ads, usually consisting only of the name of the bank, the address, and perhaps a chaste notation of the bank's total assets. All surrounded by a sea of white space. For the benefit of their big-business customers, the banks wanted to appear conservative and dignified. They did not advertise very often.

The retail banking revolution called for a new look at the bank's image and a new approach to advertising. The first step taken by many banks was a research into public attitudes. These researches promptly indicated that the man on the street considered the bank a cold, unfriendly place. Which, indeed, it *had* been when wholesale banking was paramount.

As a result, a rash of advertising resulted, stressing bank *friendliness*. A notable example was the oft-repeated television line: "You have a *friend* at Chase Manhattan."

Bank friendliness   One of the sounder *friendliness* campaigns was that of the Bank of the Manhattan Company, which strove for image-creating at the same time it sold its new retail banking services. This campaign avoided *saying* that the bank was friendly; it tried to *prove* it by the tone and spirit of the advertisements.

Cartoon characters—whimsical, everyday "little" people—sympathetically illustrated the bank's services. Copy was light and human. The cartoons were drawn small with a grease pencil on rough paper and then enlarged, giving the lines an unusual ragged effect. This caused the series to become well-known as "the grease-pencil campaign." The cartoon characters appeared in newspapers and on television. The campaign was continued for a time by the Chase Manhattan Bank after the merger of Manhattan and Chase.

Bankers Trust also combined television and print advertising very effectively. On the air, members of the bank's staff delivered the commercials. The newspaper ads showed the same people as they appeared on TV, giving similar messages. The friendly, smiling faces of the bank's actual staff—authentic, everyday people—*proved*, convincingly, that this bank was human and friendly. The ads also did a good selling job for the services.

The "friendly" image, though generally valuable to a bank, can be over-painted. New research has indicated that the consumer public, while it clearly dislikes *un*friendliness, nevertheless does not ask to be overwhelmed by bank *over*-friendliness. It wants the bank to attend to its business and be efficient. It wants its money to be safe, and correctly counted.

Selling Bank Services

Though image remains important, the basic purpose of the commercial banks' greatly increased advertising has been to *sell the new retail services*. And the banks have gone at this with hammer and tongs, apparently all of them at once. In local media of all kinds, including transportation cards, the consumer has been bombarded with nearly identical messages telling him to borrow money, or get an auto loan, or deposit his money at such-and-such a bank.

The effect of this clamor, hard sell in spirit, has been negative in several respects. The claims and offers of the competing banks, selling very similar services, tend to cancel each other out. And the competitive selling is causing image trouble in a new direction. It is destroying the old image of bank dignity and of the bank as a trustable counselor in matters of personal finance. But perhaps this image is no longer valuable in the new era of retail banking.

Other bank advertising The upsurge in retail banking advertising has apparently encouraged increased advertising in other banking spheres. Particular stress has been placed on publicizing bank facilities in foreign countries. These advertisements usually appear in color, in opinion-leader

"Bankers Trust can help you save for a Caribbean cruise, drive off with the car of your choice, fix up your home..."

Saving for vacation or other goals? At Bankers Trust interest is paid from day of deposit to day of withdrawal. Money deposited by the tenth of any month earns interest from the first.

Low-cost auto loans for new or late-model used cars are just $4.25 per $100 per year, deducted in advance. Up to 36 months to repay. Loans arranged quickly. Ask about "Charge-A-Car".

Want to fix up your home? Loans quickly arranged for such jobs as painting, remodeling, attic refinishing. Also for home furnishings. $4.75 per $100 per year, deducted in advance.

You'll find a welcome at BANKERS TRUST

Advertisement for "retail" banking services. This newspaper ad duplicates theme of television commercials. An image of humanity and friendliness is built by having the messages delivered by regular members of the bank's working staff. (AGENCY: *West, Weir & Bartel*)

and business magazines. Interesting campaigns of this type have been presented by Bank of America, First National City Bank, and Irving Trust Company.

Investment Services

Advertising for investment houses, addressed to the general public, tend to be generic, rather than competitive. The advertising sells the *general idea* of investing in the stock market. The copy is usually highly informative.

This approach can be attributed to the relatively stable relations that normally exist between a customer and his broker. Once a friendly, personal rapport between broker and customer has been established, and if the service is satisfactory, the customer may continue to do business with the same broker for many years.

Therefore, brokerage houses tend to seek their new customers from among the many people who are financially able to purchase securities, but who have not yet invested in the stock market. In times of prosperity, the number of such prospects is very large. They are deterred from entering the market largely because of timidity and ignorance of investment procedures.

This, of course, indicates a need for educational advertising. Offers of literature, or of personal advice, included in the advertising, provide a means for making contacts with the potential customers.

The brokerage firm of Merrill Lynch, Pierce, Fenner & Smith has run educational advertisements, often of a question-and-answer type, for many years. A recent ad portrayed an AT&T stock certificate, with the headline:

THIS IS A PICTURE OF A REAL STOCK CERTIFICATE.

The copy said "We're printing it here because millions of people have never seen one." The copy then went on to discuss the certificate informatively and invited readers to seek further information.

Recent advertising of the New York Stock Exchange has echoed the same educational theme, with the obvious aim of bringing new-investor prospects to its member companies. The copy, naturally, deals most specifically with the Exchange's own operations, but the ultimate beneficiaries will be its members. There are some protective public relations overtones in the copy, but these are not nearly as evident as they have been in past years, when Wall Street was more frequently under ideological attack. The informative advertising of the Exchange and of such firms as Merrill Lynch fulfills a useful public service function.

Radio market-news broadcasts are being increasingly used by brokerage houses such as, for example, Bache and Company. The action-stimulating power of this medium is well suited to stir up interest in stock purchases. Bache regularly offers literature—"recommended stock selections"—to draw inquiries.

Insurance

From the viewpoint of the advertising man, there are two kinds of insurance: (1) life insurance and (2) all other kinds.

Actually, there are *many* kinds of insurance—life, health, accident, fire, car, group, marine, liability, etc. All kinds are complex and present advertising difficulties. But the kinds *other than life insurance* usually offer specifics that the copywriter can build on and dramatize.

The most famous insurance advertising campaigns have occurred in this area, such as the Hartford Fire Insurance "fire demon" series, American Mutual's "Mr. Friendly," and the Maryland Casualty and the Travelers campaigns.

On the other hand, the specific involved in life insurance is *death*. This is a subject not easily advertised.

Life insurance is further complicated by its including several categories of insurance—straight life, term, endowment, etc., plus sub-categories of these—which can be combined in various ways to provide individualized benefits.

It started when Jane Thomas kissed him! That was when he handed her a check for the ring that was stolen.

Mr. Friendly blushed a bright red . . . and the glow began.

Then he told Tom Johnson not to worry. Tom had injured someone in an auto smash-up and might have been liable for damages running into the thousands if it hadn't been for Mr. Friendly's insurance company.

"Thank God!" said Tom . . . and Mr. Friendly felt the light coming through his serge suit.

Finally he walked into a hospital and watched a tense face become a happy face . . . happy because Mr. Friendly's company was paying for the doctor, the rent, food, and bills that would pile up while he was laid up.

Mr. Friendly left the hospital . . . shining like a neon light.

"Dog-gone it!" he said, "it's a great job being an American Mutual man . . . a satisfying job if there ever was one!"

That was when the air raid warden tapped him on the shoulder. "Hey, Mister!" he shouted, "we're having a blackout . . . you'll have to stop glowing!"

Remember Mr. Friendly when you consider insurance . . . he typifies the spirit of prompt, cheerful service you'll find in the American Mutual Liability Insurance Company. Write now for your free copy of "Watch," the magazine that helps make your home safer.

"You'll have to stop glowing!"...said the air raid warden

You're in good company when you insure with American Mutual! For this is the same organization that hundreds of industrial plants have chosen to protect their workers. Today two million families like yours command the services of our safety engineers . . . our 5,000 doctors . . . 4,000 lawyers. You, too, can enjoy the same comfort of complete protection, the same prompt help when trouble comes, the same savings. For American Mutual dividends to policyholders have never been less than 20%. Write now for "Watch," American Mutual's unique home safety magazine. American Mutual Liability Insurance Company, 142 Berkeley St., Boston, Mass.

Your helping hand when trouble comes

AMERICAN MUTUAL . . . *the first American liability insurance company*

© 1943, AMERICAN MUTUAL LIABILITY INSURANCE COMPANY

Imaginative fantasy gave American Mutual's "Mr. Friendly" campaign visibility and memorability. The lively and amusing Mr. Friendly personified the services offered by this liability insurance company. (AGENCY: *McCann-Erickson*)

You start with your family. You put them first, as always, under The Travelers umbrella—with *enough* life insurance protection. Got a car? That goes under the umbrella, too. And when your first home comes into the picture, cover that, too—to protect your property from damage, protect yourself from lawsuits. For every kind of protection you need, it will pay you to see your Travelers man (he's listed in the Yellow Pages). He'll show you the convenience and practicality of having *one plan, one man, one monthly check to pay* . . . *under The Travelers umbrella of insurance protection.*

THE TRAVELERS Insurance Companies HARTFORD 15, CONN.

The red umbrella acts as an apt symbol for the Travelers Companies which provide many kinds of insurance. Another well-known identifying symbol is Allstate's cupped hands, with the TV slogan: "You're in good hands with Allstate." (AGENCY: *Young & Rubicam*)

Because of their technical nature, these are difficult to discuss *specifically* in advertising.

Life insurance advertising   It is an axiom of the business that life insurance is *sold;* it is not *bought.*

The prospect for life insurance usually has only a very dim understanding of life insurance in the first place. And he certainly cannot be familiar with the many policy options available to him from a big insurance company. Someone

"Dad... can I have $20,000 for college?"

Look ahead a few years and imagine your own son in this picture, asking the same important question. Your answer *then* will probably depend on the financial plans you make *now*. As the costs of a college education continue to rise, most families realize they cannot afford this expense unless they prepare in advance, following a practical, systematic plan. Here's where your New York Life Agent can be of great service.

He can show you modern plans through which you can be *sure* your son or daughter will have most or even all the funds needed for college. Two New York Life policies were designed especially for this purpose: The Educational Endowment, and Whole Life with Educational Endowment Benefits. Several other cash-value *Nylic* policies can also be used to help finance a college education.

Ask your New York Life Agent about such plans. Through his intensive training and experience as a full-time career underwriter, you'll find he's well qualified to advise and serve you. A good man to know! Call him at the office nearest you. Or, for information, mail the coupon.

The New York Life Agent in Your Community is a Good Man to Know (Nylic)

New York Life Insurance Company
Dept. IN-51, 51 Madison Avenue, New York 10, N.Y.
(In Canada: 443 University Avenue, Toronto 2, Ont.)
I would like more information about your special educational policies.
I (am) (am not) a New York Life policyowner now.

NAME_____AGE____
ADDRESS_____
CITY_____ZONE____
COUNTY_____STATE____

NEW YORK LIFE

LIFE INSURANCE • GROUP INSURANCE • ANNUITIES
HEALTH INSURANCE • PENSION PLANS

Combination benefits help sell life insurance. By combining different types of insurance, New York Life can offer an educational endowment together with life insurance protection. (AGENCY: *Compton Advertising*)

must inform him, prescribe for his apparent needs. That someone is the life insurance agent. It is through the agent that life insurance is explained, individually specified, and sold.

Life insurance companies depend on their agents to sell their insurance service. They do not usually try to sell policies with advertising. They do, however, use advertising as generalized background support for the agent's efforts.

This support takes many forms, depending on the viewpoints of the advertiser companies. It may stress the *need* for life insurance. It may extol the virtues of the agent and attempt to reduce resistance against him. Or it may promote the institutional prestige of the insurance company.

It is the opinion of many experienced life insurance men that the most effective advertising is of a highly sentimental type, directed at young fathers, appealing pointedly to a father's love for his family. Or it may remind the wife of the financial difficulties faced by widows.

The most effective advertising *medium* for selling life insurance appears to be television. The emotional impact of television, and its ability to secure personal involvement, add force to life insurance appeals. In this medium, delicate personal situations can often be handled with more freedom than in print. Television is also effective with the types of insurance *other than life.*

Advertising for Hotels and Restaurants

The traditional, unimaginative way to advertise a hotel has been to show a large, architectural exterior—a view dear to the hotel owner or a real-estate operator—but the *least* interesting aspect to the prospective guest, who is much more concerned with what happens *inside* the building.

There are numerous things about hotels and restaurants that are attractive and interesting to people. It is not very difficult for an imaginative creative writer to describe a hotel with warmth and give it personality. Yet this seldom happens. It has happened magnificently, however, with the advertising for the Hotel Plaza in New York (page 268).

Humorous cartoons have values for advertising hotel service. For the Statler system during World War II, when good service could not always be maintained, the humorous-cartoon format made it possible to apologize without loss of face.

Advertising for Schools

If a school is a serious, academic, educational institution, its advertising will be extremely conservative, dignified, small in size, and strictly factual. But if the school is a *correspondence* school, a purely commercial operation, it will usually be advertised by long, hard-working, hard-selling *mail-order* copy.

Midway between these two contrasting extremes there is a third type, offering *specialized* instruction. Such as the Arthur Murray dancing schools, or the Berlitz language courses. These schools have been consistent advertisers.

Arthur Murray has been able to use television with great success, because good dancing is not only easily demonstrated before the camera, but also offers good entertainment for viewers.

The day New York almost vanished

It didn't happen all at once.
They did it very gradually.
"We can't alarm the people!" they said.
So they removed a little house here. And a great
hotel there. And then a few limestone banks
and all the cast-iron store fronts they could find.
And very quietly one night they stole a railroad
station and buried it in New Jersey.

A few people grumbled.
Some found temporary shelter at The Dakota
when Park Avenue disappeared. Others moved
to Westchester. And some completely
disillusioned out-of-towners went to Philadelphia
instead. But most people were complacent. Until
the day they discovered that their city had
been entirely replaced with glass.

Then they complained. But it was too late.
So the faces of the city grew grimmer
than they had ever been before. Clocks stopped.
And the glass began to crack.

Soon after this on one ghastly glittering
morning, an observant executive walking to work
paused on Fifth Avenue at Fifty-Ninth Street
to clean his heavy dark goggles. Squinting,
he looked around. And gasped!

There was The Plaza where he had always
remembered it. "It can't be!" he said and rubbed
his eyes. He looked again. "It *is* there!" he said.
And ran to work.

He called his wife.
"We'll go there tonight, before it's too late.
Don't tell anyone!" he hissed. So she only told
her very best friend. Soon everyone knew.

Crowds gathered. They wandered in the
lobbies. They caressed the marble, admired the
gilded cherubs. And the caryatids in the Palm
Court where palms still swayed. They feasted in
the baronial splendor of the Edwardian Room.
And discussed mergers over martinis and lunch
in the Oak Bar.

That night, they danced to *real* music
again in the Persian Room. And laughed with
Julius Monk in his red velvet world at PLaza 9-.
The lucky ones who had made reservations
retired upstairs, to spacious rooms where they
were waited on hand and foot by manicurists and
podiatrists and chambermaids and valets and
waiters with trays and florists with roses.
They loved it.

After all, people of taste are like everybody
else. They're very grateful when great demands
are met. And incurably sentimental.

Eventually word spread out of town. And
out-of-towners came again to see a part of the
city they thought had vanished. Some never
left The Plaza. They didn't have to. They had
the world on a golden chain.

The Plaza had thought of everything. It
always does.

It always will.

One of an imaginative, colorful series of ads for the Plaza Hotel in New York.
(AGENCY: *Lavenson Bureau of Advertising*)

Berlitz, using upper-echelon print media, has sold its teaching method with interesting *idea* ads. Each ad portrayed an attractive four-year-old child of some foreign nationality. If the child was Chinese, the headline read:

IF SHE CAN SPEAK FLUENT CHINESE, WHY CAN'T YOU?

The child learned Chinese at her mother's knee. The text copy told how Berlitz adapted the natural learning method of children and applied it, with improvements, to the teaching of languages to adults.

Entertainment Advertising

The advertising for show business has been astonishingly conservative. The small-size newspaper ads for legitimate theater shows are little different

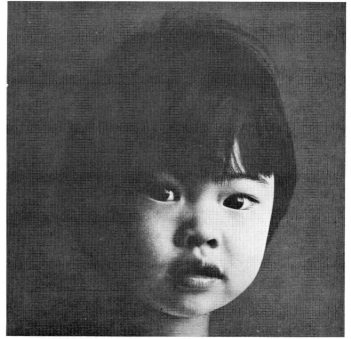

Use of the little Chinese girl's picture is not a mere trick, devised only to get attention. Actually, Berlitz teaches Chinese exactly the way the little girl learned it. The ad is a dramatization of fact. (AGENCY: The Gilbert Advertising Agency)

Never Underestimate the Power of a Woman!

Women buy more copies per issue of Ladies' Home Journal
than any other magazine on earth. It's happened
every month for over eleven years. It's happening this month, too.

LADIES' HOME JOURNAL THE MAGAZINE WOMEN BELIEVE IN

Advertising the services of media to other branches of the advertising business. This series ran for many years, sold an idea that benefited all women's service publications—but the Journal most of all.* (AGENCY: N. W. Ayer & Son)

from the public notice advertisements of the eighteenth century. They announce the name of the play, the theater, the time, plus, on occasion, one or two other details. Selling, if any, is confined to the quotation of a few laudatory words from a critic.

Movie ads are bigger and more flamboyant, but they, too, are conservative in their own peculiar ways. The style of their artwork remains the style of the early

* Ad a trademark of the Curtis Publishing Company. Reprinted with permission.

1920s. Their cluttered, vignetted layouts and their boastful adjectives belong to the same primitive period. Nothing has been changed.

Again and again, one piece of artwork is made to do for thousands of appearances in all kinds of media. Advertising consists of one ad, endlessly repeated. Even radio commercials repeat the same words. There is no campaign, in the usual advertising sense.

In fact, movies are not really *advertised* at all; they are *merchandised*. When a new movie is released, it is launched with the aid of "the book," an immense package of all kinds of merchandising material, including many sizes of mat ads and innumerable publicity releases.

The economics and logistics of show business, no doubt, are in part re-

"I don't know who you are.

I don't know your company.

I don't know your company's product.

I don't know what your company stands for.

I don't know your company's customers.

I don't know your company's record.

I don't know your company's reputation.

Now—what was it you wanted to sell me?"

MORAL: Sales start before your salesman calls—with business magazine advertising.

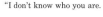 McGRAW-HILL BUSINESS PRESS

330 WEST 42nd STREET, NEW YORK 36, N. Y.

Promoting the cause of all business advertising, McGraw-Hill Business Press pointedly shows that industry's personal salesmanship needs the support of business-paper advertising. (AGENCY: *Fuller & Smith & Ross*)

Dear Sirs,
I thought you might be interested to know that I added togeather all
the money figures in your August 20th
issue, The total came out to be $1,382,184.44

yours truly
Daniel Braden

Dear Mr. Braden: You are a very ingenious
young man for adding up the money
figures in our August 20th issue (one of our
lighter issues of the year).
In all the years that I have been at
The New Yorker, I don't think that anyone has
ever done this before and we are terribly appreciative.

(Signed)
A. J. Russell, Jr.
Executive Vice President

THE NEW YORKER, No. 25 West 43rd Street, New York 36, New York • Other Advertising Offices: Chicago, San Francisco, Los Angeles, Atlanta, London

The **New Yorker** *advertises itself by being itself—and slyly makes a*
point. (AGENCY: *Chirurg & Cairn*)

sponsible for some of the eccentricities of entertainment advertising. Every show is a speculation. The play may last five days or five years. An expensive movie may flop. This makes for conservatism, a conservatism that somehow seems unfitting for a business as exciting as show business. Yet advertising excitement *is* possible, as was well indicated by the sprightly copy written by the late Billy Rose.

When Advertising Advertises to Itself

Advertising advertises its services to itself when (1) *media* advertise to agencies and advertisers and when (2) *agencies* advertise themselves to prospective-advertiser clients. This is usually done in the trade press and in newspapers. Very often, full pages of newspaper space are taken—an expensive and wasteful purchase in terms of circulation, but a relatively cheap one in terms of visibility and impact.

This advertising is created by the most talented and experienced advertising people in the world. Many *clever* advertisements have resulted. But somehow, these advertisements often seemed to lack the selling power of the ads, prepared by the same people, for their other clients.

The reason may be that the agency must pull its punches in advertising itself. It must sell itself to a wide variety of prospective clients. It is required to picture itself as perfect in *all* ways—be all things to all men. This, of course, does not make for concentrated selling power. The same difficulty occurs with media advertisers.

Where media are specialized, leading publications can take an industry-leadership position and promote their special type of media. This approach has led to memorable successes. One example was the campaign, "Never Underestimate the Power of a Woman," which the *Ladies' Home Journal* was able to run because it was so long the circulation leader among women's magazines. In another instance, McGraw-Hill Business Press exerted industry leadership in promoting the cause of *all* industrial advertising.

Chapter 29

The travel industry, all over the world, has expanded enormously in recent years. Competition has sharply intensified. And travel advertising has increased comparably.

Travel, today, is concerned with much more than merely transportation. It assumes responsibility for itineraries, cuisine, accommodations, entertainment, sport, guidance, and independent exploration. It caters to the needs of business, religion, education, and the arts.

The travel *business,* providing a multiplicity of services, and spreading in two-way fashion all over the globe, has become almost unbelievably complex. Many people take part in assisting the traveler on even a short trip.

The Two Major Areas of Travel Advertising

Travel advertising falls into two major categories, (1) carrier advertising and (2) destination advertising. This is because the funds for advertising are provided either by the carriers or by destination promoters.

The principal carriers (there are numerous, exotic minor ones) are:

- Private motor cars
- Rent-a-cars
- Bus lines
- Railroads
- Steamship lines
- Airlines

Of these, airlines and steamship lines are by far the largest travel advertisers. Carriers advertise themselves as the means of travel. They do, on occasion, advertise the destinations they reach.

Destination advertising concentrates on promoting a destination, which may be a continent, a country, a state, a city, or a special tourist attraction. This advertising is usually paid for by the interests expecting to profit from tourism, or by a government

—national, state, or local. Or by a combination of government and private groups. Destination ads almost never mention a carrier.

Advantages of the Various Types of Carriers

Each type of carrier offers special benefits to the traveler. These advantages have considerable bearing on advertising appeals.

The overwhelming advantage of air travel is *speed,* with the resulting *saving of time,* valuable to vacationer or businessman.

Steamship travel offers leisurely *comfort.* It is the most pleasant way to travel, for those who can afford to take more time.

Bus lines offer *economy.* They also reach many places not attainable with other public transportation. Tourism by bus is more highly developed in Europe than in America.

The private car and the rent-a-car provide *mobility* and *independence.* One can go where and when one pleases. The rent-a-car is much used as an *extension* of other forms of transportation.

In planned tours, it is becoming common practice to combine a number of types of transportation to cover more ground advantageously.

The Marketing of Travel

Carriers and destination promoters use a complex array of means to generate travel traffic. These include advertising, publicity and other public relations devices, sales promotion, and personal salesmanship.

An important source of travel origination is the independent *travel agent,* who provides travel advice and secures tickets, accommodations, etc. He usually does not charge his customer for his services in getting the tickets or accommodations, as he gets a commission for these from the carriers and hotels. He usually *does* charge for his time in planning elaborate itineraries.

Obviously, the travel agent's activities are of great value to the rest of the travel industry. Consequently, his goodwill is courted with advertising, sales promotion, and personal contact.

Advertising for Airlines

The advertising of airlines, particularly the large American lines, has become extremely competitive. Selling points have been developed around *price* arrangements, *equipment, safety, experience,* and *service.* Of these, *service* is mentioned most.

The rewards of this competitive advertising tend to be temporary, because competition soon duplicates any real benefit, claims cancel each other out, and all the major airlines get to be thought of as being pretty much alike.

Some of the foreign airlines, however, have countered this effect of sameness with image-building advertising. Air France has featured the gay kiosks of Paris in colorful magazine advertisements. On radio, Japan Air Lines created a distinctive atmosphere with unusual sound effects and with its quiet, dignified commercials that spoke of the "calm beauty of Japan at almost the speed of sound."

Airlines do devote part of their advertising to destinations, but not to the degree it seems they should. In this, they may be dissuaded from doing more because of the feeling that they may have too many destinations to talk about, or because their destinations are not exclusive.

Steamship Advertising

Steamship lines compete with airlines and among themselves. In competing with the airlines, steamship advertising makes much of the comforts and enjoyment of the more leisurely sea travel and its fling of luxury. "Getting there is half the fun," repeated the Cunard Line.

Copy talks about "acres of deck space" (in pointed contrast to the cramped seating of an airliner), about international cuisine, midnight snacks, pampering service, bracing sea air, ballrooms, and swimming pools. The ocean voyage is pictured as a *fun* trip, worth the time it takes. For the harried business executive, it can be an opportunity for rest.

Competing among themselves, steamship lines compete by lines and sometimes even by individual ships. They also compete by routes. Typical is the competition between the northern and southern routes to Europe. Advertising for the northern route to England, France and Northern Europe stresses *speed* —made possible by fewer miles and faster ships. Ships sailing the southern route through Gibraltar and into the Mediterranean boast of calmer waters and more days of sunshine.

In the competition between lines and ships, image becomes important.

The Italian Line strives for an image of artistic beauty, even names its ships after famous artists.

The Cunard Line has always maintained an image of good seamanship, good sea management, competence afloat. It has been greatly aided in this by its dramatic, sympathetic photography of its big ships. Cunard photographers have always seemed to understand that a ship could be visually exciting in itself.

The French Line has achieved a connotation of superb French cuisine and the sparkle of champagne. Gaiety. The French atmosphere. "France begins the minute you cross the gangplank."

The United States Lines has based its advertising and its image on its special clientele. These are wealthy, successful Americans, many with social or political prestige. They are pictured and quoted in the advertisements. Some of them sail the same ship to Europe every year.

The name, Grace Line, evokes romantic memories of Caribbean buccaneers and buried treasure associated with the geographical area served by this line and promoted by Grace Line advertising.

Role of the Destination in Carrier Advertising

Why do tourists travel abroad? Some cross the ocean to play golf. Some want to see cathedrals and art galleries, or attend music festivals. Some look for castles. Or nightclubs. But most go for a combination of things; they want to see a new country. The object of their trip is to turn a long-deferred dream into reality.

What the tourist intends to buy with his money is the *destination*, not the ship or the plane. He merely rents the carrier to get him to the destination.

In an illuminating survey of travel advertising,[1] copy researcher Johanna Rock found that of two comparable carrier ads, the one that featured destinations attracted the attention of 50 per cent more readers than an ad showing passengers en route. The destination ad got twice the copy reading. Other ads in the research confirmed the marked interest-arousing superiority of destination over the carrier.

Carrier advertisers, especially steamship advertisers, would do well to increase the amount of destination appeal in their ads. For this is the benefit the customer is seeking. He is not buying the ship. If the carrier can link its name with the benefit wanted (the destination) and can establish that "this is the way to get there," its advertising will increase its chances of making a sale.

Accuracy in Timetable Details

For those concerned with the creation and production of travel advertising, attention to the accuracy of travel details is a matter of utmost importance. Timetable items—departures, routes, dates, accommodations, prices, etc.— *must* be correct. If not, they can cause fantastic difficulties. It is wise to have proofs at least triple-checked by several persons.

[1] *Advertising Age*, Feb. 1, 1965.

French Line

YOUR GAY ENTRÉE TO EUROPE

Going to Europe? For a voyage sparkling as French champagne, travel aboard the celebrated *Ile de France* or the popular *De Grasse!*

Regardless of which accommodations you choose, on France-Afloat you will know the joys of exquisite French cuisine prepared in the grand manner . . . scintillating entertainment . . . staterooms of charming décor. And, of course, cheerful service by English-speaking stewards.

On August 23 another great ship, the 49,850-ton *Liberté*, arrives in New York harbor, flying the Tricolor for the first time. Plan your voyage for the autumn months, when England and the Continent are truly enchanting. And for a gay holiday *en route*, travel on France-Afloat! French Line, 610 Fifth Avenue, New York 20.

Gaiety, champagne, and good food contribute to image-building for the French Line. This advertising exerted a strong appeal to sophisticated people. (AGENCY: *N. W. Ayer & Son*)

French Line sailings from New York (to Plymouth and Le Havre) and minimum one-way fares: **Liberté**, Aug. 25; Sept. 14; Oct. 5, 26; Nov. 11, 29; Dec. 16; First Class, $340; Cabin, $220; Tourist, $165. **Ile de France**, Aug. 3, 19; Sept. 6, 23; Oct. 14, 31; Nov. 18; Dec. 7; First Class, $335; Cabin, $220; Tourist, $165. **De Grasse**, Aug. 19; Sept. 11; Oct. 4; First Class, $235; Cabin, $180. • Other French Line offices: Beverly Hills, Boston, Chicago, Cleveland, Halifax, Montreal, New Orleans, Philadelphia, Portland, San Francisco, Seattle, Vancouver, B. C., Washington, D. C.

Destination Advertising

The tourist cannot go everywhere at once. He must make a choice. As a result, all possible destinations, near and far, are in competition with each other for the tourist's attention, time, and dollars. Advertising becomes necessary to sell destination areas to tourist prospects.

Control of this destination advertising tends to fall into the hands of a committee. Or it may be subject to competing regional political pressures. It has the aspects of association advertising, with the faults of association advertising noted in an earlier chapter. As previously stated, the solution to a too-many-cooks problem is to delegate authority to an individual and permit him to operate the advertising machinery.

The atmosphere of Paris injected into the advertising of Air France helped to give this airline a distinctive personality. (AGENCY: *Batten, Barton, Durstine & Osborn*)

People want to see something different David Ogilvy, certainly an authority on the subject, has devoted an informative chapter of his book, *Confessions of an Advertising Man,* to travel advertising. In it, he makes an extremely basic point—that people do not travel thousands of miles to see things they can see at home.

A native of Switzerland, he pointed out, would hardly be inspired to spend

After an April shower at Buttermere, Cumberland—one of the lakes that Wordsworth loved.

Beware the sparkle of Britain's Spring!

SPRING in Britain is a heady season. It inspires giddy odes. Unlikely similes. Frightful clichés. And love.

It also has a mind of its own which it expresses by ignoring the vernal equinox. In Devon, the primroses start to pop in January. Cornish daffodils stare February in the face and chuckle. And, by the time those April showers fill the air with invisible hyacinths, you begin to believe there's a flower seed in every raindrop.

You can sense some of the sparkle of Britain's Spring merely by flicking through a calendar of events. Flat racing starts in Spring. So does the leisurely lunacy of cricket. Festivals, fairs and floral dances put a froth on your fun. And, like any fauna faced with flora, you want to grow wild. In one Buckinghamshire village, housewives celebrate Shrove Tuesday by running a pancake race!

If you *must* get practical about this irresponsible season, ask your travel agent about the latest transatlantic fares. Complete your trip by March 31 and you can get to Britain and back for $320. If that little bargain doesn't inspire spring fever, see a doctor.

FREE! Colorful 24-page fully illustrated booklet "Portrait of Britain"; write Box 172, British Travel Association.
In New York—680 Fifth Avenue; In Los Angeles—606 South Hill St.; In Chicago—39 South La Salle St.; In Canada—90 Adelaide Street West, Toronto.

In British Travel Association destination advertising, to a glamorous color photograph is added an enticing headline and cleverly written copy that manages to work in plenty of selling. (AGENCY: *Ogilvy, Benson and Mather*)

money to see mountains in Colorado. An American visiting London would be far more interested in seeing Westminster Abbey than an atomic power station. Tourists want to see something new and strange and different.

This applies to the people pictured in travel advertisements. Foreigners in exotic costumes catch the eye of an American. People who look like Americans do not.

Tourists continue to want to see the big symbolic travel attractions—the Eiffel Tower, the Rock of Gibraltar, the Bridge of Sighs, the Grand Canyon. It does not matter that these scenes have been seen in advertising many times. They are part of the traveler's dream. They should never be excluded from ads

Next time you take a vacation, uncomplicate your life.

Get out of glamorous Paris. Drive your car onto that amazing French train that beds-down cars as well as drivers and then speeds to the South. Disembark at Avignon in the heart of lazy, sunny Provence and drive a leisurely pace through provincial France, Roman France and a lot of relaxed, sunburned towns.

This is France's artists' country. Music's everywhere. And every photograph you take is an impressionist painting. You can shed your coat and tie, here. You can bicycle and keep your dignity. You can learn all there is to know about wine and cheese and bouillabaisse. You can fall in love, here. You can even stay forever.

For list of beautiful old inns and facts on Provence, write Dept. NY-1, Box #221, N. Y. 10. French Government Tourist Office, New York, Chicago, Los Angeles, San Francisco, Miami, Montreal.

Emphasis on visual impact, combined with a clever headline, gives interest and personality to destination advertising of the French Government Tourist Office. (AGENCY: *Doyle Dane Bernbach*)

because a copywriter or art director has become bored with them. The customers do not share this boredom.

Advertising for Britain

The "Come to Britain" advertising prepared by Ogilvy, Benson and Mather for the British Travel Association is outstanding in the field of destination advertising, not only for its creative excellence and its sound strategy, but also for its impressive continuity, year after year.

The interesting headlines and well-written copy of this campaign have already been discussed. Also worthy of notice is that the text copy of this series is loaded with factual information. Typical prices are given for meals, lodgings, theater tickets, drinks, admissions, shopping items, car rentals. By being specific, the copy removes hazy doubts, brings the tourist nearer to translating his dreams into action.

Another characteristic of the campaign is its *dragnet* selling. It reaches out for everybody. It projects appeals to business executives, golfers, the literary minded, hunters, music and theater lovers, sightseers, food lovers, Shakespeare fans, motor tourists, history buffs, status seekers, people seeking a rest, shoppers, drinkers, boating enthusiasts, honeymooners, art collectors, antique collectors, to mention a few.

What can you possibly do for an encore?

Bravo!

India is for people who suspect they've seen everything. It's an unexpected and delightfully different encore. A land as exciting as Lancers wheeling in close formation cavalry drill. As tranquil as a high lake in Kashmir. As glorious as the Taj Mahal itself. For colorful brochures about India, her modern hotels and travel facilities, see your Travel Agent or write to the Government of India Tourist Office.

New York, 19 East 49th Street. Chicago, Palmer House. San Francisco, 685 Market Street. Toronto, 177 King Street, W.

The Government of India Tourist Office injects a fresh note into destination advertising by presenting its age-old marvels as something new. (AGENCY: *Pritchard, Wood*)

Destination Advertising for France

The destination advertising of the French Government Tourist Office is noted for its *visual* excellence. Layout and illustration display artistic flare and smartness. Headline *ideas* are exciting.

The campaign has not promoted Paris, but rather the rest of France outside of Paris. Apparently the promotion of Paris has been left to French carrier advertising.

Destination Advertising for India

A fresh and lively approach to destination advertising has been provided by the Government of India Tourist Office. Keynote of the copy is the statement, "India is for people who suspect they've seen everything."

One advertisement shows, at the top, a small, square photograph of the Eiffel Tower, with the headline:

WHAT CAN YOU POSSIBLY
DO FOR AN ENCORE?

Under this is a much larger photograph of the Taj Mahal, and under it the second headline:

BRAVO!

Another ad in the series shows the leaning tower of Pisa at the top, with the headline:

SO WHAT ELSE IS NEW?

The large picture below is of the Oriental Red Fort of the Emperor Shah Jehan at Delhi. The second headline:

DELHI

Ten

ADVERTISING TO PROMOTE ACTION

Sometimes advertising has been called upon to initiate public action of one kind or other. It attempts to do this by arousing and marshaling public opinion.

It has been thus employed to force a change in a traditional industry practice that affected the public. It has also been used by citizens, or groups of citizens, to protest against government policies. Or to attempt to influence government policies. Or to urge or oppose the passage of legislation.

A rapidly expanding exemplification of action-initiating advertising is advertising to elect political candidates.

Characteristically, this type of advertising leans to emotional appeals. Its language is strong and its visual presentation does not hesitate to be bold and daring.

A classic example of advertising to change an industry practice was the newspaper advertisement with a cartoon illustration and the headline:

Chapter **30**

ACTION-

INITIATING

ADVERTISING

A HOG CAN CROSS THE COUNTRY WITHOUT CHANGING TRAINS—BUT YOU CAN'T!

This was one of a campaign of newspaper and magazine ads instituted in 1945 by Robert R. Young, chairman of the Chesapeake & Ohio Railway. It pointed out that a hog could be shipped from coast to coast by railroad without changing cars, but that transcontinental passengers were forced to change from one railroad to another at Chicago, St. Louis, and New Orleans. Vigorous copy, attributed to Edwin Cox and Draper Daniels of Kenyon & Eckhardt, called for "action to end this inconvenience to the traveling public . . . NOW!"

The campaign enlisted much editorial support in the press and on radio. As a result, major railroads, which had previously claimed that through service in and out of Chicago was impractical, reversed their stand and announced that such service would be provided.

The Advertising of Protest

Large newspaper advertisements with such messages as a protest against the war in Vietnam, or some other governmental action or policy, have become increasingly common. These may be placed and signed by a single wealthy individual, or more often, by groups of individuals who have contributed to the cost of the space. Long, all-text copy presents a viewpoint on which the group agrees. Lacking the dramatization, the repetition, and the continuity needed to change opinions, such one-time advertising efforts obviously are limited in effectiveness.

A continuing, color magazine campaign, now almost forgotten, once had force enough to have possibly had some influence on our country's history. This was the World Peaceways campaign, running in 1936, that gave voice to widespread pacifist feeling in the years immediately preceding America's entry into World War II.

One advertisement depicted a disabled World War I veteran in a wheelchair. The headline read:

HELLO, SUCKER

After referring to men who promoted war for selfish reasons, the copy said, "We were all suckers. The lovely ideals we fought for turned out to be a mess of slogans, with the noble ring of an empty tin can." And again: "And suckers we'll be again if we are not careful. The machinery of war is grinding again— the propaganda" . . . "the appeal to emotions, the subtle coloring of news."

Political Advertising

In the Johnson versus Goldwater presidential campaign, each candidate was reported to have spent approximately 4 to 5 million dollars in advertising, by far the greater part of it television advertising. In New York State, Senator Robert Kennedy is said to have reported an expenditure of $1,200,000—70 to 80 per cent of it for television in the last five weeks of the campaign.

Advertising to elect a political candidate has grown enormously in volume in a few years. It has also improved its techniques, becoming far more professional. It is no longer satisfied with the stand-up or sit-down presentation of the candidate making a speech. In television, particularly, it acts out and dramatizes the issues of the campaign.

The startling impact of this approach was demonstrated in the commercials prepared by Doyle Dane Bernbach for the Democratic National Committee. One of them opened with a little girl counting petals she plucked from a daisy.

A Hog Can Cross the Country Without Changing Trains—But YOU Can't!

The Chesapeake & Ohio Railway and the Nickel Plate Road are again proposing to give human beings a break!

It's hard to believe, but it's true.

If you want to ship a hog from coast to coast, he can make the entire trip without changing cars. You can't. It is impossible for you to pass through Chicago, St. Louis, or New Orleans without breaking your trip!

There is an invisible barrier down the middle of the United States which you cannot cross without inconvenience, lost time, and trouble.

560,000 Victims in 1945!

If you want to board a sleeper on one coast and ride through to the other, you must make double Pullman reservations, pack and transfer your baggage, often change stations, and wait around for connections.

It's the same sad story if you make a relatively short trip. You can't cross that mysterious line! To go from Fort Wayne to Milwaukee or from Cleveland to Des Moines, you must also stop and change trains.

Last year alone, more than 560,000 people were forced to make annoying, time-wasting stopovers at the phantom Chinese wall which splits America in half!

End the Secrecy!

Why should travel be less convenient for people than it is for pigs? Why should Americans be denied the benefits of through train service? No one has yet been able to explain it.

Canada has this service . . . with a choice of two routes. Canada isn't split down the middle. Why should we be? No reasonable answer has yet been given. Passengers still have to stop off at Chicago, St. Louis, and New Orleans—although they can ride right through other important rail centers.

It's time to pry the lid off this mystery. It's time for action to end this inconvenience to the travelling public . . . NOW!

Many railroads could cooperate to provide this needed through service. To date, the Chesapeake & Ohio and the Nickel Plate ALONE have made a public offer to do so.

How about it!

Once more we would like to go on record with this specific proposal:

The Chesapeake & Ohio, whose western passenger terminus is Cincinnati, stands ready now to join with any combination of other railroads to set up connecting transcontinental and intermediate service through Chicago and St. Louis, on practical schedules and routes.

The Nickel Plate Road, which runs to Chicago and St. Louis, also stands ready now to join with any combination of roads to set up the same kind of connecting service through these two cities.

Through railroad service can't be blocked forever. The public wants it. It's bound to come. Again, we invite the support of the public, of railroad people and railroad investors—for this vitally needed improvement in rail transportation!

Chesapeake & Ohio Railway · Nickel Plate Road
Terminal Tower, Cleveland 1, Ohio

Action-initiating advertising appeals to the emotions, strives to build up indignation or anger, as in this newspaper advertisement for the Chesapeake & Ohio Railway and the Nickel Plate Road. (AGENCY: *Kenyon & Eckhardt*)

Her childish count gradually becomes a man's voice doing a countdown. At zero, the screen flashed with an atomic explosion.

Then was heard the voice of Lyndon Johnson, saying: "These are the stakes . . . to make a world in which all of God's children can live . . . or go into the dark." The commercial ended with an exhortation to "Vote for President Johnson on November 3."

Other commercials dramatized, negatively, statements and attitudes attributed to Senator Goldwater, or his supporters. One displayed a social security card being torn in half on the screen. Another portrayed a map of the United States with the sawed-off Eastern seaboard floating out to sea.

Of course, all candidates appear before TV cameras and radio microphones as *news*, or in interview programs, at every opportunity. The dramatized "issue" *commercials* provided something *additional* to the candidate's speech-making.

It is notable that no print advertising was included in the budget of the Democratic National Committee. That was left to local Democratic groups. The choice of television for national advertising was guided by the desire to reach a mass audience, plus awareness of television's power to project an emotionalized message.

Local political advertising   In the New York City mayoralty election won by John Lindsay and in the preceding Democratic primary, the total advertising expenditure was estimated to be *at least* several million dollars.

In this local election, television played a less dominant role than in the national election. Radio, which could be prepared quickly and was flexible and economical, became a favorite medium. In addition to commercials in English, voter appeals in Spanish and Italian were broadcast from foreign language stations.

Other effective local political media were subway posters, outdoor posters and billboards, and especially, fleets of sound trucks. A memorable subway poster consisted of a photograph of shirt-sleeved candidate Lindsay walking vigorously down a city street. Its caption, quoted from the newspaper column of Murray Kempton, read:

> "He is fresh
> and everyone else
> is tired."

In the past, action-initiating advertising has appeared relatively infrequently. But its use seems to be increasing. As more people realize that the advertising pages are open, for a price, for the promotion of ideas as well as for the sale of goods, use of this kind of advertising should increase still more. It offers interesting possibilities for the future.

INDEX